D1563387

THE AMERICAN EXPERIMENT

THE
AMERICAN EXPERIMENT

BY BERNARD FAŸ

in collaboration with

AVERY CLAFLIN

KENNIKAT PRESS/Port Washington, N.Y.

....

THE AMERICAN EXPERIMENT

First published 1929
Reissued 1969 by Kennikat Press

Library of Congress Catalog Card No: 68-8211
SBN 8046-0142-9
Manufactured in the United States of America

FOREWORD

This work is a study of the incubation, development and significance of a new civilization—that of the United States. It makes no pretense to historical completeness, nor is it, in the manner of Bryce, an exhaustive treatise of the minutiae of democratic government. Its object is to trace in architectural lines the rise and promise of the first civilization to develop under the observation of a humanity sufficiently endowed with implements to record it adequately.

After a brief critical sketch of governmental machinery there follows a panoramic description of the great modern nation: its work, its play, its moral qualities and prejudices, its emotions, beliefs and ambitions. This section is perhaps the most significant part of the book. Here are reviewed the qualities of American life today which contribute to an original civilization—qualities not found in histories or documents, but in business life, politics, the press, educational institutions, churches, the arts, amusements, and in the general reaction of individuals to all of these. This is followed by a study of the effects which the old and new worlds have had upon each other. A summary points out the salient features of American civilization which Europe might advantageously adopt or adapt to its own purposes.

The collaboration of Mr. Faÿ and myself which produced this volume began in 1917 on the battlefields of Verdun. Those first discussions and comparisons of the old and new worlds have been many times amended and revised. Constant study and observation have added new material and brought the work into its present form.

AVERY CLAFLIN.

NEW YORK
January, 1929

CONTENTS

THE AMERICAN EXPERIMENT

CHAPTER I

THE AMERICAN EXPERIMENT

Seen from Europe, that is to say from a great distance, America appears to be something very big, but quite simple: a huge buzzing machine which produces everything in quantities—automobiles, social and political theories, millionaires, and movie films. It contains no historical monuments worthy of the name, but it has its sky-scrapers; and people who have seen them are as proud as though they had beheld the great sea serpent. Finally, America is famous because, though wine is prohibited there, by way of compensation every one jazzes, has money, and wears silk shirts. A brilliant and gaudy vision, a confused and mighty clamor; and this is about all that Europeans know of the United States.

Of course, there are a few scholars and a select number of well-informed persons who learned something of the famous American democracy from their school books, and since then have gleaned from newspapers and magazines a few facts about American politics. For them the names of Washington, Jefferson, Franklin, of Lincoln, Roosevelt, and Wilson summarize the history of the new world and evoke a vision of the oldest and most prosperous democratic government; the only one which ever succeeded in obtaining the absolute loyalty of its people or in meriting their gratitude. These well-informed persons know no more. Nor do they feel there is anything more to be known. They agree with Stendhal, who said a century ago: "A free government is one which does no harm to its citizens, but

3

which, on the contrary, affords them security and peace. But that in itself is by no means synonymous with individual happiness, which can be attained by each person for himself. People would be sluggish indeed who could be made happy simply by being secure and undisturbed. We confuse these things in Europe, particularly in Italy, since we are accustomed to governments which do us harm. It seems that our greatest joy would lie in being rid of them—in which we resemble an invalid suffering from some painful disease. The example of America suggests nothing to contradict this. There the government does its work very well and harms no one. But it seems as though destiny wished to disconcert and refute all our philosophy, or rather to accuse it of being unacquainted with human nature in its totality. For many centuries the unfortunate condition of Europe has prevented any real experimentation; yet we perceive that when the Americans have disposed of governmental misfortunes, they seem to have done away with a part of themselves. The wells of feeling appear to have dried up; they are just, they have common sense, and they are unhappy." [1] While approving of the early American Government and its principles, Stendhal could not accept the result as satisfactory. Similarly today, although citing the political evolution of the United States as an irrefutable argument in favor of popular government and majority rule, Europeans will scarcely concede the top rank to American civilization. A vague doubt persists, a feeling that in the obscurity surrounding these notions there may lurk some vitiating error or inaccuracy. Majority rule may not have been the chief factor in the development of the United States.

A much smaller group of Europeans has recently come to look upon the United States as an apostle of the idea of federation. They pictured the wealth and prosperity of the

[1] Stendhal: *De l'Amour.*

new world. Professors of economics, bankers, international
traders all began preaching the gospel of coöperation. Even
the term "Federalism," never very popular in Europe, was
recalled with deference when the victors of 1918 attempted to reorganize the economic life of the old continent.
"Agree among yourselves. Emulate the United States, whose
federation of forty-eight states created a gigantic market to
every one's advantage." President Wilson, as patron of the
League of Nations, had already made similar declarations
and had sought to demonstrate that the United States owed
their greatness to a firm resolve to agree among themselves,
to remain united despite all difficulties or conflicting interests. Such a doctrine, promulgated at a critical juncture
by a man of immense authority, the virtual dictator of 110,-
000,000 people, and commander-in-chief of 4,000,000 fresh
troops, made a profound impression upon all serious-
minded people and was not forgotten. Those who at the
present moment are advocating a United States of Europe,
a Pan-Europa, or a European Customs Federation were inspired, and are now encouraged and sustained, by the American example. Neither the Swiss nor the Dutch Confederation covers a sufficiently large territory to permit of comprehensive generalization. The term "empire" was more accurate to describe Austria and Germany; witness the latter,
after the flight, disappearance and deposition of its emperor,
remaining an empire as a final protest. The United States
alone has continued as a federation for a century and a
half, and prospered thereby. Its one serious crisis—the
Civil War—ended in a federalist victory. And now the
nineteenth century standard-bearer of democracy comes
forward as the emblem of a universal federalism.

The cause of federalism would be further advanced had
not certain obscure but powerful attitudes spread persistently through the masses of Europe during the last three

or four years. The strength of the United States was adequately demonstrated by the war. Every one admired it and was thrilled to contemplate the adolescence of a new world power—sinewy, youthful and generous. The post-war period sustained and extended this power. With its fleets and its money, with its bankers exploring and exploiting every corner of the globe, the United States stands out as sovereign arbiter of our time. Following Assyria and Egypt, Rome and Byzantium, Spain, France, and Britain, it sends forth countless hordes bearing half the gold of the entire world as a treasure, as a weapon, and as a menace. The spectacle begins to strike terror. Europe is worried, and even while cringing, it spies out the errors and shortcomings of the young giant. One sentiment, profounder than all others, is still shadowy and hidden. Yet though it is but vaguely manifested, it already affects the actions and dominates the imagination of Europe. It has done no more, however, since Europe has not defined its attitude logically; its real opinions have not yet been extricated from an amorphous mass of notions, misstatements, and hunches. Land of opulence, declare some; land of democracy, say others; again they cry, land of federalism and pacifism. But all their sonorous and uncertain phrases hold little weight when opposed to this one sharp emotion. A hateful fear of the United States is spreading and may eventually submerge all other feelings.

Such an attitude is not without its inconveniences and dangers. If firmly embedded, it is liable to distract Europe to such an extent as to make it oblivious to its own essential interests. It may create a barrier between Europe and America which would be very difficult to surmount and would divide the white races into two hostile camps, incapable of mutual understanding or collaboration. At a time when tired and bleeding Europe is most in need of encouragement and optimism, nothing would dishearten it more, or lead more effectively to a fatalistic acceptance of the worst disasters. Aided by human inertia it would quietly build up a most deplorable situation whereby it would precipitate the very results it pretends to foresee and avoid. Nothing would arouse the United States more strongly against Europe than the sense of being misunderstood and hated. There is no more peremptory reason, no better excuse, for treating another nation inconsiderately or even brutally than the knowledge that such treatment is expected and that the expectation has given rise to many uncharitable opinions. This severe and cynical judgment, which not a few Europeans hold against the United States, can cause worry and distraction in Europe, and can irritate America by belittling its sense of greatness and of moral nobility and by questioning its respect for other nations and its taste for friendly relations. It can do no good, but the evil it conceals —as yet barely discernible—is infinite. And therefore it must be ceaselessly combated. It must seem absurd and despicable to persons who have come to the United States as citizens, guests, or friends; who have felt the warm, rich, generous, sturdy pulse of life which beats through the forty-eight states from Atlantic to Pacific; who have found hospitality there, and affection, as well as all they love best: beauty, love of beauty (not exactly as in Europe, but not so different), activity, delight in action, greatness, nobleness, ambition, and a passion for the immense, the infinite, the perfect, and the sublime. No one can fail to be struck by the abundance of good will and of praiseworthy intentions manifested everywhere. Undeniably, nothing is finished; no goal has been attained. There are no eternal monuments, for such are never found until the idea or achievement which they commemorate has long become a thing of the past. The biggest and handsomest structures of the new world are its railway stations and ports, places where one goes when going somewhere else. To that end they were built. One day they will be destroyed to give place to larger terminals or for some other purpose, but today they exist; and in their vastness, utility and perfect adaptation they are beautiful. Similarly, throughout the country, beauty has assumed no final form, but gleams from innumerable spangles. One must be stubborn, indeed, or else hypocritical, not to concede to the new world a powerful allurement, not to admit the headiness and exhilaration of its life. To see nothing but an octopus, or a cry-baby, or the working-out of a doctrine, is to belittle strangely this wilderness made into a nation through the indomitable will and industry of the white race.

How is it possible to neglect or misunderstand this extraordinary achievement which lies beneath our very eyes and which is all the more thrilling since legend and reality are still close at hand and constantly mingling? We have an unparalleled opportunity to observe the incubation and efflorescence of a new civilization, the offshoot of our own —and we would seem to reject that pleasure, to spurn that instruction offered for the first time to a humanity endowed with books, machines, libraries and newspapers enough for recording and assimilating so gigantic and slow-moving a phenomenon. The pleasure of understanding and knowing should alone suffice to make us more patient and discerning. In the formation and development of the United States we are to see the operation and testing of all the principal forces which Europe has worked out since the sixteenth century, the most powerful and renowned mechanisms invented by Mediterranean and Atlantic civilizations. Perhaps the most notorious of these is democracy—what might be called the great formula for coagulating masses of people and keeping them compact. In earlier times men could be held together in peace by the mention of God and His power, or of the power of one individual; that sufficed to intimidate or bewitch them—at any rate to maintain amity. But for the last two centuries, the masses of mankind have been ensnared, frightened, or charmed, solely by their own powers and numbers. This alone delights and thrills them. Talk of anything else makes them belligerent. They have been given so exalted an opinion of themselves, and have become so accustomed to relying upon themselves, that now all wisdom, power, insight, and even good seems vested in numbers. Democracy reduces all problems to arithmetic and all decisions to a matter of computation. If nine-tenths of the people vote for a law, it is supremely just; if six-tenths vote for it, that law is adequately just; but if only three-tenths vote affirmatively, it is iniquitous. All forms of democracy may exist—aristocratic, as formerly in Venice and in England; royalist, as was the case in Poland; communist, as in ancient Sparta—all gradations may be adapted to democracy, provided the principle of numbers is respected and the crowd, the majority, the greatest number remains final arbiter. A product of mathematics, the multiplication table, and the diffusion of primary education, democracy has made sensational progress. One would have said in 1918 that it had conquered the world. Its era of greatest success was opened by the American experiment, which refuted all accepted theories and revealed to the eyes of astonished philosophers and amazed populaces that a democracy could be established in an immense territory whose population was to exceed many millions. The American experiment was decisive. It exercised the most profound influence on that other major experiment, the French Revolution, to which, on the whole, it was superior, since it realized a solid and more durable achievement with less glory and less bloodshed. From 1776 to 1926 the United States remained a great democratic republic without excess or weakness. It advanced with regular strides, apparently in step with its principles as originally defined. The holy land of democracy, one might say. At the present time, when this doctrine, after seeming to triumph over all its ancient enemies, is attacked by a new adversary—communism—which substitutes faith in a special class and in physical exertion for faith in numbers, America is the sheltering rock of democracy, safe it would seem from all assaults of Bolshevism and socialism.

However, the United States· is far from being the land of one pervasive idea. The philosophers who explain all phases of life in America in terms of a democratic instinct are quite off the track. Democracy was made to serve here, just as various other principles and rules of action were employed when it seemed advisable. At the Constitutional Convention in 1787, when opposing factions were evenly matched, and Washington and Franklin watched each other with misgivings, what policy was finally adopted? Not that of majority rule, which seemed too obscure, too indeterminate and dangerous. A compromise was adopted; the American Nation was built not on a theory of majority rule, or obedience to higher authority, but on one of the harmonious interworking of separate interests. The Constitution of 1787 is not the masterpiece of wisdom or logic it is often said to be. On the contrary, it discreetly refrains from considering a good many problems and courageously avoids broaching certain grave difficulties. The delegates realized that, first of all, a working agreement was necessary which would permit concerted action while still allowing a certain latitude to divergencies of desire, intention, custom, and tradition. So the new nation was created with a central national government whose functions were strictly limited and whose will was sovereign only in a restricted domain. Nor could the majority impose its will everywhere; thanks to the states, some measure of autonomy and self-assertion was left to local groups, individuals, and special interests. The organization which these eighteenth century patriots organized and anticipated is both democratic and federative. It corresponds fairly well to Proudhon's definition: *"Foedus,* federation, from the Latin *foedus,* genitive *foederis,* i.e., pact, contract, treaty, convention, alliance, etc., is a convention by which one or more chief townships, groups of townships, or states, bind themselves reciprocally and equally to each other for one or several particular ends, whose burden then rests specially and exclusively upon the delegates of the federation. The essence and character of the federal contract—to which I call the reader's attention—is that by this system the contracting chiefs, townships, counties, or states not only bind themselves reciprocally and mutually to each other, but reserve individually, in forming the pact, more rights, liberty, authority, ownership, than they give up. In sum, the federal system is the opposite of the hierarchy or administrative and governmental centralization which characterizes imperial democracies, constitutional monarchies, and republics." [2] Where democracy tends to strengthen the ties of a nation and intermingle its citizens, federalism allows play, space, ventilation, and gives a large degree of latitude to the individual. He is not always obliged to yield or conform to the will of the majority. That is why the French Revolution, desiring a pure democracy, refused to accept the principles of federalism and even looked upon the word as treasonable. On the contrary, the United States esteemed both systems equally, employed them side by side for 140 years, proving thereby that it was more interested in concrete utility than in doctrinal purity, and was less

[2] Proudhon, *Du Principe Fédératif.*

interested in political consistency than in employing all means at its disposal to facilitate and sustain life on the new continent.

The United States has outgrown democratic principles and strict federalism as well. It abandoned them, not impatiently or disparagingly, but through a need for action, and thanks to a fortuitous independence of mind which is never entirely obsessed by logic or theory. People have busied themselves in vain to find the United States a strong proof of this or that principle. The doctrinaires of three centuries have eagerly examined this young race for subjects of dissertation and argument. They found some at first, but generally ended in hopeless entanglement; because further study demonstrates that principles and doctrines have been used as supports or stimuli, but never as limitations to activity, desires, or aspirations. There is no dominant or constant method; no fixed goal except to live and become greater; no unvaried formula except never to stop, whether times are good or bad, but to keep on, to be aggressive, to forge ahead. This also explains why strangers are fascinated, and are tempted to stay and work here, becoming imbued with the country's nervous enthusiasm. The United States will never be understood or esteemed and loved by any one who is seeking for strict logic in its activities or expects to find in its people and their attitudes that rational perfection which Europe thinks it possesses—and has perhaps attained.

It is this race, throbbing with life, which we have tried to study in these chapters. We make no pretensions to an exhaustive analysis of American life in detail. That is beyond our powers and perhaps beyond any human powers. We have tried in all humility to show what principles and doctrines have served to develop a great nation, and what forces—often obscure and shapeless—have employed these formulae for their own expansion. Today, when the world is trying to resolve some of the thorniest problems of organization, it should be of some interest to see how the United States adapted both democracy and federalism to its purposes, and what benefits resulted. This is not a theoretical or imaginative discussion, but a study of the United States in action, of its utilization of doctrines and ideas, of its personality, and of the increasing fullness which distinguishes in ways of its own this gradually maturing civilization.

The American experiment instructs us as to the functioning of democracy, its value as a mode of living, its adaptability and chances of enduring. It arrests our attention, our curiosity, and our solicitude, since it is the only federation known to have extended over a whole continent and to have lasted more than a century. But most of all, the American experiment attracts us by the richness, the peculiar quality, the novelty of that strange accident, the birth of a nation and its development to the highest degree of terrestrial power in less than two centuries. Far more than any theory or thesis, that immediate reality, so ardent and so full of promise, fascinates us.

What a delight it would be to add a little to that youthful nation's knowledge and appreciation of itself; and what still greater delight to persuade a few Europeans that there is much strength, as well as wisdom, to be gained by being disinterested enough to comprehend.

CHAPTER II

THE AMERICAN RACE (1607-1801)

It is generally believed in Europe that the United States has no past. This opinion is one of the principal causes of error in our judgment. It leads us to see an edifice without fundamental solidity, a civilization without tradition, whereas the United States has behind it not only its own past, but the vast ancient heritage of Anglo-Saxons, Latins, and Indo-Europeans as well. The former is not extensive —covering only three centuries—but it was so crowded with events, it followed so unusual and individual a course, that its influence, its true duration, is really much greater than the passage of years would indicate. The conquest of a virgin continent; the founding of a new group of states; rivalry with the most prosperous peoples of Europe; an immense and unexpected victory which suddenly gave the young nation a prestige equal to that of the most prosperous monarchies—such factors are striking, and are comparable to the greatest events of history. Like Asia at the time of Alexander, and Europe during the great invasions, the new world lived hard during its first century of colonization. That pregnant era has left an indelible imprint upon the present. Alone among Western nations, the United States has maintained an eighteenth-century constitution which it reveres almost as much as the Ten Commandments. It studies, emulates, and zealously perpetuates the past of which it is so proud, and wherein it sees its early title to glory. No other country has so many historical and genealogical societies. Certain of these, notably the American Historical

Association, have attained country-wide renown. No other people today can boast of so thriving and brilliant a school of historians. The nation is proud of them, both on their own merits and as the apostles of a brilliant epoch.

Furthermore, an eighteenth-century formula is frequently cited as basis for its present policies. Washington's Farewell Address still remains the official injunction against collaboration with Europe. The civilization which is thrust upon the immigrants, the Americanism which is preached by politicians and patriotic societies, is still the civilization of the Fathers—a seventeenth and eighteenth century doctrine. Those two centuries bequeathed to the nation a vast store of customs, of material, intellectual, and moral tendencies, which still seems essential to its development. All this goes to make up what may be rather inadequately termed the American race. Any such word as "culture" or "patriotism" is too narrow and fails to designate a phenomenon which has material as well as spiritual effects. "Tradition" is too intellectual, too negative. It disguises, rather than reveals, the active and creative nature of American life. We spoke of "race" because the term comes closest to the essence of the heritage. We do not mean that the seventeenth and eighteenth centuries created a uniform type of American, but they did establish a set of peculiarities common to the entire country, affecting body and mind, arising from material circumstances (colonization and primitive life) and from historical developments (status of Britain's American Colonies, the Constitution, etc.). It would be difficult to understand the structure of American society, or even the mentality of the individual, without a precise conception of antecedents. We shall try to give this succinctly, but without omissions.

When speaking of colonies, a Frenchman visualized trading posts which a nation had established for its own commercial, military, and political advantages. Such was the origin of nearly all French colonies—particularly in Canada. The State organized the colonies, developed and protected them, in its own interests. In Canadian history up to 1763 we constantly find traces of French patriotism, the intervention of the French State, the resources of His Majesty.

It was quite different with England's North American colonies in the seventeenth century. The English State did seek to turn them to the best possible account, but the colonists followed their own paths without bothering much about the mother country. They had left home not as knights errant, nor in search of the golden fleece, but purely to avoid persecution, to find a less unbearable type of life than in England where the ruling powers were so harsh in their antagonism. The dissenters who founded New England obtained capital in London. All initiative came from their group, not from the government which, without being hostile, was content to ignore them. The thousands of English who emigrated to North America between 1630 and 1700 (from 200 to 1,500 left annually for Virginia alone) were almost all exiles, refugees and malcontents. At that time the economic situation in England was very unsatisfactory: wages were low, farmers and workmen were suffering and consequently quite willing to try their luck in a new land. Catholics persecuted by the Anglicans and Puritans; Puritans harassed by Anglicans; Anglicans and Royalists routed by Cromwell; Irish maltreated by the Protector following their resistance; and Cromwell's soldiers themselves after the Restoration—such were the varied groups of emigrants who shipped to America and whose loyalty and devotion to the crown was obviously not excessive. The mother country retained so little hold on them that they sometimes refused to fight for her, as for instance, the Virginians in

1695-96. At that time the French were threatening to invade the province of New York. The English government demanded that all the colonies should unite in defense of the one in danger. The Virginia burgesses replied that such a course was impossible, claiming that the enrollment of troops for service in New York would so alarm the young men as to lead them to desert the colony, and would even prompt many of them to abandon wives and children. No effective assistance was obtained from them. Many of the immigrants in Virginia were poor servants, indentured to their masters for seven years, thus exchanging misery for servitude. Likewise in New England, the Puritans formed only a small minority. In Massachusetts about the middle of the seventeenth century only two out of every fifteen immigrants belonged to the established church. The other thirteen were even hostile to it. In preference to joining the church they made considerable sacrifices, such as renouncing their political rights. So it is apparent that the English colonies were originally neither a national creation nor, properly speaking, a vast religious enterprise, although both elements were present. It has been said with more accuracy that "the American colonies in their infancy were largely commercial undertakings engaged in by companies and groups of individuals." However, this statement must not be understood nor explained by the often misused formula of reducing everything to terms of economic phenomena. This factor is important and indicates the motives of those who organized the English expeditions to America, and the conditions which impelled such emigration. But the actual departure of emigrants and their definitive establishment in the new world cannot be accounted for without taking into consideration another intellectual and emotional factor—the state of uncertainty. This heroic and audacious wager in which the colonists staked life and possessions on

the promise of an unknown continent, tempted Sir Walter
Raleigh; likewise it attracted the Puritans; nor did it have
any less appeal for the poorest farmer who crossed the turbulent Atlantic. This great migration which peopled North
America is in no way comparable to the barbarian invasions
of Europe, though they marked too the overrunning and conquest of a continent. The Barbarians descended upon a civilized world, whose wealth was known and catalogued in advance; they forsook arid, inhospitable plains for a meridional
climate and fertile, sunny, well-worked land. Their slow and
irresistible advance was based on calculations, certainty, and
a kind of ferocious prudence. On the contrary, the conquest
of North America by the white race was curiously intangible and dreamlike. What did those poor folk know of the
Vinland they were setting out for? A vague, fascinating
imagery filled their minds; but what did they really know,
save that an immense waste of ocean must be traversed to
reach—more hardships? That absorbing spectacle of dangers
wittingly faced, that open-eyed plunge into the abyss, that
faith in an unknown land, is one of the most vividly imaginative phenomena to be found in the history of humanity. It reveals the extraordinary courage and the peculiar
intellectual qualities of these hardy pioneers.

To choose America in the seventeenth century was to
risk all, without the guarantee or reassurance of the past.
To be sure, the Europe they left behind was a frightful
nightmare. It still reeked with the havoc and destruction
wrought by the religious wars: England was smouldering
from the conflagrations started by the Wars of the Roses;
France was burdened with the interminable conflicts between Catholic and Protestant; Germany had been ravaged
by the Thirty Years' War; and throughout Europe the
seething turmoil of hatred and strife centered about the
House of Hapsburg. The continent had never before known

such disorder. The Renaissance had brought about an excessive enervation, stimulating men's daring, driving them to the limit of human endurance, raising insurmountable barriers between them—as can be appreciated by recollecting that Calvin and Rabelais were contemporaries, that Milton followed abruptly on Shakespeare, that Locke wrote while Bossuet was preaching. The Reformation caused each man to face an issue which went far beyond religion, since fortune, happiness, liberty and life, all depended upon his choice. The Catholics were persecuted in England; in France they were the aggressors. The sole idea upon which all agreed was the right to hound one's religious adversaries. The most ardent reformers were the most intolerant. When the Puritans got the opportunity they proscribed Catholics, Quakers, and Anglicans alike, to clear the ground for their church. Finally, the brusque changes caused by the adoption of Roman law in many parts of Europe, led to a new confusion and to much bitter conflict, since they affected the everyday life and immediate interests of the individual. Difficulties, fears, and dangers lay at every turn. None the less, omens of a new order of things could be seen in the magnificent works of art produced by England, France, and Italy, in the glory of the French Monarchy, with its wit and classic literature, and in the increasingly solid and prosperous British Empire. As the arts flourished and prosperity increased, the parties, sects, and factions fought more intensely: for the victor gained spoils of untold value —as witness the Amsterdam of 1640, the Versailles of 1660, and the London of 1700.

To withdraw from the game when such stakes were involved, to renounce what they already possessed or looked forward to, and to take a primitive continent in exchange was certainly audacious. It was a long and perilous voyage. The mortality on board was fearful. One ship is said to have lost 130 out of 180 passengers. A traveler of the times, William Copps, describes conditions: "Betwixt decks there can hardlie a man fetch his breath by reason there ariseth such a funke in the night that it causes putrifecation of blood and breedeth disease much like the plague."

Notwithstanding, the cost of passage was exorbitant—a minimum of six pounds sterling—much more than the poor folk of the seventeenth century could afford. But even if they did scrape together the passage money and escape the terrors of the voyage, there remained the hardships of the first months in America. The shores of the wilderness, rockbound, wooded, or swampy, offered meager hospitality. Massachusetts or Virginia, it made little difference. The Northern cold led to pulmonary complaints, while the Southern heat caused fever and debility. Over half the Mayflower colonists succumbed in the first year. In Virginia, five out of six servants died in a similar period. This was so well known that all chroniclers of the times mention it. Molina declared in 1613 that of 300 settlers, diseases had claimed one half. Evelyn wrote: Old Virginians affirm that during the first years of the colony, the toll of maladies was 100,000—which seems exaggerated. In addition there was the dread of famine and Indians. If the New Englanders, during their first winter, had not found and pillaged the corn of the savages, they could hardly have survived. It is said that 1,800 persons starved in Virginia in 1636. The Indians of the regions which are now the United States and Canada seem to have been less civilized than those further south, although not lacking in belligerency. However, the Puritans were quite ready to defend themselves—and not with Evangelical mildness. Moreover, they had the good fortune to get their first settlements well established at a time when the Indian tribes, decimated by plague, were quite demoralized. The Indians of Virginia resisted more stubbornly and often jeopardized the very existence of the colonies. In October, 1609, there were five hundred settlers, but by May, 1610, disease, famine, and Indian depredations had reduced the number to sixty. Such were conditions in Virginia during the first thirty years; subsequently they improved. But the climate was neither pleasant nor salutary for Caucasians—which is one reason for the introduction and rapid spread of the negro throughout the Southern colonies.

The colonists were not properly equipped to face such hardships and dangers. Separated from the mother country by a hundred days of ocean, they received supplies most irregularly. What they did succeed in getting was generally sold by the ship captains at exorbitant prices. During most of the seventeenth century, the English government, absorbed by the quarrels between King and Parliament, and by the Revolution, gave no real help to the emigrants, who were forced to rely principally on themselves. The companies which had fostered the expeditions still gave assistance, but they were not willing to make substantial investments, and their zeal was wavering. Moreover, the colonists would have frowned on too great solicitude on the part of the companies or the state, being jealous of their independence and eager for gain. The Puritans of Massachusetts distrusted the England from which their faith had been banned. The Southern planters were latently and then openly in conflict with the mother land, whose conception of their rôle was quite different from their own. London looked upon Virginia as a source of the raw materials needed for its industries and navy—lumber, cereals, glass, etc. The Virginians, finding these products to be but moderately remunerative, preferred to cultivate tobacco, which speedily brought them wealth. Both James I and Charles I tried to discourage this tendency, urging the planters not to persist in the cultivation and use of tobacco, "an evil habit of late times," an exaggerated luxury, a useless expenditure and a vice. They failed; but Charles II, through commercial ordinances which permitted exports of tobacco to England alone, very nearly succeeded in ruining the trade.

Although exposed to a ruinous climate, to Indian attacks, and famine, and receiving little aid from the remote and meddlesome central government, Britain's North American colonies were none the less successful. By the end of sixty years their progress was so marked that all the outcasts, persecuted, and malcontents of Europe aspired to a refuge among these prospering emigrants. A large group of French Huguenots, driven from their country by the revocation of the Edict of Nantes, went to America, where they established themselves in the province of New York and at Charleston. Many German dissenters did the same; and likewise the English Quakers, who found such freedom as they would never have dared even to hope for in England. English America already had its own personality, distinct from that of England. It is hard to delineate, but some traits are clear. Though loyalty to the English government was not much in evidence during the seventeenth century, still English civilization reigned supreme. Every one spoke English and used the commercial and social customs of England. No one had yet thought of separation. The original characteristics were quite unconscious, the results of circumstance and environment. First of all, each individual had a much more important rôle than he might have played in England. Land had little value unless cultivated. Workmen were essential to prosperity. All kinds of sacrifices were made to obtain them. They were paid four or five times as much as at home. At the expiring of their indentured service they were given lands. And still there were not enough. They could not be forced; they had to be attracted. From the very outset people found in America a land extraordinarily favorable to their individual development. Every man who was physically and morally fit could make a place for himself. In Virginia a frank and almost brutal individualism was the rule; the same spirit in New England seemed imbued with a mystic, religious, and democratic fervor. To the Puritan immigrants law and society were but tools to enforce the supremacy of God. His Providence was ever present, and no man should make a single move not in conformity with His wishes. This was the bulwark of individualism, providing an incentive to build limited communities ruled by the will of God—which is to say, by the will of the strongest or the most adroit. Thus what later became known as the democratic spirit was already manifesting itself both in the importance of the individual and in the tendency to form compact groups ruled, not by a man, but by the will of God as interpreted and defined by an élite or majority. A new concept was introduced, and the sovereign lost power. The pilgrims of the Mayflower drew up and signed a social contract to govern the choice of magistrates and the enactment of laws. This was natural to them, as similar documents were habitually drawn up by dissenting churches. Custom and religion watched over the cradle of the English colonists' first great democratic act.

However, the democratic tendency which later struck the French "philosophers" of the eighteenth century so forcibly was not the only characteristic of the Anglo-American civilization during the seventeenth and eighteenth centuries; neither was it the most important nor the most original. America, whose Indians were so close to the heart of Rousseau and of Chateaubriand, also possessed social conditions approximating the "state of nature." It would be wrong to think that the moral proclivities of the white race in the new world were the same as those which the great Genevan attributes to men who are free of the social, emotional, and intellectual servitude arising from complex human relationships. When the colonists moved away from the coast to explore and cultivate the interior, they found themselves dispersed over an immense tract and virtually released from every bond of society. But their contact with nature, far from being a long poem of love and peace, was a constant struggle, a perpetual danger: wild beasts, Indians, weather, and rivers were all hostile; nature and the elements were inimical. The settlers were alone. Frequently they even had to make their own tools. Such were the frontier conditions which, for nearly three centuries, were to exercise the most profound influence upon the individual and the groups in America. The struggles against the wilderness were the most trying and dangerous between 1630 and 1780; for thereafter, pioneering, without losing the thrill of conquest, was rendered less perilous through better equipment and weapons. But during the early period the settlers had to develop and expend an amazing amount of energy. Still they lost nothing by it. Purified by solitude, tested and strengthened by effort and sacrifice, ennobled by triumphs of which they were justly proud, the Americans grew to be one of the most powerful races in the world. Trapped between sea and virgin forest, the American received an education which would have made the Roman envious. Massachusetts farmers, weary of cultivating arid lands wrested from the wilderness, took to the sea, where for many years their ships plowed the North Atlantic, undismayed by fogs, tempests, and turbulent waters. Such new conditions, a life at once so full and original, a comradeship with forest and ocean, could not fail to produce a great people and engender a fecund civilization. By developing human personality, the American wilderness made the initial and essential contribution to the formation of powerful aristocracies.

Virginia—the oldest colony—was the first, and most skilled, in developing a local nobility. The class was not, as is too often stated, an offshoot of the English aristocracy. The number of English nobles who emigrated to America was very small, and its members did not prosper. The Virginian aristocracy was born in Virginia. One might say that it sprang from the soil as a by-product of tobacco. A large majority of the Virginian immigrants came from the servant class in England: poor, honest folk, as a rule, often of good extraction. There was also an important contingent drawn from the English bourgeoisie. Virginian aristocracy developed out of these two groups. It was primarily composed of wealthy men who became in time veritable lords of the land.

Tobacco cultivation was enormously remunerative between 1612 and 1629, and made a good many people wealthy. But as tobacco exhausted the soil very rapidly, big profits could be procured only by the possession of great domains. Consequently many growers were obliged to drop back into the ranks of the people. Those who could organize and manage vast plantations increased their resources and power. Virginia possessed no roads or convenient ways of communication other than rivers and inlets which, fortunately, were deep and numerous. There were no towns of importance, each plantation being a center in itself. The growers sold their tobacco directly to the exporters, who often duped the smaller men. When the commercial restrictions of Charles I reduced the value of tobacco, many of the settlers faced starvation. The wealthy sold their product as best they could and awaited better times.

With the seventeenth century, Virginia saw a rapid influx of negro slaves which England, having at last built a navy large enough to cope with the Dutch, imported from Africa. This lowered the cost of manual labor and caused the poor whites still further impoverishment. As a result, there was considerable emigration from Virginia to more hospitable territories. Remaining behind were the seigniorial lords who ruled proudly, a middle class rich and courageous enough to maintain a certain independence, the slaves, and a few poor whites, abject and helpless, despised even by the negroes. The evolution of that aristocracy is so curious and neglected as to warrant some scrutiny; it enables us to observe how a kind of feudal system was evolved. Select, for example, the illustrious Byrd family. William Byrd, the first of the name, living in the second half of the seventeenth century, was a resourceful merchant. He grew tobacco for export. In return he imported rum from the Barbadoes, as well as sugar and ginger. Then he brought over white servants from England and disposed of them at a high figure. Writing to one of his English agents he said, "If you can send me six, eight or ten servants by the first boat, at not too high a price, I will be able to buy you first-grade tobacco. It is barely obtainable except in exchange for servants." Byrd likewise sold various commodities to other settlers, such as cotton, glass, lead, medicines, and he bartered with the Indians for furs. He was thrifty, even to the extent of sending his old wigs to London for renovation. When he dabbled in politics, he did so for profit. He held several lucrative offices. By the time he died, his estate had grown to 26,000 acres.

His son, William Byrd II, was also a business man, though not so sharp; he was more imaginative, occasionally careless and imprudent. His ventures were often highly speculative and not always successful. Though politics was not profitable, he took it up for his amusement; he liked to be of service and to figure in the public eye. Thus he became one of the Commissioners selected to determine the boundary between Virginia and Carolina. His writing shows talent and wit.

William Byrd III had still less business instinct. He could not manage his fortune and at one time was so burdened with debts that he very nearly had to sell his estate. But, at length, by mortgaging a hundred and fifty-nine slaves and his silver plate, he overcame his difficulties. William Byrd III was considered a great gambler and racing man of weak though brilliant character. In the French and Indian Wars he served as colonel and was considered a good soldier. He was a kind father and a man of great wit. Exhausted by his adventures and harassed by financial difficulties, he died in 1777.

At that period there was no more brilliant aristocracy in the world than that of Virginia. Even Europe was impressed by the society which produced Washington, Commander-in-Chief of the Revolutionary armies, Jefferson, who drew up the Declaration of Independence, Patrick Henry, one of the principal instigators of the Rebellion, and the noisy Lees, so zealous in behalf of liberty. These gentlemen owned splendid houses with delightful furnishings which are still admired today, carriages, and an infinite number of servants. Their homes were veritable towns which could supply every need. And finally—the supreme luxury—they were philosophically inclined, and were not at all antagonistic to democracy, as they considered themselves its natural leaders. In such an atmosphere the ablest minds of the American Revolution were born and bred.

Conditions in New England, though different, possessed a number of like characteristics. A decidedly original civilization had arisen here also. The first decades of its history present a rare example of absolute theocracy. The elements of the colony were far from homogeneous—speculative

English capitalists and Puritan settlers. But within a short time the former class was squeezed out and the latter assumed control of a government established to suit their own preferences. The civil and judicial organs of Massachusetts had been designed for trading posts and were controlled by London bankers and merchants. But the management was soon transferred to America where, in the hands of Puritan clergy and magistrates, it became the fulcrum of a new government. To participate in the election of magistrates one had to be a freeman, a title which was conferred only on regular members of the official church of Massachusetts. This Puritan church was known in New England as Congregational. But the majority of the colonists were not members in good standing. While not opposed to its principles, a great many people refused to submit to certain disagreeable requirements. It was not enough to accept the doctrines of the Congregational Church and to desire to lead a holy life in communion with the church, but each person was expected to have heard some personal, intimate, and tangible call of God, whereby he had been persuaded to acknowledge his sins and to desire regeneration. His conversion had to be publicly confessed by the proselyte, who appeared before the whole congregation to describe in minute detail how he had felt the action of the Holy Spirit upon him. Discouraged by such regulations, seventy-five or eighty out of every hundred colonists preferred to forgo participation in the government, so that a very small class was left in a position of dominance. It becomes obvious that Massachusetts was actually ruled by a very few men despite its apparent democracy, when we note how continuously the principal members of the council held office. Bradford was assistant to the governor uninterruptedly from 1632 to 1679. Then he was elected governor and occupied that position until the dissolution of the govern-

ment established under the first Massachusetts charter in
1684. Between 1630 and his death in 1648, Winthrop was
governor, deputy governor, or assistant. Dudley retained
one function or another during his whole sojourn in the
colony. Endicott was governor every year but one between
1649 and 1664. This aristocracy was quite distinct from that
of Virginia, where possessions and financial prosperity were
the basis of all honors and privileges. In Massachusetts
throughout the seventeenth century the ruling group was
primarily religious in character. Among its most illustrious
members were the Mathers, all Congregationalist ministers,
who worked indefatigably to strengthen theocratic power in
the new world, and who waged an incessant battle against
heterodoxy and sin. Richard Mather was born in Lan-
cashire in 1596. Intelligent and sober, he prayed to God
thus: "My heart relented with tears—that God would not
deny me an heart to bless him, & not blaspheme him, that
is so holy, just, and good; though I should be excluded
from his presence, & go down into everlasting darkness &
discomfort."

He received a good education, and was a clergyman in
England until his Puritan convictions obliged him to seek
refuge in the new world, where his fine qualities were much
admired and gained him a position of influence and prestige.
Four of his six children became ministers—the third, Increase, being numbered among the colony's most distinguished citizens. Like his father he was a zealous worker, a
lover of books, and a man of profoundly mystical disposition.
His son represents him to us as a sort of visionary who constantly received forebodings and divinations of the future.
"He had for diverse Lords-Days," wrote Cotton Mather,
"made the Death of that Miserable King [the Indian monarch, Philip] a Petition which in his Public Prayers he
somewhat Enlarged upon. But on one Lords-Day he quite

forgot it; for which Forgetfulness I will remember, that I heard him wondering at, and Blaming of, himself in the Evening. However, he was more Satisfied, when a few Hours after, there came to Town the Tidings, That before *That* Lords-Day, the *Thing Was Accomplished.*"

Throughout all his biblical preoccupations, Mather conserved an ardent though gloomy conception of life. When the Indian wars led the settlers to massacre the savages pitilessly, he demanded publicly that they should put to death the son of the leading chief, a child of nine who had been captured with his mother. He explained that although David had spared the life of little Hadad, greater severity would have been to more advantage and the colonists should profit by his example. As a matter of fact the people of Massachusetts disregarded his exhortation and sold the child into slavery. Mather's rôle was of considerable importance when the Hanoverians became established upon the throne of England and gave a new charter to Massachusetts. He exerted all his influence in behalf of the former theocratic constitution. Though unsuccessful, he had the consolation of seeing all the functionaries chosen from among his friends and in accordance with his wishes. This relieved somewhat his bitterness at the curtailment of the clergy's political supremacy, which the Crown had in effect destroyed, replacing the old system of suffrage by one based on land tenure. As President of Harvard, Mather continued to maintain his social and political eminence until the eighteenth century. Cotton Mather, the next in line, was hampered by the decline of the Church and by his own excessive piety. Haunted by the idea of hell, by hate and fear of the Devil, by the conviction that Satan was everywhere seeking the ruin of souls, Cotton Mather inaugurated the most curious attack of nervous and mystical hysteria which the new world has ever known. Having come to America to serve God and to found a state under His guidance, the Puritans lived in great dread of the Devil. Their hardships and their wild environment prepared them to accept the weirdest tales without surprise. In 1692 it happened that strange things were taking place in Salem. Children, afflicted with ailments of apparently preternatural origin, accused certain persons of having bewitched them. A superstitious panic soon gripped the entire region and spread from there throughout Massachusetts. On Mather's advice the governor organized a special tribunal of the worthiest Puritans to examine these cases! It reviewed several hundred in all, convicting and hanging a number of unfortunates. Others died under torture. George Burroughs, a preacher of renown who had studied at Harvard, was one of the victims. He met death with great dignity in the midst of a populace which was hesitant but feverishly excited. When the governor lost heart in this procedure, Mather's struggles against the Devil became still more impassioned. A poor woman of Boston, Margaret Rule, who was persecuted by the Evil One, was next the object of his attention. Except for an occasional bit of rum, he deprived her of food and drink; he prayed beside her, and during her attacks, he examined her body with a minuteness and audacity that would have shocked all but a saint. Gradually the public began to feel that all this was being carried too far. A reaction against witchcraft trials set in. The Mathers were sharply attacked, and the Puritan aristocracy lost many important offices. Increase was forced out of Harvard, and Cotton, despite his zeal, his industry, and his enormous erudition, never held government office. Mournful events beset his last years. Married three times, the father of fifteen children, and the author of several hundred works (sermons, treatises, etc.) he burnt himself out with his vehemence. He would prepare for all important occasions by fasts and all-night vigils; he was constantly awaiting God's instructions and watching for opportunities to repulse the wiles of Satan. Before taking a wife he prayed and fasted. All great events in his life were characterized by trances and mystic ecstasies. The Angels brought him counsel and succor, although, according to his journal, he felt bound "To *Conceal* with all prudent Secrecy whatever *Extraordinary Things* I may perceive done for mee, by the *Angels,* who love *Secrecy* in their Administrations. I do now believe," he added, "That some Great Things are to be done for mee by the *Angels* of God." Despite his queer ways and inordinate vanity, Mather was a good man with good intentions. At times he succeeded, as in his advocacy of inoculation, which was then regarded with much suspicion. But more often his ardent temperament was a handicap to him, and his aristocratic convictions, amidst a society which was about done with the ascendancy of the ecclesiastical coterie, denied him the position which his intellectual qualities merited. A few days before Mather's death, Benjamin Franklin is reported to have visited him. On taking leave, he was conducted through a gloomy corridor. Suddenly the old pastor cried, "Stoop!" Young Franklin, not quite comprehending this exhortation to humility, marched along and promptly bumped his head against a projecting beam. Whereupon Mather assured him that there were times in life when he would find stooping an admirable means of avoiding trouble.

Thus before the theocratic aristocracy vanished it gave a final succinct word of advice to the generation which was to replace it in guiding the destiny of the colonies. From the early eighteenth century until the Revolution, the leaders in social and political life were largely drawn from a wealthy and refined merchant class, whose good graces were sought by the English government. But the merchants tended to hold aloof, preferring to retain their contact with their own people. This commercial and financial "nobility" dominated New England from 1700 to 1770; and today those old Boston families which still survive, such as the Lowells, Otises, Cabots, and Saltonstalls, show distinct traces of their former power and solidarity. What a contrast between them and the settlers along the western frontiers, who were independent and democratic, and who rivaled the Indians in cunning and ruggedness. This upper class was not strictly provincial. It also produced centers of refinement in New York and Charleston. Moreover class distinctions were quite willingly recognized and maintained throughout the coast colonies. At Harvard students were seated according to social position. The future revolutionary tribune of Massachusetts, Adams, was placed fourteenth in a class of twenty-four. Conditions were the same farther south, although there the wealthy were plantation owners, in contrast to the merchants and bankers of the North. Many of their names are still familiar: Massigault, Laurens, Rutledge, in South Carolina; Ludlow, Carter, Randolph, Fairfax, Blair, in Virginia; Van Rensselaer, Phillipse, Van Cortlandt, Livingston, the landed gentry of New York State; Van Dam, Cruger, Walton, Ludlow, in New York City. Even in Pennsylvania it was said of the rich Quakers: "Through the possession of the finest lands, and the exporting of provisions to the Antilles, they established imposing fortunes. Their leaders managed by masterly organization to dominate the colony for many years, and administered it to the advantage of the Quaker aristocracy of the three eastern counties."

It would be inaccurate to compare these upper classes of eighteenth-century America to the English or continental nobility. The fact that there were no actual titles must be taken into account. While class distinctions were real, they were never officially or systematically encouraged, nor acknowledged as an end in themselves. It was a living aristocracy, amorphous, perhaps incapable of crystallization. The doors were always open to fortune and to that benevolent notoriety acquired by public service. The wealthy American of good family possessed an incontestable superiority over his fellows; he could easily obtain an official position whence he might influence the government to his personal advantage. But he could not close the door behind him. He could not prevent the young men who were successful from entering his class. This developed a fluid group of powerful, dexterous and courageous men, while those who lacked such qualities found it very difficult to maintain their posi-. tion. The sole undisputed social privilege of this class was an education at Harvard, Yale, Kings College (Columbia), Princeton, William and Mary; in England, Oxford, Cambridge; or on the continent, Geneva for Protestants, Saint Omer for Catholics. The only other advantage through which the American aristocracy maintained its ascendancy and influence was its contact with Europe, first with England while she was still the mother country and arbiter of the colonial destinies, and later with France and Spain at a time when contact with these peoples became desirable. After its own fashion America participated in the vast international and intellectual movement which stimulated all aristocracies of the eighteenth century. The American aristocrats who rose to a position of public prominence in the colonies were nearly all ardent internationalists. The most striking example was Benjamin Franklin. Son of a candle-maker whose children outnumbered his dollars, when very young he went to London, where he developed his knowledge of printing, literature, and the ways of the world. Returning to America, young Franklin managed by his tireless energy, rare intelligence, and a peerless precision and application of mind, to acquire an exceptional standing in Pennsylvania. As printer and editor he soon outstripped all his American colleagues. Franklin was a child of the people, but he possessed all the instincts of an aristocrat. He amassed a substantial fortune and was able to indulge freely his keen penchant for science and philosophic speculation. With his ability to interpret as well as to understand, and his insistence upon seeing with his own eyes at a time when so many savants were content with theorizings and deductions, he discovered a number of fundamental truths in physics. He popularized the scientific experimentations in which the upper classes of Europe took such delight, thus creating a new relationship between the two worlds. The University of Philadelphia, the American Philosophical Society and the first American fire companies were founded by him. Swimming was made more general and popular through his efforts. His fine qualities and address won him friendships in the most distinguished circles, as well as a number of lucrative positions. This man of humble extraction was in truth better received and more justly appreciated by the aristocracy of England and the continent than by democratic America. Twice, indeed, his position in his native land was nearly compromised; first, by his popularity in England, and then by his extraordinary success in France. His dazzling career there was due to his friends among the philosophers and to the great ladies, duchesses and princesses, who imposed his creed upon the ministers of state. Franklin loved the people, but he feared their violence and detested crowds. With a sincere desire to aid the poor, he sponsored radically democratic theories, but he appreciated the rights of intelligence and knew the value of government by the strong. In his own family he founded a sort of dynasty; his son became Governor of New Jersey and his grandsons astonished Paris by acting like young lords and dandies.

The Adams family in Massachusetts offers an analogous instance of social advancement enhanced by the growing wealth of the colony and consecrated by the Revolution. After beginning his career as a schoolmaster, John Adams assumed an important rôle in the Continental Congress, was first Minister to England and second President of the United States. Up to the present, the Adams family has maintained its preëminent rank: John Quincy was President; Charles Francis, Minister to England during the Civil War; Henry and Brooks, authors of much distinction in the generation just past; Charles Francis II, writer and railroad builder.

Thus, social, political, and economic conditions all contributed to form a natural aristocracy in America which the acceptance of limited suffrage as a principle seemed to confirm. Moreover, it appears to have been tacitly agreed that political preferment should go to the most prominent citizens. At any rate, since such positions were usually but meagerly lucrative, the aristocracy had no difficulty in maintaining its official standing. In nearly all the colonies an upper chamber represented in particular those well-established and powerful families which had come to be looked upon (among themselves, at least) as a legitimate nobility. It guarded their prerogatives against the encroachments of the people's rising ambitions. This antagonism must be taken into consideration if we are to understand the American situation between 1700 and 1770. A double conflict was emerging: first, all America, rich and poor alike, opposed the English in an effort to diminish the Crown's participation in colonial government; second, the long-established families clashed with the newer immigrants, the wealthy and aristocratic seacoast provinces with the pioneer and democratic West.

The cities were both economically and socially a product

of the merchant class, and the merchants could retain firm control so long as the cities did not grow too rapidly. The malcontents moved west to free territory. Here the democratic leaders were formed; here arose a spirit of discontent with both England and the urban aristocrats—it might be termed the democratic instinct in its virgin state. When the cities assumed greater proportions, and constant immigration transformed them into dense centers of the proletariat, a more demagogic, more brutal spirit of democracy was fomented. Included in this category were those Bostonians who, on various occasions during the eighteenth century, tarred and feathered the English customs officials.

This was the element which was so intensely stirred by the various kinds of religious and political dissenters arriving from Europe after 1760. These immigrants were no longer merely fleeing from persecution; they were articulate reformers advocating one doctrine or another with unrestrained zeal. One of them was Thomas Paine, who eventually attained a position of great influence. With little culture and no profound philosophic gifts, and with too much liking for whiskey, this unfortunate man turned from a wretched life in England to become in no time a leader of the American populace. His virulent but adroit pamphlet, *Common Sense,* appealed to both class prejudices and nationalism. Copies of his writings were circulated by hundreds of thousands. In Philadelphia between 1776 and 1780, he was even considered a "Father of his Country." The newcomers were in effect able to speak with greater freedom than members of the submerged classes who had been here longer and who frequently found themselves obligated to the wealthy by ties of gratitude or through sheer poverty. In this way the large cities soon became as revolutionary as the frontier. Another matter is of vital importance in tracing the evolution of ideas in eighteenth-century America. While the laity was working and struggling to free itself from the political and economic tutelage of England, the American churches, particularly the New England Congregational Church, were fighting Anglicanism and its efforts to introduce a hierarchy which would set the power of the bishops in the New World alongside the authority of the Crown. It is quite obvious how this conflict would make the Congregational Church more popular and give it a democratic front. Indeed, this dispute between two reformed sects which had both been guilty of so much intolerance would not have promoted democratic feeling so effectively had not the New England church been engrossed in a liberal evolution. No more hell, no more eternal damnation, said the new doctrine. A very curious phenomenon of intense religious feeling, known as the Great Conversion, gave the American churches a more democratic and emotional appeal. At a time when amusements were rare, when popular interest in religious matters was very great and sermons were listened to with rapt attention, it was far from negligible to have pulpits occupied by apostles of equality and liberty. Even though their words had a strictly theological significance, they could not fail to influence, both directly and by analogy, the social and political ideas which were then under formation.

The revolution which separated America from England was an outburst of religious feeling, democratic leanings, and nationalism—the revolt of one human type against another. For a century and a half the relationship between the colonies and the central government had been strained, not strained to the breaking point it is true, but the times of perfect cordiality were rare and of short duration. Since the population was largely composed of dissenters who received little aid from the State, it is obvious that complete autonomy could have been their one authentic ideal. Of course, between 1689 and 1763 the English colonists did prove their loyalty in many encounters with the French. Rivalry with Canada obliged the New Englanders to look to England for assistance, just as the Canadians were forced to remain faithful to the monarch who supplied them with necessities. Many great Americans of the eighteenth century, including Washington and Franklin, served under the English flag. What their ancestors would have been most reluctant, or might even have refused, to do, these men agreed to without hesitation—such was the identity of interests. One might have expected such a situation to make for absolute loyalty to England. In fact the London government was so convinced of this that when the nation emerged proud and victorious, and conscious of its national unity, the veritable dictator of a Europe whose peoples still slumbered under the yoke of kings little disturbed by questions of patriotism, it sought to bring back into the body of the nation these colonists who, though originally recalcitrant, had recently given many proofs of valor and devotion. That was a grave mistake. Once the danger had passed and Canada was wrested from the French, and no other menaces clouded the horizon, Americans gradually lost interest in England. Even a certain hostility arose; and French emissaries arriving in increasing numbers, found attentive ears. When the King of England or his ministers spoke of their common country, Americans were inclined to shrug their shoulders. Many writers look upon this as evidence of a maturing spirit of democracy, a point of view which is not quite accurate. A careful study of the disputes between England and the colonies indicates that the latter protested against Parliamentary authority but acknowledged the sovereignty of the King. The Bostonians refused to pay the levies of Parliament, yet their appeal was directed to the Crown. While asserting that they were beyond the jurisdiction of the two

Houses, they still owned allegiance to George III. It was only by trying to force them into the sphere of national politics that England caused a revolt. But once the revolution had begun, all the elements of disorder utilized it to their own advantage. The democratic crisis became very acute after 1776. Nevertheless, one must not forget that before then it was the anti-English sentiment of the local aristocracies, the boycotting of English products by American merchants, which gradually prepared the revolution, made it possible and necessary.

For a correct interpretation of this great event certain facts must be borne in mind. During the colonial wars, the settlers and the British soldiers had fought side by side. But the former never accepted nor understood the insular definitions of English patriotism. However, their resistance to it was of a kind which was to be seen throughout eighteenth-century Europe. The American who sought to get rid of an irksome national bondage was no exception; the exception was the Britisher, who was conscious of political, ethnic, and moral unity at a time when such sentiments existed nowhere else.

In spite of their democratic tastes the colonists had shown no prejudices against a local aristocracy and the authority of the King. Nor did they turn against these social factors until the conflict became violent. It was a second revolution engrafted upon the first. There is another singular characteristic of the American Revolution. From start to finish it was directed by men of means or of exceptional intellectual capacities. Frequently, the two were combined. Washington and Jefferson were leading plantation owners of Virginia. Franklin was wealthy and for thirty years had been the outstanding figure of Philadelphia. The Carrolls in Maryland, the Livingstons, Morrises and Schuylers in New York, all belonged to the colonial nobility. John Adams was a

distinguished intellectual; Hancock a prominent merchant,
etc. Then there were the Deanes in Connecticut, the Lees
in Virginia, the Laurenses in Carolina. Excepting Thomas
Paine, who had just arrived from England, not one of the
revolutionary leaders rose directly from the lower classes.
There were few of those fantastic military careers which
made such a memorable showing in France twenty years
later. Throughout the war, Washington was a veritable military dictator; correct, prudent, and wise, to be sure, but
nearly independent of Congress. The French Court negotiated directly with him and offered subsidies without Congressional action. The historians of the nineteenth century
were so impressed by the French Revolution and by the
doctrines of modern democracy, that they have credited the
American revolt with certain traits which it did not really
possess. The latter was totally eighteenth century in character. In all probability it was launched by a minority and
imposed upon the country by force. It was prepared for
by the well-to-do and educated (ministers, journalists, lawyers) and put into effect by the most audacious and far-
seeing members of this group, with the aid of a mob which
was not always aboveboard. There were indeed many admirable examples of patriotism, but these were always
attributable to a minority; with as many as 2,000,000 inhabitants to draw from, Congress never succeeded in maintaining an army of more than 20,000. Nor could it levy
taxes or raise funds in America sufficient to carry on the
war. Wherefore the absolute necessity of a French alliance.
Those who fought did so with rare heroism. One need but
recall the winter at Valley Forge, where Washington and
his army held out despite their lack of clothing and supplies.
LaFayette declared, "I shall never forget your soldiers so
handsome in their nakedness."

In all these particulars the American Revolution was much

the same as it would have been had it taken place at Geneva, the Hague, or any other mercantile center of Europe. The underlying factor was the will of the race to organize a world of its own. Between 1770 and 1785 patriotism was not nearly so keen as the feeling of common racial and cultural interests. Sailors and pioneers fought equally well under the orders of aristocratic merchants and landowners. Franklin and Washington were genuinely new types and they amazed the whole world. The American race was becoming articulate. Europe was gradually becoming aware of the existence of a new human category—Americans.

When victory was finally achieved and the time came to profit by it, the Americans were sorely perplexed. At this troubled moment of vacillation and turmoil, the turbulent, envious, and usually powerless elements which we have come to term democratic, gained a foothold.

The war had been costly and these expenses had to be met, though the idea was repugnant to rich and poor alike. Taxes were excessive and gave rise to many disputes. The currency had depreciated. In many places commerce was in new hands. Immigrants arrived in swarms at every port, then drifted westward. Several states which had formerly been Anglican found difficulty in reorganizing their religious life, with the result that the practice of church-going was interrupted, particularly in the South. The royal governors with their garrisons had disappeared. The nation was represented by a powerless Congress—and most of the provincial administrations were enfeebled either by equal-rights constitutions as in Pennsylvania, or by the masses which, having learned the use of violence, now threatened to turn against their leaders.

On the other hand war profiteers, landholders who had grown rich on post-war conditions and immigration, lawyers, journalists, business men who had served as high army officers or civil officials for eight years and had come to like it, were tempted by the thought of power; and they hoped to profit by modifications in the old aristocracy, which party strife and Tory sentiments had grievously weakened. At length several encounters involving bloodshed provided the motive, encouragement, and opportunity to settle the question. The aristocratically inclined grouped themselves together and imposed the Constitution of the United States upon the majority. No more than three years were required to persuade or constrain the multitude. Following a preliminary convention at Annapolis where the need for a united nation was clearly stated for the first time, a second gathering at Philadelphia laid out a plan. All states except Rhode Island sent delegates. The most distinguished and influential citizens were brought together: Washington, Franklin, Madison, Monroe, Jay, Hamilton, Gouverneur Morris, etc. But even these great minds could not readily come to an understanding. Franklin and others with democratic leanings looked in this direction for a regeneration of the world. Many like Hamilton were convinced that the American experiment had conclusively proved the mediocrity of democratic institutions. They would have preferred a king. We now know with certainty that a group composed chiefly of influential New Englanders and dominated by Rufus King and Gorham, considered asking Prince Henry of Prussia to come over and rule America. Gouverneur Morris was dreaming of an aristocratic republic.

These men, the wisest and strongest in the land, were hopelessly at odds. Yet they represented the only hope; if they failed to agree, there was little chance of America becoming a powerful nation. This point marks the intervention of that mysterious and potent element, that happy fatality, which seems to dominate American history. Beyond individual differences, beyond their faith in democ-

racy or monarchy they felt a stronger instinct which impelled them to achieve something positive at any price. They
resorted to a compromise which satisfied no one, neither the
conservatives who found the new government too weak, nor
the radicals who looked upon the Constitution as an open
door to tyranny. From an abstract point of view, this document may indeed seem singularly meager. It creates a nation,
since president and representatives are elected by the entire
people; but it pretends to maintain states' rights by equal
representation in the Senate. It organizes a democratic elective system, but the voice of popular suffrage may be severely
constrained by the president's authority to veto Congressional initiative, to choose ministers, to appoint justices of
the Supreme Court and a host of lesser functionaries. The
permanent Supreme Court is aristocratic indeed. The system
of balanced powers—executive, legislative and judiciary—
comes not from Rousseau, but from the liberal theory of
Montesquieu, whose heart it would have delighted. It is truly
an eighteenth-century masterpiece, with that delicate machinery and logic which charmed our ancestors in both
Europe and America.

On the other hand the Constitution possesses a number of
wholly original characteristics. Most apparent is a tendency
to define strictly the limits of its own power. Of all great and
famous constitutions, it is the briefest and least complicated.
It strives to encroach as little as possible upon the life and
ambitions of the individual; we might say that it has less
respect for democracy than for human beings. It curbs
the dominion of the collective will over the individual. To
appreciate the originality of this attitude, one must remember
that the late eighteenth century made a cult of government
and had firm faith in constitutional instruments. Was it not
Turgot himself who exclaimed, "Give me a good government and I will make good men"? But the Constitution of

the United States respected persons and previously established institutions; it restricted its domain to politics and administration. It contains but seven articles in all:

I. Congress and its powers.
II. The President and his authority.
III. Organization of the Judiciary.
IV. Relations between states.
V. Power to amend.
VI. Supremacy of the Constitution.
VII. Ratification.

No country ever succeeded better in defining and limiting the scope of politics. No encroachment upon other realms, social, intellectual, religious, or emotional. Even economic life is but indirectly mentioned. In contrast with all other legislators from Solon to Cabet, the Americans seem to have lacked the necessary imagination to produce a grandiose document; whether through wisdom or insufficiency, they were content to follow the best political recipes of the time. Such prudence and moderation, such respect for the actualities of life, stood out in strange relief against the precocious and exhaustively imaginative work done by the French legislators between 1788 and 1800 (five constitutions of fifty pages each). The aging century was shocked at the poverty-stricken imagination of the Americans. French philosophers regretted that they had not proffered the aid of their genius. They had marvelous ideas to recommend, a thousand and one sublime suggestions for ennobling the document. Even the Americans were not overly proud of their political offspring. Wise old Franklin wrote several contrite and mournful letters to his European friends expressing his hopes that the Constitution would be completed and perfected by subsequent additions. What disturbed the brilliant minds of Europe most was the difficulty of ascertaining in which body sovereignty was really invested. Everything was checked and balanced. In fact the Constitutional edifice was expressly constructed so as to give no one the impression that he held supreme power. This was a source of much speculation in Europe. How could a people exist in such a state of delicate and unstable equilibrium? America, they said, was certainly headed for despotism or anarchy.

Of course, nothing of the kind occurred. The Constitution, which had adopted the theories of Montesquieu and the traditions of English law, was above all the product of American soil and American stock. Its greatest quality is the full latitude in living which it allows, and the unchecked opportunity it affords for the nation to expand. It seems like a bare outline in contrast with European constitutions which are virtually moral, social, and political encyclopedias of the nations which possess them. But the American code affirms very little with finality. It points out no one path to the exclusion of others; it leaves the future a free hand and an unfettered heritage.

This rare and precious quality did not need to be sought after; it thrust itself upon America. The need to analyze, ponder, and justify one's actions by logic, characterizes the most complex centers of civilization, but is not felt by a race trained in the school of nature. The finest accomplishments of the United States have been the result of intuition or necessity. It would seem that Providence, in bestowing less leisure and less competent powers of reason upon America, had endowed it with a clear and judicious instinct.

At any rate, when the document was finally adopted in 1788, two schools of interpretation immediately arose. One, invoking the name of Washington, demanded authority; the other cried for liberty in the name of Franklin. The two real leaders, both great men and aristocrats, were Hamilton and Jefferson. The former was still a young man but newly established in the country, of modest origin and of keen acquisitive intelligence. Better than any one else he understood his time and the laws which governed the economic world. He perceived that prosperity depended upon the activity of a few and the discipline of many. To a man of his intellect, the masses appeared stupid. He dreamed of founding a great monarchy, or at least an aristocracy for his colleagues and a dynasty for his children. With that in view, he sought to organize a strong central authority with wealth, culture, and birth as its basis. He believed in neither the sovereignty nor the wisdom of the people; he was a skeptic in religion, like many of his time, and held a somewhat cynical view of the world. Nothing seems to have claimed his admiration save a human being endowed with his most brilliant attributes—genius, power and authority. He would have liked to see such a person ruling over a docile people in a prosperous and mighty land.

Jefferson was an aristocrat by birth, culture, environment, and career. Born among wealthy surroundings, his dazzling political life took him to the court of France, where with his friend LaFayette he advocated theories of limited monarchy. He loved books, good wine, power, and women, and detested turbulence. He never fought, and intensely disliked being worsted in any sort of encounter. He was the proud son of an aristocratic merchant family which had maintained its influence in Virginia for upwards of a century. He was a reader of philosophy, French in particular. Though he believed in God, he had little religion other than a cult of progress and democracy. His faith in the latter, like some people's faith in God, was compounded of much fervor and great ignorance.

To Jefferson democracy was a faith, but he retained that American sagacity which was to make him a great president and an illustrious philosopher. He aspired to a democracy of individuals wherein every one would have his place and the means to live after his own fashion. Hamilton was an aristocratic nationalist; Jefferson a democrat with little patriotism (in theory).

But destiny juggled with these men in a strange manner. Hamilton thought he had founded a nation with the Constitution of 1788. However, it was soon discovered that many, and perhaps even most, did not share this conviction. The United States was still frequently looked upon as a federation. Between 1795 and 1800, when quarrels over foreign policy divided the nation into two camps (pro-English aristocrats and pro-French democrats), the legislatures of Kentucky and Virginia passed resolutions affirming the right of states to withdraw from the Union whenever they saw fit, and proclaiming that the source of sovereignty was not in the federal nation but in the states. This interpretation brought the entire achievement of 1788 into jeopardy again. It remained a menace which no one dared or could face squarely until the Civil War. And not until then did the United States truly take on the aspect of a nation. Previous to this the country cannot be said to have possessed real national unity. It is strange that the United States has never been able to find a suitable name. Italy, France, Spain, Germany, England—simple proper nouns—aided materially in establishing the unity of those nations. Such words are both emblems and definitions. The only simple formula which can be, and which is, applied to the United States is America. This is most significant, as it reveals the position of the United States, which had so much difficulty in becoming a nation, but which represents a continent, a civilization, and a race.

When Jefferson became president it was expected that he might transform the United States into a true democracy

in keeping with his principles, a weak central power and
feeble government with a strong and sovereign people. But
from the very beginning it would seem as though the demon
of America exerted a much more potent influence upon him
than all his theories, proclivities, and passions. His first
message was an appeal for national peace and union. He was
in a position to give striking evidence that the United States
had changed its objective and was rallying about the standard of democracy. The essential test of this would have
been a reconciliation with France and French doctrine. Under
various pretexts, which were probably sincere but were certainly inspired by instinct, Jefferson consistently discouraged
a French alliance. No changes were made in the Constitution, nor was the power of the central government diminished. To be sure, he assisted certain local democrats in their
struggles against the old aristocracy, but this long-winded
combat would have ended satisfactorily enough without his
aid. A comparison of Jefferson's philosophy with the achievements of his presidency reveals inconsistencies verging on
the ludicrous. In fact, as chief executive he definitely quashed
the possibility of a French alliance, confirmed the authority
of the central government, and assisted in the extraordinary
expansion of his country.

Such was the United States at the outset of the nineteenth
century; a hybrid country, half national and half federal,
where a merchant aristocracy still prospered in the sea-ports,
and a society was developing further inland which called itself democratic because it was distrustful of the old aristocracy, though it actually aspired more to liberty than to
equality, more to power, wealth, and independence than to
patriarchal fraternity. While discussion of democracy was
becoming more and more animated, social inequalities still
remained very great. For nearly thirty years the Virginian
aristocracy governed the nation; in New England and the

Atlantic states the upper classes maintained their ascendancy.

The United States was already a magnificent country, with a splendid race of men ennobled by danger, stimulated by continual struggles with nature, and aided by a Constitution and a social organization which would not hamper the spontaneous development of groups or individuals. America was a land of strong and ambitious men who were working together, turning their backs upon Europe and blazing their way through the virgin forests.

CHAPTER III

THE AMERICAN TERRITORY (1803-1865)

The educated European must naturally view most aspects of American civilization with a grain of condescension. For him its juvenile and pragmatic conceptions are fresh and enthusiastic, but alas, they are but the prelude to inevitable disillusionment. On the other hand, no traveler can fail to be impressed by the vast American continent. Size is the most striking quality in the United States. The oft-noted happiness of the people seems derived from the sunlight, fresh air, and spaciousness of the youthful domain. Wealth, physical well-being, and inexhaustible resources which make this nation the most fortunate in the world, are drawn from the continent whose immense plains, mountains, valleys, and lakes contain more treasures than ever before belonged to a single people. As a result, a close contact with nature was maintained all through the nineteenth century, bringing with it undeniable health and strength. This is the source of that youthful paganism which surprises and fascinates the Europeans. Space also led to tolerance. Not that Americans are more patient or less obstinate than others, but they had the means of avoiding and ignoring one another. They were free of that stifling congestion which has done so much to discredit democracy in Europe by making one feel that at each moment he is being elbowed, watched, pushed, or driven by fellow men whose slightest movements react through the whole dense mass like an inadvertent tap on a gong. In comparison with America, Europe seems like a series of barriers. Every hundred miles brings a change of race, genius, climate,

art, religion, and beauty. Here space is more akin to time—
a powerful, unchanging dizziness. Few variations, no frontiers, no limits; for differences develop so gradually that they
are scarcely perceptible. The value of this space does not derive from the variety of designs which human ingenuity has
traced upon it, but from its purity. Its vastness has rendered
it almost impermeable, and seemingly inexhaustible. Between
Ogden and Omaha one travels for a whole day over a country where the railway stations are posts driven into the sand.
The sun sets on a solitude as barren as the Sahara.

The importance of space in the shaping of the American
mentality and physique is the legacy of Jefferson. It would
certainly not have become so great a factor without the acquisition of the Louisiana territory. But there is no evidence
that Jefferson ever wanted or expected to purchase the
whole region. He was, of course, annoyed when Spain gave
Louisiana back to France in 1880. A powerful nation at the
back door could have no other effect. Moreover, this blocked
the Mississippi and stirred up what little restlessness in the
West was still dormant. Jefferson handled the situation
with his customary astuteness. In a letter intended to be read
by the French leaders he declared, "The day that France
takes possession of New Orleans fixes the sentence which
is to restrain her forever within her low water mark. It
seals the union of two nations which in conjunction can
maintain exclusive possession of the ocean. From that
moment we must marry ourselves to the British fleet and
nation." Pinchon, the French minister, was thoroughly
taken in and promised to endeavor to obtain a reopening
of the Mississippi. Apparently Jefferson did not intend
to go much further; for Monroe, whom he sent on a special
mission, was instructed to bid up to ten million dollars for
New Orleans and the Floridas only. On the other hand
Napoleon was laying his plans and it would be idle to think

that Jefferson's threat carried much weight with him. His project for fortifying the Western empire had come to naught after the disastrous expedition to San Domingo, the key to it all. So, rather than risk its capture by Great Britain, he resolved to get rid of the colony entirely. In conference with Barbé Marbois, who was to handle the negotiations, he declared, "Irresolution and deliberation are no longer in order. I renounce Louisiana. I cede not only New Orleans, but the whole colony without reserve." Marbois was to obtain at least fifty million francs in return. Monroe had no instructions to acquire this immense area; and it is doubtful whether Jefferson, the leader of the strict constructionists and proverbially a timid man in action, would have dared of his own accord to assume a power far beyond any which the Federalists had ever exercised before. However, Monroe took it upon himself to exceed his instructions and make the purchase. Temporarily, at least, Napoleon drove a good bargain. He got ten million francs more than the figure he had set, to say nothing of the private claims up to twenty millions which the United States was to take over. He won a certain amount of good will, and he kept Louisiana from England. But the United States gained an empire which, according to Napoleon, was destined to humble the pride of England.

No one knew just what was to be done with this new territory. And for some time the question did not suggest itself except in a speculative way. But gradually the development of this vast region came into prominence under the head of internal improvements. And in spite of glaring faults, the ways in which this task was handled are a triumph of federalism.

The logical and natural method of developing a territory was through the central government. As early as 1770 Washington realized that until the West was linked with the East by practicable highways, no consolidation was possible. He had plans for a canal from the Ohio to the Potomac which would open a direct waterway between the Mississippi valley and Europe. The Revolution diverted his attention from this project for some years, but eventually he returned to it. In 1785 he obtained a charter for the canal from the Virginia legislature. But his elevation to the Presidency obliged him to defer his plans once more. In connection with this idea, he also thought of a national capital built upon converging thoroughfares, to be at once the military, commercial, administrative, and educational center of the nation. He considered a national university as an indispensable adjunct "to spread systematic ideas through all parts of the rising empire." But during his presidency it was difficult for him to carry out the canal project upon which the others depended. And Washington died, leaving his schemes still in embryo. Jefferson next toyed with the idea. His message of December, 1806, suggests a constitutional amendment to enable Congress to apply the surplus revenue "to the great purposes of the public education, roads, rivers, canals and such other objects of public improvement as may be thought proper." The amendment was not adopted, and Jefferson was unwilling to go into the scheme on a large scale without it. But the real ardor of internal improvement passed into the competent hands of John Quincy Adams. In his career from 1807 to 1828, we see more clearly than anywhere else the embodiment, the evolution, and the catastrophic defeat of the theory of constructive centralization. In February, 1807, Adams offered the following resolution to the Senate: "That the Secretary of the Treasury be directed to prepare and report to the Senate, at their next session, a plan for the application of such means as are constitutionally within the power of Congress, to the purposes of opening roads, for removing obstructions in rivers,

and making canals; together with a statement of the undertakings of that nature now existing within the United States
which, as objects of public improvement, may require and
deserve the aid of the government." The next year this same
resolution (under another name: Worthington) elicited
from Secretary Gallatin a report on a complete national
system of roads and canals. The project was being backed
by the oratory of Clay when, unfortunately, the threat of
war turned attention to other channels, and the subject was
dropped for a decade. In 1817-18, however, the problem
came up again. New York, Pennsylvania, Maryland and
Virginia, each wanted the lion's share of Western commerce. Owing to their continued haggling over proposed
routes, little was accomplished. So the West, the most interested party of all, urged the federal government to take
charge of the whole project. The constitutional scruples
of Madison and Monroe arrested matters at this point, and
the financial panic of 1819 left the treasury in such a
wretched condition that nothing further was considered until
1822. In that year, a bill relative to the tolls of the Cum-
berland Road was passed by Congress but vetoed by Monroe. He accompanied the veto with an absurd disquisition
reasserting his scruples and at the same time indicating a
loophole through which Congress might get around them.
Congress took advantage of this, and during the next two
years appropriations for internal improvements were actually
forthcoming: an Act appropriating funds to repair the Cum-
berland Road (connecting the Potomac with the Ohio),
another for the improvement of harbors, and a third, more
comprehensive, authorizing a survey for roads and canals
for commercial, military, or postal purposes of national
importance. Thus when Adams came to the presidential
chair the policy of internal improvement was well under
way; and he was prepared to develop to the utmost his

fondest ideal—a scheme for constructive centralization, scientifically administered.

To recount Mr. Adams' tribulations and dismal failures would gain us nothing; nor could we explain them satisfactorily by merely pointing out his tactless and uncompromising methods which alienated so many of his potential supporters. It is probably true that his radical explanations would have seemed more appropriate and would have been less critically received had they come from a Senator rather than from the executive; yet the final outcome could hardly have been much different. Adams did achieve something. He spent over two and a third million dollars for roads and harbors. This was more than twice the expenditures of all previous administrations combined. Also, he contributed greatly to the Chesapeake and Ohio canal movement. But there were three tendencies so powerful that few men (and Adams was not one of the few) could have withstood them: 1—The South was growing uneasy about the slave question. It feared Adams' loose constitutional interpretation as a precursor of abolition. 2—Adams was devoted to the cause of science and had one of the best scientific minds in the nation. But ironically enough, the scientific development of the steam engine spelt ruin for his network of canals and roads. 3—The American people, though favorably inclined towards the policy of internal improvements, was far from willing to concede that the work should be done by the central government in the most efficient and scientific manner. The states fought over conflicting programs, and corporations squabbled for federal patronage. Party rivalry was bitter. In one instance, where Ohio had requested land for canals, each party, fearful lest the credit go to the other, passed a bill in conformity, so that Ohio received twice the land asked for. The problem became more involved, and the President, attacked on all sides, losing friends constantly by his unwillingness to compromise, and forever haunted by the Jacksonian war-cry of "Bargain and Corruption," was powerless. His cause was lost and there is something pathetic in his lurid defeat of 1828. Nine years later the thought of it was still bitter to him. "The great effort of my administration was to mature into a permanent and regular system the application of all superfluous revenue of the Union to internal improvements which at this day would have afforded high wages and constant employment to hundreds of thousands of laborers, and in which every dollar expended would have repaid itself fourfold in the enhanced value of the public lands. With this system in ten years from this day the surface of the whole Union would have been checkered over with railroads and canals. . . . When I came to the presidency the principle of internal improvement was swelling the tide of public prosperity, till the Sable Genius of the South saw the signs of his own inevitable downfall in the unparalleled progress of the general welfare of the North—I fell and with me fell, I fear never to rise again—the system of internal improvement by means of national energies."

What Adams never fully understood was that the tremendous latent power of the nation was turned in another direction. He believed his failure due to incapacity; and at the very end of his life he inveighed against this weakness with a kind of sublime curse—a mixture of conceit, impotence, and contrition worthy of a Shakespearian villain. "If my intellectual powers had been such as have been sometimes committed by the Creator of man to single individuals of the species, my diary would have been, next to the Holy Scriptures, the most precious and valuable book ever written by human hands, and I should have been one of the greatest benefactors of my country and of mankind. I would, by the irresistible power of genius and the irrepressible energy of will and the favor of Almighty God, have banished war and slavery from the face of the earth forever. But the conceptive power of mind was not conferred upon me by my Maker, and I have not improved the scanty portion of His gifts as I might and ought to have done. . . . May I never murmur at the dispensations of Providence." Probably it never occurred to him that both he and his predecessors (Jefferson included) had administered the government democratically in imagination only, and federally not at all. But it now seems clear that such was the case. Until 1828 the nation's political leaders came from the aristocracy of the Massachusetts merchants and the Virginia landowners—the Massachusetts and Virginia Dynasty. Their ideal of government was lofty. Each of them had the public weal uppermost in his mind. But the theory that the people should *be governed* (instead of governing) was injected so powerfully by Hamilton into the actual application of the Constitution that even Jefferson could not stem it. Moreover, all the presidents from John Adams to his son had seen extensive service in Europe. This caused a certain conventionality of attitude and a leaning towards old world precedents in cases where there were no American ones to follow. Had the country not increased beyond the original thirteen states, the Virginia and Massachusetts Dynasty might have persisted until it was disrupted by slavery. The people had become accustomed to aristocratic leadership and took it for granted. In fact, the tendency to imitate England was very marked. Often, but not always, it was involuntary. State boundaries had already lost their significance, and federalism was becoming a mere figure of speech. But a system founded upon a glaring fallacy was doomed the moment it met with definite opposition. How could an aristocratic, central government prevail when based upon a democratic, federal constitution?

How could an educated and refined class keep the reins
when confronted by voters who had just grasped the theory
that every man was competent to govern? How could the
intelligent labor for the common good when the first fruits
of their work—freedom, education, and resources—had
whipped the ambitious into frenzied struggles for personal
emolument? Hamiltonism could only have maintained itself
by force or by fraudulent deprivation of voting privileges.
Neither alternative was resorted to. So the defeat of 1828
routed the aristocratic utterly and irretrievably—at least,
for seventy years.

During the Massachusetts and Virginia Dynasty, the state
divisions had somewhat gone to seed and the federal principle was lost from sight. But it subsequently reappeared
under the more natural and far more significant divisions
of slave states and free states, trans-Allegheny and cis-
Allegheny. Here at last was an opportunity to put federalism
to the test. Hitherto the nation had been small, economically
undeveloped, and subject to the domination of one class.
Disagreements arose either from opportunism or from differences of personality. The country was now split into
sections, latitudinally and longitudinally, by geographic,
biological and economic distinctions of the utmost consequence. The effort to keep those sections under a single government despite their divergent ideas and interests, consti-
tuted a problem over which the country wrangled for thirty-
seven years. Federalism triumphed, but not without bitter
strife and many violent upheavals and reverses.

Government for the merchants and landowners had
gained such momentum that it was many years before
Jeffersonian democracy could make enough headway to
overthrow it. But the change was coming. Against cis-
Allegheny there arose trans-Allegheny, the new West. The
belligerency of these frontiersmen, the result of a turbulent

and exhausting life, was noted from their first appearance in Congress. Jefferson wrote of Jackson: "His passions are terrible. When I was President of the Senate, he was a Senator and he could never speak on account of the rashness of his feelings. I have seen him attempt it repeatedly and as often choke with rage." Impatient of unwieldy formulas and traditions, the Westerners resented the rule of trained statesmen and officials. They felt as competent to govern as to fight. And with the vision of their country's future greatness before them, they resented the thought that its progress was being impeded by the political cabals of the East.

Friction began on the land itself. The national government considered the public domain as a source of revenue and sold pieces of it to settlers on credit. The settlers invariably spent all their capital on the first installment and relied upon loans, profits, or sales to cover the balance. A debtor class was created which naturally looked upon its creditor, the government, as an oppressor. This enmity took form in the idea that the public lands belonged to the people and not to the government. Then the Panic of 1819 made the situation intolerable. Money had always been scarce in the new West. Loans to the settlers came largely from banks whose financial methods were far from sound and whose assets and collateral were largely frozen in the land. So long as times were normal they got along well enough. But postwar conditions in the East brought matters to a head. In reaction to the economies of the war, this section indulged in the usual orgies of speculation, extravagance, and inflation. The United States Bank, the official fiscal agent, was swept along in the current until the middle of 1818, when it saw that in order to avoid ruin it must resort to a vigorous deflation. This drastic measure affected the smaller institutions and placed a severe burden upon the people. In the new lands the situation was particularly bitter. Loans were called and mortgages foreclosed. To cover their debts thousands of settlers were obliged to part with their hard-earned possessions. By this process the national bank in Cincinnati came to own a great section of the city—hotels, cafés, warehouses, stables, iron foundries, residences, and vacant lots. Throughout the West the bank was known as the monster, and antagonism to the "engines of aristocracy" became extreme. Abstractly one would say that the internal improvement system of John Quincy Adams might have been an excellent solution, perhaps the best solution, for Western distress. But the Westerners were in no mood to be guided by a man of the class which Adams represented. Moreover, they did not want to be governed, in even the best possible manner; they wanted to govern themselves.

They found their champion in Andrew Jackson. Turner styles him "the very personification of the contentious, nationalistic democracy of the interior—a six-foot backwoodsman, angular, lantern-jawed, and thin, with blue eyes that blazed on occasion"; a "choleric, impetuous, Scotch-Irish leader of men; expert duellist and ready fighter." The incarnation of an indomitable will, his true genius was that of a commander. In the war of 1812 he was made a general, though he had not the slightest knowledge of military science. Yet he made recruits fight like veterans, and at New Orleans he won the most brilliant victory of the war. On the other hand he was grossly ignorant. His education had been rudimentary, and he never sought to improve it. He had no use for knowledge and never really understood any political or economic problem. To Adams he was a "barbarian who could not write a sentence of grammar and hardly could spell his own name." But his fiery nature fascinated the popular imagination. When cornered on a question of policy his advocates needed only to reply "Hurrah for Jackson," and the masses found the rebuttal all-sufficient. Although he professed to be one of the people and owed much of his support to the creed that the people should govern, the country has never known a more tyrannical ruler. All his actions were characterized by domineering and high-handedness. Thanks to his hold on the people he bulldozed Congress as no one else has done before or since. But are we to see Jackson's era merely as the triumph of Western violence over Eastern culture? Merely a retrogression from monarchical eminence to tyrannical ignorance? Are we to regard Jackson as so many do—an unintelligent man who had luck or genius enough to spot winning issues? In one sense this is exact, but a closer scrutiny reveals him as the founder of a new era.

We are reluctantly forced to conclude from a historical examination of democracies that the majority always seeks its own level; that mediocre leadership is the rule rather than the exception. Indeed, superior talent is of some disadvantage to a democratic executive; such a man, by sponsoring some comprehensive scheme of his own, will often steer too far from the average will of the country, where a less endowed chief, by advocating one measure or another as the occasion arises, will come closer to a representative policy. The merits of federal democracy will never be fully appreciated until this view is accepted. The career of Andrew Jackson furnishes an excellent example of what can be done within the limits of the American Constitution.

Jackson had two exceptional traits. Aided by his astute lieutenants, Van Buren and Kendall, he divined admirably the currents of popular sentiment. Also he possessed the indomitable energy and will to put through his projects even when confronted by the most stubborn resistance. Keen enough to sense popular dissatisfaction with the development of centralization, he apparently concluded that certain powers should be diversified as much as constitutional limits permitted. This is clearly a federal point of view; and even though Jackson rarely used the word "federal," he consistently fought the centers of power and scattered their resources. As he has not been given due credit for the institution of practical federalism, we should note how his principal acts are a reflection of popular sentiment and assume more unity and coherence when viewed in this light.

As fiscal agent of the government, the Bank of the United States was a protected monopoly whose profits accrued to private individuals. Jackson was suspicious of banks in general, and as he had not forgotten the days of the panic, he distrusted this bank in particular. It seemed too aristocratic to a man of his tastes that such an institution should continue in power, and he resolved that the bank must be destroyed. Thus, when Biddle applied for a recharter, he encountered an emotional resistance such as no logic or financial reasoning could withstand. The bank was not rechartered. It lingered until the expiration of its old charter in 1836. Then it reopened simply as a state bank. But before it expired Jackson administered one more blow by removing the federal deposits from its custody. He placed these in various institutions which were selected for political reasons and were dubbed "pet banks."

Another decentralizing process began in 1835. Prosperous times had brought the government an excess of revenue which wiped out the public debt and left an ever-increasing surplus. The natural policy would have been to expend this on internal improvements. But true to his federal instinct, Jackson preferred to return the unnecessary income to the states. He distributed twenty-eight million dollars to them in the form of loans without interest.

Also, there were the public lands. To Adams these represented a vast potential wealth which the central government should improve—or judiciously dispose of to its own profit. Jackson thought otherwise. The new lands belonged to the people. Accordingly he reduced prices in various ways; with unbounded munificence and recklessness he made grants, sales, and gifts to states, corporations, and individuals. In all he disposed of over sixty-three million acres of public domain. Jackson's tyranny lay in his ability to force through his pet measures despite fierce opposition. And the opposition from Clay, Calhoun, and Webster was formidable. But a federalist tyrant, a tyrant who diffuses power rather than accumulates it, is a rare blessing. Though he insisted that the central government should not function for its own advantage, he did uphold its sovereignty— also a truly federal attitude. When South Carolina attempted to nullify a national decree, Jackson's rage was terrible. "I will hang the first man I lay my hand on engaged in such treasonable conduct, upon the first tree I can reach."

The one truly indefensible act that can be laid against Jackson was his practice of building up the Democratic Party by the bestowal of offices. Perhaps he believed that one set of persons should be kept in public office as a sort of aristocracy. Nevertheless, it may be argued that a spoils system of one kind or another is practically inevitable in any new democracy. Jackson inaugurated one in this country primarily because he established a great party. Any other man in his position could hardly have done otherwise.

Under Jackson the crisis of trans-Allegheny versus cis-Allegheny was met and successfully weathered. The result was not beyond criticism, and many individual actions were quite unpardonable. But on the whole justice was done. The under dog became uppermost, and where the pendulum of power had been in the East it now swung to the West. Great credit for this achievement is due to Jackson and his advisers. For preventing the worst, perhaps more credit is due to his opponents. Adams had predicted that the Union could not last another twenty-five years. Had the leaders of the opposition sulked and attempted to foster discontentment, an irretrievable split along the Alleghenys might have resulted. But they accepted defeat with great patriotism and relinquished their personal preferences to the good of all.

As their efforts did not avert a rupture between the North and the South, federal principles hardly gained so conclusive a victory as in the East-West controversy. For forty years leaders fought over the question of slavery and, despite the intense feelings of the contingencies behind them, compromised their differences. Civil war did not result until one party refused to compromise, refusing the most advantageous conditions which could be offered without sacrificing all semblance of justice.

It is customary to begin a discussion of this question by asserting that in the early days of the new nation all thinking men of both the North and the South believed slavery to be an evil which should be eradicated in due course of time. This seems reasonable enough. Indeed it must always have required a generous seasoning of self-deception to think of slavery as anything but an evil. Thus, when there was no particular advantage connected with the institution, slavery waned. But the cotton gin was invented. Thereupon the possession of cheap cotton pickers became an immense pecuniary asset. To expect the consciousness of a moral evil to outbalance brimming coffers was too much. Slavery must be preserved, said the Southerner, evil or no evil, union or no union. This made the Northerner bristle with indignation. He knew the moral side of the case, for it had been drummed into him by preachers and pamphleteers. It was a good reason for complaint. But had this been all, his sympathy for the negro would perhaps have gone little further than his feeling for the Armenians today. But he was deeply jealous of the Southern money bags. The Southerner had discovered perpetual motion—had found a way to make money and live in clover without doing a stroke of work. But there was here one underlying factor which, since it was of no use to the Northerner, he was determined to destroy. Rhodes figured that in 1850, "of the large planters owning more than fifty slaves, whose elegance, luxury and hospitality are recited in tales of travelers, over whose estates and lives has shone the luster of romance and poetry, there were less than eight thousand." As the total population of the slave states at that date was over nine and a half millions, this situation created a formidable oligarchy. It is not strange that the Northerners should have been galled by such conditions; and the feeling was aggravated by the Southerners' natural superiority in political matters. Politics was the logical vocation for the young man of the South whose fortune and position were inherited and who needed to learn no trade or profession to insure their perpetuation. Again citing Rhodes: "The sons of the wealthy almost always went to college, and there they began to acquire the knack at public speaking which seemed natural to the Southerner. The political life of their states was early opened to them, and by the time the promising young men were sent to Congress they had learned experience and adroitness in public affairs. If they made their mark in the national House or the Senate, they were kept there and each year added to their usefulness and influence. The aspirants for political honors being almost wholly from the small privileged class, it was not difficult to provide places for those eminently fitted. Moreover, the men who wielded the power were convinced that continuance in office was the proper reward of those who had shown capacity and honesty. The absurd practice which prevailed

at the North, of rotating their representatives in the lower
house in order to make room for as many as possible of those
who had political claims, never gained foothold in the South.
This was, indeed, one reason why the South won advantages
over the North, in spite of its inferior numerical strength."

As the arguments were marshaled, the South again had
the better of the case. Their chief support came from the
very letter of the Constitution, to wit: the federal government is formed by compact between sovereign states; the
activity of the federal government is limited to the powers
delegated by the Constitution; it has no right to pass conclusive judgment as to the extent of its own powers; but
the states, as parties to the compact, have equally the right
of determining whether the Constitution has been observed
or violated, and of deciding on the proper mode of redress.
This last clause is strained, to be sure, but the argument as
a whole would certainly have been approved by the framers
of the Constitution. The opposition had a more difficult time
of it. As we see it now, they had as their basis the practical
federalism which had grown out of the Constitution—the
averseness to centralization, the tendency to compromise,
and the utility of the national administration for these purposes. But such tenets did not form good debating material.
So against the states' rights doctrine of Calhoun, Webster
preferred to put "the people of the whole United States
acting in their collective capacity." Such a foundation was
even more flimsy. Webster's "people of the whole United
States" had never collaborated in this way, nor had they
anything to do with framing the Constitution. But he made
a brilliant argument and backed it with his sublime oratory.
"It was a glorious fiction," says Professor MacDonald, "and
it has entered into the warp and woof of our Constitutional
creed; but it was fiction nevertheless." Indeed, though poor

logic, it was good practical federalism. Webster felt instinctively that the general weal should transcend the special good of eight thousand.

Henry Clay was the hot-headed, youthful statesman whose oratory had precipitated the war of 1812. Though in the course of years he gathered the rich wisdom of experience, he never was accused of being an intellectual. But never was there a more staunch American, never was there a man who better understood the country as a whole. Indeed, his genius was of a sort which any nation at any time could find of service. Clay had his own opinions on all current topics; some were accepted, although generally he was on the losing side. But the characteristic which distinguished him was his sense of compromise. People think differently, and are stubborn in their views. Nowhere is this more apparent than in parliamentary debates. If the difference is serious, a victory of one side may be sublime, but a prolonged deadlock or a war is a sure loss to every one. Three times Clay encountered such a situation, and each time he proposed and put through a compromise measure. He was called the Great Compromiser.

"The Missouri question is the most portentous one that ever threatened the Union," wrote the aged Jefferson. And indeed from 1818 to 1821 the debate as to whether Missouri should be admitted as a free or slave state racked the nation to its foundations. Until Maine applied for admittance the balance of free and slave states was even. But the latter viewed with alarm the increasing population in the North and its resultant preponderance in the House. The entry of Maine, giving the North a majority in the Senate also, fanned the resentment into open resistance. The South proposed to offset Maine by admitting Missouri as a slave state. To the people of the North this came as a brutal shock. Instead of eventual extinction, as envisaged by the Constitution, an unlimited extension of slavery confronted them. The thought that the fair territory of Louisiana might be peopled with slaves was a grim one. But the South was in dead earnest; so Congress finally authorized Missouri to frame a slave constitution with the understanding that all future states cut from the domain above 36° 30′ should be free. This quieted matters until the Missouri Constitution appeared containing a clause which discriminated against free negroes or mulattoes. Immediately dissension flared up and raged so violently that the country trembled. Congress was helpless until Clay appeared upon the scene. In committee he offered a compromise resolution:

1. Missouri should pass no laws prejudicial to the entrance of any citizen from another state. This was for the North.

2. After assenting to this formally, Missouri should thereupon become a state. This was to prevent further Congressional disturbance.

3. Missouri should not be deprived of any of the rights and privileges constitutionally exercised by the original states. This was for the South.

It was not immediately adopted. But Clay persevered with zeal and skill. He did not limit himself to speeches, but made a man-to-man canvass, persuading and beseeching with impressive sincerity, until at length he formed a slight majority. Thus the first phase of the agitating conflict came to a peaceable termination.

The second episode occurred in 1833, and Clay was again the mediator. But the controversy, though bitter, was so one-sided that a compromise was more easily obtained. It must be noted that the leadership of the South had shifted from Virginia to South Carolina. The utterances of Hayne, Lowndes, and Calhoun formulated the most advanced opinions of the slave states; and although time was required for them to seep through, they indicated the course which the whole section would ultimately follow. The nullification dispute of 1832-33 resulted from the high protective tariffs of 1828 and 1832. Neither of these bills did much credit to the economic sense of the framers. In fact, political considerations made them far more obnoxious than was necessary. South Carolina in particular found them onerous. The export of cotton was her principal source of revenue. This created for her large balances in foreign countries, mainly in England. On account of the tariff her purchases of goods manufactured abroad cost more than did similar purchases made by the Northerners patronizing their local industries.

Calhoun's states' rights doctrine had by now taken a vigorous hold upon South Carolina, and the legislature of that state resolved to put it to the test. Accordingly a state convention was called which proceeded to declare the tariff acts of 1828 and 1832 null and void. Jackson's wrath was followed by action. He ordered General Scott to Charleston and issued a proclamation refuting the right to annul. His arguments were all borrowed from Webster and made an excellent impression on the country. Calhoun, who had expected other Southern states to follow his lead, was stunned by the formidable opposition. He himself could not compromise, and Webster would not. Accordingly Clay was sought out and after some debate agreed to work for a settlement. The result of his skill and address was a bill which gradually reduced the tariff, until after nine years a uniform rate of 20 per cent. was attained. The bill was passed; and shortly after, South Carolina repealed the nullification ordinance.

The events leading up to the compromise of 1850 were similar in character to those preceding the Missouri Compromise. By war and by treaty another vast tract had been added to the Union, comprising what is now Washington,

Oregon, California, Idaho, Nevada, Utah, Arizona, New Mexico, Texas, and parts of Wyoming and Colorado. The situation was infinitely complicated but with the usual issue at bottom. Texas had become a slave state and California had applied for a free constitution. What was to be done with the intermediate territory, then called New Mexico? Congressional controversy waxed furious for the better part of a year, one Senator threatening another at the point of a revolver. The triumvirate appeared for the last time. Calhoun was so weak that he could not read his speech. His arguments were familiar and even commonplace to the Southerners, many of whom were now out for a more radical stand. Clay offered a compromise, and to the amazement of the North, Webster supported him. As finally effected this compromise conceded more to the South than to the North, and demonstrated that in application the federal system was gradually becoming warped by the pressure of circumstances. The idea of a separate Confederacy was finding many supporters in the South. And obviously, whereas it was simple to unite the slave owners for the defense of their own property, it was nearly impossible to consolidate all degrees of Northern sentiment upon a moral issue—an issue which in reality only affected them as the basis of some one else's prosperity. We see what a change had taken place since 1833 by the fact that Webster thought the Union sufficiently endangered to forsake his traditional principles and urge a compromise. However, the result of the compromise was excellent. Whatever moral sentiment remained unsatisfied, the thing itself had a semblance of finality. Prosperity ruled, and every one seemed happy. Clay's dreams of another compromise to maintain peace for thirty years seemed on the verge of fulfillment. But the Great Compromiser died; and when a new crisis arose in 1854 there was no one of his capacity to settle it.

Stephen A. Douglas wanted to be president. He was powerful in the North, but to attain his ambition he sought to acquire the Southern Democratic vote as well. Hence he advocated the extraordinarily untimely doctrine that the 1850 Compromise vitiated the Missouri Compromise, and that as a consequence the unsettled parts of Louisiana territory should be free or slave according to the dictates of the settlers. This doctrine was enacted in the Kansas-Nebraska Bill and subsequently upheld by the decision of Chief Justice Taney in the Dred Scott case. Northern indignation against both of these issues was so intense that the South became disgusted. According to the North, the Southern oligarchy was ruling the nation; according to the South, if the national administration could not prevent these infernal outbreaks against its own enactments, they would create a government which could. The separatist movement gained strength with each conflict, and as it grew it demanded greater concessions and became more obdurate. At length by 1860 the question of slavery had given place to the question as to whether secession should be permitted. Until then the Southerners had had enough control in Congress to keep their actions within legislative bounds. But the initial victory of the Republican Party and the entrance of Lincoln made them realize that the balance of power had turned against their oligarchy. Immediately secession began. In a panic, Senators and leaders of thought sought wildly to mediate, even if this should entail greater concessions to the oligarchy. The most important plan was the Crittenden Compromise. As a boundary between slave and free states it proposed to extend to the Pacific the line of 36° 30′ agreed upon in the Missouri Compromise. The Senate appointed an excellent committee of thirteen to consider it. The Southern delegates would have accepted it. But it fell through and the influence which brought about its rejection came from Abraham Lincoln. "Entertain no proposition for a compromise in regard to the extension of slavery," he wrote at the time. "The instant you do they have us under again; all our labor is lost and sooner or later must be done over. . . . The tug has to come, and better now than later." After that, conflict was inevitable.

If we take the stress of the times into consideration, it is difficult to criticize any of Lincoln's actions. It seems that he practically always did things as well as they could be done. Yet given the magnitude which his figure and his precedent have assumed in our traditions, we should perhaps regard him more critically. Lincoln believed first of all in the sovereignty of the federal government. Secondly, he thought that slavery was wrong and that it should be restricted by the central power. Slavery is a moral evil; but the Constitution had been at great pains to avoid stating that the federal administration has authority to enforce the moral code of one section upon another. Such a precedent, furthermore, would be bound to subvert any federation sooner or later. Slavery might have been handled differently. Lincoln's own theory of gradual emancipation with compensation, if applied by such a man as he, would have been a thousand times preferable to civil war. But it was conceived a decade too late. Emancipation, which he finally proclaimed as a war measure, amounted to a capital tax of $4,000,000,-000. The general Unionist antagonism to Southern oligarchy required that its power be curtailed. But it was a far cry from this to the capital tax; this was precisely the sort of outrage against minority rights which a federal system ordinarily guards against. Lincoln had the capacity to avert civil war and might have added a brilliant page to federal history. But fate did not bring him upon the scene until the South had already become partial to the idea of secession. Had there been no interval between Clay and Lincoln, our history might read differently.

But once the immense territory was acquired and colonized from coast to coast, the nation, less thrilled by its size than terrified by its diversity, and eager to break down all barriers which might thwart unification, resolved to attain moral and economic unanimity, whatever might be the cost. Thus one of the essential principles of federalism was sacrificed. But it had not served in vain. It had brought the United States men and territories which would never have been acquired under a more strict national organization. It had maintained a fertile and stimulating state of freedom in a people who required above all the opportunity to work and develop. Without the adaptability of federalism, without Clay and his compromises, the United States would never have obtained dominion over its vast continent. This extension, this spaciousness, which is so much a part of American civilization and so essential to every American citizen, was one of the inestimable gifts of federalism to the great Republic. Even Napoleon, with all his power and genius, with the unbounded devotion of his adherents, could not accomplish the same for France.

CHAPTER IV

THE AMERICAN NATION (1866-1920)

Before 1860 the United States was a federal republic. After 1865 it was a nation in the modern and European sense of the word. Federalism did not die; rather it passed into the texture of the nation. Whatever grievances one section may now feel against another or against the nation as a whole, it entertains no thought of obtaining satisfaction, or even ameliorating its condition, through autonomy. Since the Civil War the great administrative end has been to develop a national spirit, to foster a unity and activity which would place the nation in the foremost rank among civilized peoples. The natural boundaries have been crossed and all parts of the continent welded into a flexible nation. The matter of space is no problem for the time being at least. In place of vast tracts of fertile wilderness peopled by a few indomitable pioneers, there are now millions of their descendants, forming a mass, dense yet elastic, classified yet free—a mass which, as regards well-being and happiness, has no equal. To advance in fifty years from the rank of Mexico or Sweden to that the greatest nation required singular energy and rare good fortune.

Ambition in America is as vast as the land itself. There is enough space for each individual to give free rein to his desires. Neither frontiers nor rigid class boundaries arise, as in Europe, to render his dreams chimerical. It is not at all fantastic to imagine superb destinies and strange metamorphoses in a land where proportions are so immense. The nation has developed, along with the spirit of adventure and

75

optimism, an ambitiousness which is quite inconceivable in Europe. Nowhere else does a vast mass of human beings show so little inertia. Each individual forms a part of the nation as separate drops of water are integral to the ocean. The surface of society, to continue the figure, is just as turbulent, with its swells and dips. Those whose initiative has brought them to the fore today are but perilously perched. A few generations hence their offspring will be lost in the slough of obscurity. Evidently each crest must represent a power of tremendous vitality. What prevents it from becoming a tidal wave? Nothing but the fact that the bulk of the nation, though fluid and agitated, possesses a center of gravity. When a crest mounts too high, the inertia vested in the federal government begins to pull against it. And eventually it sinks again.

In the last fifty years there have been striking clashes. The opponents against which the federal government has pitted itself have ranged from the most important numerically (the party) through the most powerful economically (the corporation) to the most significant morally (the individual). Often the federal side of the case has seemed inexcusable, and the intelligent public has looked upon it as a jumble of inefficiency, stupidity, and ignorance, with right and justice all against it. But in the long run, as the historian reviews the past, the government's defense of tradition grows consistent, and rich in fundamental wisdom.

An interesting fact is to be noted here. The aggressors whom the government successfully curbed were not subversively inclined. That is, they sought to attain their ends by recognized means. They were certain, astute, and procured the assistance of the most skilled intellects. Often they paid for legislation or got around the law, but they were rarely defiant. They did not attempt to undermine the central administration. There have been few radical agitations to obtain more than local or temporary prominence. This is probably due to the fact that ambition seeps even to the lowest levels, and persons of ability among the masses usually prefer to obey the urge of ambition as individuals rather than as class leaders. This is fortunate, for it must be admitted as a defect of the American government that as yet it has devised no particularly effective scheme for coping with destructive groups. The fact that such groups have not accomplished more seems to bear out the hypothesis that, all other things being equal, man prefers good to evil and order to chaos. But the few lawless groups which have had capable direction obtained positions from which the ordinary administrative and judicial forces were powerless to dislodge them. The infamous Tweed Ring, which defrauded New York's taxpayers of sums estimated at from $45,000,000 to $200,000,000, was finally destroyed by a press campaign, through information gathered by the New York *Times* and the cartoons of Thomas Nast in *Harper's Weekly*. The Philadelphia Gas Ring was partially overthrown by a citizens' committee of one hundred. But the most amazing band of all, the Molly Maguires, whose murderous activities terrorized the anthracite coal region of Pennsylvania for over a decade, was only brought to justice through individual effort, the tireless aggression of a railroad president and the skill and courage of a private detective. In audacity and foulness the story of this society sounds like a tale out of Renaissance Italy.

The anthracite coal field in Pennsylvania covers less than five hundred square miles, an area whose center is about seventy-five miles from Philadelphia and a hundred from New York City. It is hard to imagine a more dismal country. Arable land is scarce, and what little there is, is not fully utilized. The surface is rough and jagged. Building sites for collieries are often difficult to obtain. The exigencies of coal mining require that large bodies of men be gathered at given points. But it is only a step from these thickly settled patches to desolate mountain ranges. The mining population is largely foreign-born, and it presents an appalling sight to any one who is not accustomed to it. The men live in coal and breathe coal. Coal dust has penetrated every pore of their bodies. This, added to the pallor from life underground, gives them a diabolical appearance which nothing in their life serves to mitigate. Their leisure hours used to be passed in saloons amid drunkenness and brawling. Life under such conditions was truly worth little, hardly more than the taking of it. So indeed it appeared in 1875, when, for a period of ten years, murders of the utmost atrocity had been occurring without retribution, murders which were coolly planned upon the slightest provocation and executed with increasing boldness.

The Irish population in the anthracite region outnumbered that of any one other nationality. After centuries of oppression the Irish had come to regard any resistance to authority as praiseworthy. The relation between boss and miner hardly tended to change this attitude. As early as 1855 it was rumored that a secret society existed which avenged the grievances of its members by blood. And it is certain that seven years later the fiendish operations of the Molly Maguires were a dreadful reality against which the police, the administration, and a highly excited populace were helpless.

In June, 1862, a breaker boss named F. W. S. Langdon, had made himself unpopular with his men. In the course of an angry altercation he denounced one of them violently. Later in the day he was found dying. He had been beaten with stones and the fatal blow was apparently dealt with a hammer. A few arrests were made, but there was no evidence and no trial.

In December, 1862, about two hundred armed men attacked the collieries of William Goyne. They raked the fire from under the boilers, stopped the engines, and allowed the mines to flood. Then they beat and mauled about fifteen employees, attacked and closed the colliery store. They remained on the scene for over two hours, and as they left, uttered threats of vengeance should the colliery be opened without permission.

In November, 1863, George K. Smith, a coal operator, was suspected of having given the federal government information concerning the district enrollment. One evening, not feeling well, he had retired. A man called and insisted upon seeing him. As he came downstairs, a crowd rushed into the house and commenced shooting. Smith was instantly killed. No evidence was obtained to convict any one.

In August, 1865, David Muir, a mine superintendent of excellent character, fair-minded and popular, was attacked by three men in early morning. He was shot and stabbed several times and died immediately. Although the murder took place on a highway within earshot of many people, its perpetrators escaped justice.

In January, 1866, Henry H. Dunne, superintendent of one of the large coal companies, was murdered on the highway in the late afternoon. Although news of the crime spread rapidly and several people saw the murderers leave the scene, their identity was not discovered. The coal company employed detectives and offered a large reward to no avail. The assassins were not punished.

In October, 1868, Alexander Rae was waylaid and robbed. He was thought to have been carrying a mine payroll. He was not; and the robbers, apparently to vent their disgust, murdered him. Rae was a charitable man, who took great interest in the welfare of his workers. Three men were arrested and tried. But although at least one of them was guilty, their alibi was so skillfully contrived that they were all acquitted.

In December, 1871, Morgan Powell, a boss, was murdered in the center of a town in early evening. The murderers escaped.

This revolting list, chosen at random, is but a small fraction of the crimes committed by the Molly Maguires. Such a state of lawlessness was a serious handicap to the mining industry. The murder of capable bosses, the frequent destruction of property, and the flooding of mines (the two latter offenses, though not always committed by Mollies, were encouraged by them) brought severe losses which affected every one. The greatest sufferer was the Philadelphia and Reading Railroad, with its subsidiary, the Philadelphia and Reading Coal and Iron Company. The president of the railroad, Franklin B. Gowen, saw plainly that the law was powerless before the Mollies and resolved to pursue extraordinary methods to bring about their extermination. Accordingly he put the case in the hands of the Pinkerton Agency, which sent a young Irish detective to the coal region with instructions to join the Molly Maguires and obtain information as to their organization, plots, and crimes. James McParlan was the man.

It is difficult to do justice to McParlan. His experiences add a chapter to human adventure rarely paralleled in modern times. In two years McParlan penetrated nearly to the center of the Molly organization, won the confidence of many leaders, prevented crimes while pretending to abet them, warned victims, and gathered a mass of detailed information so complete and cogent as to withstand grilling cross-examination later on by keen lawyers. He pretended that he had killed a man in Buffalo, and was a fugitive from justice—an honorable situation from the Molly point of view. To account for his income when he was apparently

out of work, and to give a reason for his movements about
the district, he let it be understood that he was a counter-
feiter.

The climax came in September, 1875. The usual Molly
procedure had been one of reciprocity. That is to say, the
Mollies of one district would agree to kill a marked man
in another district, and the Mollies in the second district
would commit some murder in return. This made identi-
fication difficult and facilitated alibis. In exchange for the
assassination of policeman Yost, the Mollies of his district
were expected to kill a mining boss, John P. Jones. McParlan
saw to it that Jones was warned, and he succeeded in post-
poning the attempts of his group indefinitely. Unfortunately
another group was plotting this same crime and succeeded
in accomplishing it one morning near a crowded railroad
station. The murderers fled to the mountains and eluded pur-
suit. About five miles away, however, they stopped for rest
and refreshment. They were seen here by a young law
student who was examining the hillsides with a spyglass.
He collected a party which approached the criminals from
two directions and easily captured them. The trial was a
time of intense excitement. A good deal of evidence became
available and the prosecution, spurred by the energy of
Gowen, was prepared in great detail. The murderers, on the
other hand, relied upon their usual defense of alibi. But
something went wrong. It became clear to the lawyers for
the defense that the other side knew too much of their case
in advance. They feared that they also would be implicated
if the perjured witnesses were used to establish the alibi,
and this point was abandoned. The first trial resulted in a
verdict of murder in the first degree, the first capital sentence ever pronounced against a Molly Maguire. The suspicions of the lawyers, however, soon crystallized into a
rumor that there was a detective among the Mollies and

McParlan was singled out, although just why is still a mystery. Of course, his murder was prescribed. But McParlan showed his nerve in the face of it all, and boldly denounced his accusers. Furthermore, he demanded a conclave of prominent Mollies to hear him. This was more or less agreed to, but the intention was to take his life beforehand. "For God's sake have him killed," said a prominent Molly, "or he will hang half the people in Schuylkill County." Four times at least, he escaped from his would-be assassins by the narrowest margin. At length he became convinced that his mission was so well known or strongly suspected that he could be of no further use where he was. Accordingly he returned to Philadelphia. From then on, the downfall of the Molly Maguires was rapid. Arrests and convictions followed in quick succession, due largely to the damning testimony of McParlan. By the end of 1877 the society was destroyed, never to reappear in the anthracite region.

This bloody tale shows post-war conditions at their worst. The instinct of lawlessness and violence which a great conflict always unchains is not readily suppressed again. Patriotism, by causing the murder of the nation's enemies to be looked upon as a praiseworthy act, will often encourage individuals or groups to give vent to the desire for vengeance or to unscrupulous ambitions. As any nation would have done, the American people became restive and difficult to manage after the Civil War. While the central government, in emerging victorious from the conflict, was more firmly established than ever, it was actually menaced by an accumulation of sectional difficulties which assumed serious proportions through the powerlessness of the local authorities. The federal government could hardly have settled these difficulties, since the Constitution placed police control beyond its jurisdiction. Moreover, it was never a case of section against section, but of one locality divided against itself.

The defect would lie in the local government of one particular district. This applies equally to the Molly Maguires, the
Tweed Ring, the Gas Ring, and most other public scandals
of the United States. As a matter of fact there seems to be
a greater disparity than necessary between federal government and the government of states and municipalities. As
the first had no hand in the establishment of the others,
it can hardly be held responsible for their misdeeds. Incapable or corrupt local government seems to be a vice which
is inherent in modern democracy. Even Bryce reluctantly ad-
mits this: "—the Machine and the whole organization of
Rings and Bosses. This is the ugliest feature in the current
politics of the country. Must it be set down to democracy?
To some extent, yes. It could not have grown up save in a
popular government; and some of the arrangements which
have aided in its growth, such as the number and frequency
of elections, have been dictated by what may be called the
narrow doctrinairism of democracy." One of the worst features is the fact that any well-organized society is a potent
factor politically. Even a ridiculously small body of voters
which can be counted upon to vote *in toto* one way or the
other, is always catered to by candidates. Thus local elec-
tioneers never breathe a word against even so vile a body
as the Molly Maguires. Worse still, in 1875, when lawlessness was at its height, it is said that the Molly vote was
actually purchased by the Republican Party. It is difficult
to state precisely whether these wheels within wheels are
changing for better or for worse. In the case of New York
City, for instance, there seems to have been a slight improvement. Tammany is still supreme, but Croker was not
so flagrantly corrupt as Tweed, nor Murphy so bad as
Croker. And the new boss, Olvany, appears in a better light.
But there is still so much room for improvement that the
case seems hopeless for the present. Bryce, however, judg-

ing from England's experience, is more optimistic. He seems
to consider powerlessness and corruption as evils attendant
upon one stage of political development. He believes that
eventually they are outgrown. Let us hope he is right.

The lesson of the Civil War was well appreciated. Eleven
years later, corrupt election returns from several states
placed a Republican in the Presidential chair when the office
should have gone to a Democrat. A technicality in the Constitution was used to prevent a reëxamination of the returns and the result was allowed to stand. One wonders
whether there is any other nation in the world where this
would have been accepted without violence, where peace
could have been preserved despite a rank injustice to the
majority of the voters.

The Hayes-Tilden campaign of 1876 was the most excit-
ing the country has ever known. Grant's eight years had
been most unsatisfactory in many ways. The rehabilitation
of the South had been bungled. Grant had not availed himself of his opportunities to promote civil service reform.
Finally the Crédit Mobilier, Belknap and Custom House
scandals, with the Panic of 1873 (though not attributable
directly to Grant) restored the Democrats to their pre-war
strength. The new candidates were Rutherford B. Hayes,
Republican, and Samuel J. Tilden, Democrat. Hayes was
governor of Ohio. He was not brilliant, and every step forward had been made by dint of perseverance and unbend-
ing purpose. His judgment was sound, not intuitively so,
but as a result of intelligent reasoning. A college graduate
(Kenyon), he was a good student, with a respect for educated society. "Slow in thought, speech, and action," says
Rhodes, "when once he made up his mind, he was inflexible
and not tormented by vain regrets." He was an excellent
example of the type of man best fitted to guide a federation.
Tilden was governor of New York. He had good business

acumen, and as a corporation lawyer he had made a fortune. Some say he was scrupulously honest and bore an honorable part in the overthrow of Tweed and in combating other instances of state corruption. Hayes' campaign was undoubtedly the better organized of the two, which placed his chances on a par with his opponent's. Still the contest was to be an exceedingly close one, with New York apparently as the pivotal state.

Excitement on election day and during the night was intense. But when it was learned that Tilden had carried New York, and likewise New Jersey, Connecticut, and Indiana, it was reckoned that the solid South would elect him. The next morning almost all papers conceded this. But the New York *Times* dissented. In a later edition it claimed that the South was not solidly Democratic, that South Carolina and Louisiana had gone over to Hayes, and that Florida was still doubtful. The electoral vote then stood 184 for Tilden and 181 for Hayes. Florida's four votes could give Hayes a majority of one. Three days later it appeared that South Carolina honestly belonged to Hayes, but that Tilden had popular majorities in both Florida and Louisiana, assuring his election. But there was doubt. It must be remembered that these states were still under the carpet-bag régime. Corruption was rampant among the negroes, and their Northern ringleaders made the most of their opportunities. One of the measures passed to keep the Republican strength in the South superior to that of the Ku Klux Klan, empowered the state election boards to throw out votes on grounds of intimidation or fraud. By this means a Tilden majority of 90 in Florida was converted into a Hayes balance of 925. The case of Louisiana was more flagrant. Tilden's majority on the face of the returns was between 6,300 and 8,957. The Returning Board consisted of four disreputable Republicans. J. M. Wells, the chairman, was, according to General Sheridan, "a political trickster and a dishonest man." His record was appalling. Thomas C. Anderson was as corrupt, though not so clever. Casanave, a negro, was an ignorant nonentity. Kenner, another negro, had been indicted for larceny. This body proceeded to throw out the votes of 2,042 Republicans and 13,250 Democrats. This elected Hayes. But the story goes that, before making the final return, Wells offered to sell out to Tilden for $200,-000. The popular vote stood 4,300,000 for Tilden and 4,-036,000 for Hayes. Of course the Democrats objected strenuously, and soon Congress was all clash and turmoil. The dispute eventually narrowed down to this: In case of a contested ballot, did Congress have the right to go behind the official certificate of a given state to ascertain the honesty of its figures? In a slightly different form, this was the states' rights issue again. But with true historical irony, it was the Democrats who were attacking the doctrine now and the Republicans who defended it. The situation was desperate. We shall be "brought to the point," said Goode of Virginia in the House, "where one party or the other must make an ignominious surrender, or we must fight. Are the gentlemen prepared for the latter alternative?" A cry of "Yes" burst from the Republicans. A Louisville paper said that 100,000 unarmed citizens would march to Washington to maintain the rights of Tilden. A prominent Southerner declared that 145,000 well-disciplined Southern troops stood ready to fight for him. Rhodes, after a thorough study of the period, is certain that the country was on the verge of another civil war. "The number of men out of employment and in want owing to the depression of business, the many social outcasts in the community, whom the railroad riots seven months later disclosed, constituted a formidable army who were ready for any disturbance that might improve their condition or give them an opportunity for plunder. The

mass of adherents on each side, which was clearly indicated
by the closeness of the vote in many Northern states, shows
what a terrible internecine conflict would have followed a
bloody affray on the floor of Congress." Despite the stress,
enough legislators kept their heads to bring the conflict
to a conclusion. A committee of fifteen was chosen, five
senators, five representatives, and five justices of the Supreme Court. There were seven Democrats and seven Republicans, with the political hue of one justice remaining in
doubt. He turned out to be a Republican and his vote sustained Hayes' election. Upon seeing how the matter ended,
the Democrats were keenly disappointed and greatly enraged.
But at this moment an act of sublime magnanimity insured
a peaceful termination to the dispute. Forty-two ex-Confed-
erates, members of the House, "solemnly pledged themselves
to each other upon their sacred honor to oppose all attempts
to frustrate the counting of the votes for President" and
"did not propose to permit a second civil war if their votes
could prevent it." Still it was a dangerous crisis. The Hayes
election was not confirmed until two days before the expiration of Grant's term.

The significance of the Hayes-Tilden controversy can
hardly be overestimated. The settlement of a vital conflict
was effected where none had seemed possible. But the outcome can hardly be considered a triumph of democracy, for
more than half the voters believed that a gross injustice
had been committed. On the other hand, a verdict which
denied Congress the right of prying into state affairs was
clearly a reaffirmation of the spirit of the federal Constitution. Moreover, the moral point raised here is of considerable
importance: we have the choice between a rigid code upholding an unfair result, and a fair judgment involving an
infraction of the code. But a moment's consideration is
needed, however, to make it clear that the maintenance of

the code outweighs the triumph of right. After all, there is no such thing as absolute justice. Justice is a convenient term for expressing the relation between a circumstance and a standard. The problem is not to deliver a just decision, but to ascertain the circumstance and determine the standard. A violation of the standard opens the door to chaos.

In some ways the Hayes election was the greatest victory American federalism ever won. No opponent is more formidable than a popular majority in a free country, particularly when its passions are roused, as in this instance. But the government keenly realized its responsibility, and made a superhuman effort.

Political parties are not solidly constructed in the United States. During a presidential campaign, the sectional leaders hang together if they can, but such homogeneity is only temporary. There is rarely a national boss, and party ambition does not run to great projects. On the other hand there have been many smaller groups whose ambitions were boundless, and with whom the government was soon to find itself in constant and stubborn conflict. When Jackson gave away the public lands, he virtually said that the natural resources of the land belonged to those who would take trouble to acquire them. That was the policy to which the greatest American fortunes are due. Money was amassed primarily by obtaining, developing, and marketing the great natural resources of the country. Beyond the original decision that profits should accrue to the individuals and not to the nation, the government, as such, has had little to do with actual development except in the conferring of franchises. But the individuals and groups that obtained grants and franchises from the government obtained fortunes. Until recently at least, land and transportation have been the greatest sources of wealth in this country.

In the earliest days the owners of great feudal estates

in and about New York, the Van Rensselaers, for instance, amassed what were large fortunes for those times. Then came a period of merchantmen and shipbuilders. Some famous names appear among these: Samuel Adams, John Hancock, Robert Morris. Among the New England families who came into prominence then are the Cabots, Peabodies, and Brookses. Peter Chardon Brooks of Medford, with $2,000,000 was the wealthiest man of the region. But by far the richest man up to 1830 was Stephen Girard of Philadelphia, shipowner and principal stockholder in the Bank of the United States, a rapacious miser, who astonished every one by willing about $7,000,000 to charity. Then came the great fortunes in city lands, acquired by purchase, fraud, speculation, bribery, and what-not: Astor, Goelet, Rhinelander, Longworth, and Field. The Astor fortune was the largest of these and probably reached $450,-000,000. Next, which brings us up to the period under consideration, come the railroad fortunes: Vanderbilt, Gould, Sage, Hill, Harriman, Huntington, and Crocker, to name only the principal figures. The benignity and prestige which clothe these names today incline us to forget the scandalous ways in which their fame was acquired. A good many tricks, fair neither in love nor war, were currently resorted to. One bout between Commodore Vanderbilt and Tammany is amusing. In 1863 Vanderbilt wanted to secure for the New York and Harlem Railroad a perpetual franchise on a line from the battery to Union Square. To that end he proceeded to buy the Aldermen on the City Council. But as the franchise promised large profits, others too were eager for it. In particular there was George Law who was busily at work bribing the State Legislature. As this was the higher body it appeared that Law would win. At this stage the Aldermen, who thought nothing of double-crossing, took a hand. Said they, the New York and Harlem stock is now quoted at about $100. Suppose we pocket Vanderbilt's money and pass the franchise. That will send the stock up. Then the Legislature will act for Law and we shall have to annul the Vanderbilt grant in conformity. As a result the stock will fall heavily. Now if we sell short on the rise and cover during the slump we can make several fortunes. They acted accordingly, and almost everything went as they had predicted. But Vanderbilt was a resourceful fox. Apparently some of his brokers had been approached with short offers, for he soon caught on to the game. He secretly bought up every scrap of the stock that was available, and the price, instead of dropping, rose and rose. The Aldermen were caught. They had to cover their $90 sales at $179, while the Commodore pocketed millions.

An acquisitive disposition is unfortunately accompanied by greed and envy. Formerly, at any rate, the temptation to acquire more wealth through legislative manipulation was strong and frequently yielded to. On the other hand envy of the rich became rampant among the less fortunate, and this was not mitigated in the least by splendid public gifts of great value. The wealthy tended to become a special class, the interests; for in the main, legislation affected them as one body. As a result a group of men, located for convenience in New York, came to constitute an oligarchy which was far more powerful than the cotton growers had ever been. Public sentiment turned more and more strongly against it. Yet nothing effectual was done to curb its power. The labor unions attempted to do little beyond strengthening their own rights, and were not particularly successful even in this. Of course it was some time before the federal government, conservative as ever, could take action. On the face of it, there was nothing illegitimate in amassing a fortune; and besides, there was a good chance of profit for unscrupulous

legislators. Yet the growing popular aversion to this new
centralization of the "interests" maintained a clamor which
would compel attention sooner or later. As the issues crystallized, two ideas appeared which might be of service in combating the great fortunes. First, the combination of similar
companies under one directorate so as to destroy the natural
economic effect of competition, seemed morally wrong.
Second, since the very wealthy had more property requiring protection, they should pay more taxes than the poor.
Intelligent men pondered over these ideas for some time,
and at length they were embodied in law. The Sherman
Anti-Trust Act was passed in 1890, and the Wilson-Gorman
Tax Bill in 1894. But something more than legislation was
necessary. The income tax was declared unconstitutional
by the Supreme Court. Why, it is not easy to comprehend,
for a previous court had passed upon the legality of such
a tax and it had actually been collected during the war and
until 1872. This blow was a severe one and no more was
heard of income taxes for over fifteen years. The anti-trust
law was a good one, but difficult of enforcement. The interests employed the best lawyers in the country to find ways
of getting around it. They were so well entrenched that a
good deal of courage was required to attack them. Besides,
the lobbyists at Washington exerted their tremendous influence to the limit. As neither Harrison, Cleveland nor
McKinley cared to put his hands into the hornets' nest,
the Sherman Act remained pretty much of a joke until
1901, when it received vitality in the hands of Theodore
Roosevelt. From then on it became the famous "big stick"
which curbed the avarice of more than a few millionaires.
This alone should warrant devoting a few pages to Roosevelt. But in addition, he must be regarded as one of the
principal creators of the present national ideal in America.

He and Wilson have best represented the tendencies which have come to the fore in the last forty years, and which are the directing forces of the present.

At the close of the nineteenth century, politics was a much maligned profession. The wealthy considered the politician as little above the jailbird. The proletariat believed him considerably below—about on a par with the Wall Street magnate. Popular ambition lay elsewhere than in politics. The captain of industry was the idol, and the amassing of a great fortune seemed the ultimate end. In fact the country was creeping towards a stage of development which, if unchecked, was certain to entail a social upheaval. The able and ambitious were busy acquiring wealth by fair means or foul. The aristocracy of the old families had been submerged beneath the deluge of great fortunes. The Civil War had impoverished the Southern families who had helped make Newport a fashionable resort. They were no longer able to afford the luxury of a summer on the shore, and the page in the Sunday papers devoted to society found the "breaking-in" entertainments of the new rich more akin to the popular novel conception than to the sober traditions of the descendants of the patroons. Often the two classes were united by marriage, and wealth soon became the ruling criterion of the social world. Then as the great fortunes came into the hands of the second and third generations, all incentive to work disappeared. Then men were usually without professions, and what is worse, their sole concern was with sports, social relations, and vices. They took not the slightest interest in intellectual pursuits of their own, nor in the intellectual achievements of others, unless it happened to be the fashion. The wealthy lived on a scale of unparalleled material extravagance, squandering their inheritances, vying with one another in purchases and entertainments, with little thought of the future. At this stage Theodore Roosevelt appeared. His entrance into politics was somewhat of an accident, but that is of no importance. The fact that he, an aristocrat, entered this field successfully was perhaps his most significant achievement. It led the general public to regard the politician more favorably. Today a gentleman may hold office without necessarily losing all claim to respectability. To Roosevelt politics was a tempting prize. He had enough money, but he adored the limelight, power, the opportunity to fight, the national prominence given to all his actions. Through sheer exuberance of animal spirits he was obliged to keep in a constant state of activity. This soon had its effect upon the nation. To quote Stuart P. Sherman: "Then came the impact upon the national character of the Rooseveltian personality, persuaded that there are a hundred things more interesting than making money, all worth while: hunting grizzlies, reforming, exploring, writing history, traveling, fighting Spaniards, developing a navy, governing men, reading Irish epics, building canals, swimming the Potomac with ambassadors, shooting lions, swapping views with kaisers, organizing new parties, and so on forever. Under the influence of this masterful force the unimaginative plutocratic psychology was steadily metamorphosed." Roosevelt's career should at least demonstrate that politics is a far more attractive outlet for an able man's energy than business, a field which is already overcrowded. He sought to reinvest the profession of governing with the prestige it had enjoyed under the old Federalists.

Although this may be his chief glory, at the same time Roosevelt had certain well-defined governmental policies to which he devoted much of his time. He held that the failure of ancient republics was due either to the exploitation of the poor by the rich when they were in power, or the robbery of the rich by the poor under reversed conditions. The function of the state should be to serve as buffer between these two factions; to restrain one or the other without prejudice whenever it exceeded the limits of justifiable conduct. The rôle of the chief executive he conceived as follows, to use his own words: "I believe that the efficiency of this government depends upon its possessing a strong central executive, and wherever I could establish a precedent for strengthening the executive—I have felt not merely that my action was right in itself, but that in showing the strength of, or in giving strength to, the executive, I was establishing a precedent of value. I believe in a strong executive; I believe in power." Incidentally these convictions were very characteristic of Roosevelt. Once he had made up his mind his beliefs were almost fanatical. Happily they remained reasonable until his later years.

In actuality Roosevelt used his governmental buffer almost entirely in behalf of the common people. This does not conflict with his conception of government as mentioned above, for the great interests were becoming inordinately powerful. Nevertheless had conditions been different, he would have had a much harder time of it. Roosevelt succeeded just so long as he championed the people and the people's ideals. For seven years he had the popular vote. With it behind him he successfully fought the trust, Congress, and the political bosses—the most powerful elements in the country. To be sure his consummate political skill was largely responsible for his victories, but nevertheless, had he not had popular backing to begin with, the rest would have been impossible.

Roosevelt's fight against the trusts was a brilliant one and, as far as one can see, it was not prompted by selfish motives. He thoroughly believed that the family and the protection of private property formed the bases of civilization. He was firmly opposed to any kind of socialism. On these fundamental propositions most financiers would have agreed with him. Roosevelt's disapproval of trusts arose because he believed that great industrial organizations gave too much power to a few and nullified the opportunities for individual development in too great numbers of people. Acting upon this principle, in 1901 he instituted prosecution against the Northern Securities Company for violation of the anti-trust act. The Northern Securities was a holding company whose principals were James J. Hill and J. Pierpont Morgan. Its object was to bring the Northern Pacific, the Great Northern, and the Chicago, Burlington & Quincy railroads under the same control. In sum this meant a permanent monopoly of the northern routes from Chicago to the Pacific, and eliminated competition on through traffic. A circuit court decided in favor of the government and the Supreme Court confirmed their decision. The latter gave a 5-4 verdict, and as one of the concurring justices differed in some degree from the other four, it was popularly said that the government had won by $4\frac{5}{8}$ to $4\frac{3}{8}$. It has sometimes been said that had Roosevelt desired, he could have obtained better results through coöperation than through antagonism. This is probably not true. The financial interests were honorable in their way, but decidedly selfish. It is doubtful whether any one could have obtained results from them by gentler methods. In conference with the president, Morgan is reported to have said, "If we have done anything wrong, send your man (the Attorney-General) to my man (a prominent lawyer) and they can fix it up." Afterwards Roosevelt said, "That is a most illuminating illustration of the Wall Street point of view. Mr. Morgan could not help regarding me as a big rival operator, who either intended to ruin all his interests or else could be induced to come to an agreement to ruin none." Be that as it may, Roosevelt would never have won such public applause by compromising with the interests. He told the rich they were corrupt, and he threatened to jail them. He invented the Ananias Club into which he put all men whom he considered liars. The public enjoyed these methods hugely and considered the man who dared employ them in the presidential chair as their true friend. Roosevelt appreciated the value of this attitude and sought to strengthen it on every occasion. He boasted of his friendship with miners, farmers, cowboys, and prizefighters. Perhaps it was quite natural for him to do this. If so, he had an innate political genius, for no more successful method of vote-getting has ever been devised.

Roosevelt was particularly successful in his dealings with Congress. Yet his success was largely achieved through the application of a very simple formula. He kept hammering at it with elaborate programs of action. Congress by nature does not approve of too much action, and so found itself constantly at odds with the president. He was always very careful to explain his side of any controversy in very definite and forcible language, and in such a manner that it would immediately receive national attention and usually national approval. Congress, on the other hand, was too inarticulate to address itself to such an audience, and therefore often found itself in the dilemma of being obliged to vote against the opinions of its electors or to allow the president to have his own way. It generally did the latter.

Had Roosevelt been more consistent in his thinking he would probably have extended his conception of the state to his dealings with foreign countries. It does not require any great stretch of the imagination to see that he might have advocated a strong international organ to smooth out differences between nations, very much as he believed that the state executive should arbitrate class differences. In his later years, to be sure, he did recognize the value of

certain of Mr. Wilson's ideas, but his own foreign policy
was modeled on quite different lines. Roosevelt considered
the nations of the world not as members of one family, but
rather as a number of entirely distinct families, each one
being made up of a central power enlarged by colonial
possessions, dependencies, and spheres of influence. The history of his foreign relations is to a great extent an account
of his attempts to enlarge and strengthen the American unit
of power. In other words, Roosevelt was an imperialist
with a grandiose conception of an American empire, which
Sherman says made the Kaiser's dream of Mittel-Europa
"look like a postage stamp." Roosevelt believed the Spanish
war to have been inevitable, though he never said exactly
why. With such a hypothesis, the acquisition of Porto Rico
and of the Philippines, together with the Cuban protectorate,
must appear equally inevitable. Which they certainly were,
with Roosevelt in office; as was also the annexation of the
Hawaiian Islands and the leasing of the Canal Zone. Of
course, he was able to justify all of these measures on political, diplomatic, or humanitarian grounds. Mr. J. A. Hob-
son, the English economist, maintained that the acquisition
of more territory and the strengthening of the American
spheres of influence were due to a desire on the part of
the trusts to secure new and protected markets for their
surplus products. The economic trend may eventually prove
this to be true, but on the other hand, Roosevelt was not
exactly in the habit of making gifts to the "interests"; and,
after all, his Pan-American ideal seems to offer a sufficient
explanation. Although little blood was shed in the course
of this aggrandizement, it by no means follows that Roosevelt would not have had recourse to force upon even a slight
pretext. The development of the navy under his rule was
amazing, and his sending of the fleet around the world was
a more open display of militaristic power than the Kaiser

ever dreamed of. When the troubles over Panama came to a head, Roosevelt observed Bunau-Varilla's intrigues with complacent amusement. After Panama had announced its independence, American warships prevented the landing of the troops which the Colombian government had sent to put down the rebellion. The Roosevelt government immediately recognized the republic of Panama and negotiated with it for a lease of the Canal Zone. Pulitzer of the New York *World* attempted to expose the crookedness of this deal, and Roosevelt promptly set the Department of Justice on his trail. Although the courts decided in favor of Pulitzer, the whole truth was not revealed. In later years, Roosevelt stated to W. R. Thayer that had he not been able to come to terms with either Colombia or Panama, he would have seized the Canal Zone by force in behalf of civilization.

However, Roosevelt did not limit his threats of force to weaker powers. The discovery of gold in the Klondike had revived the dispute between the United States and Canada about the Alaskan boundary. The joint commission appointed by McKinley had failed utterly to come to an agreement. As the irritation continued, Roosevelt decided to settle the matter once and for all and to settle it in favor of the United States. A commission was appointed consisting of three Americans, two Canadians and one Englishman. The matter was finally settled by Lord Alverstone, the English representative, who voted with the Americans. It seems possible, however, that the British government ascertained Alverstone's views before selecting him, for Roosevelt had taken pains to give Justice Holmes of the Supreme Court, who was abroad for the summer, a letter which he was to show "indiscreetly" to Mr. Chamberlain, Mr. Balfour, and two or three other prominent Englishmen. In closing this letter he stated, "I wish to make one last effort to bring about an agreement through the Commission, which will enable the people of both countries to say that the result represents the feeling of the representatives of both countries. But if there is a disagreement, I wish it distinctly understood, not only that there will be no arbitration of the matter, but that in my message to Congress I shall take a position which will prevent any possibility of arbitration hereafter; a position which will render it necessary for Congress to give me the authority to run the line as we claim it, by our own people, without any further regard to the attitude of England and Canada. If I paid attention to mere abstract rights, that is the position I ought to take anyhow."

But Roosevelt's most striking diplomatic successes arose from his conflicts with a man whom he began by admiring greatly and whose methods and ideals vastly resembled his own—Wilhelm II. In his first plans for German hegemony, the Kaiser believed that through commerce and corruption he would secure the aid of both North and South America, but when President Cleveland reaffirmed the Monroe Doctrine in 1895, he was seriously disturbed, for he had contemplated planting German colonies in Central and South America and already had about four hundred thousand Germans in Brazil. By way of retaliation he sought to harm this country in secret at every opportunity. At the beginning of the Spanish war he attempted to form a naval coalition with France and England. Fortunately England balked and Mr. Balfour replied to the Kaiser, "No: if the British fleet takes any part in this war it will be to put itself between the American ships and those of your coalition." In fact it was probably because the English commander stood ready to back Dewey at Manila that the German squadron did not attempt to seize the islands. A German commander who was there declared recently that following instructions from Berlin the fleet had actually stripped for action.

For a long time the Kaiser had been desirous of getting

a foothold in America. When the likelihood that the Panama Canal would be constructed became a certainty, he redoubled his efforts. The people of Venezuela owed considerable sums of money in Germany, England, and Italy, but the creditors could collect neither interest nor capital. The Kaiser hit upon the plan of getting England and Italy to join him in making a naval demonstration at Caracas or Porto Cabello for the obvious purpose of collecting their debts, but with the ulterior motive of establishing a German garrison on the South American coast. Roosevelt perceived the ruse and also found out that both England and Italy were quite willing to arbitrate. Thereupon he told the German ambassador, Holleben, that unless the Kaiser consented to arbitrate the Venezuelan dispute, the American fleet would be sent to defend that country against any German attack. Holleben replied that his Imperial Master had refused to arbitrate, and as his Imperial Master could not change his Imperial mind, there could be no arbitration. A week passed and the ambassador had no further advices. Roosevelt then told him that *he* had changed his mind and that Admiral Dewey would leave for Venezuela a day earlier than he had intended. Before cabling this, Holleben consulted with the German consul-general in New York, who was well acquainted with both Roosevelt and Dewey and who assured him that the latter could blow the whole German fleet out of the water in half an hour. In a day and a half Holleben was able to inform the president that his I. M. consented to arbitration.

Roosevelt was a masterly diplomat and an eminently successful politician. One cannot but admire his material achievements. It is therefore a little startling to realize that the ideals which he preached and the goals toward which he aimed are today largely gone from the American character. They remain as a brilliant tradition, but are no longer an active force. This is usually the fate of the practical man, and Roosevelt preached little which he did not hope ultimately to achieve by his own power and during his own lifetime. He was emphatically not a philosopher, and could never see the value of pure ideas. His thoughts were such as could leap into materialization almost as soon as they were conceived; and, conversely, he was incapable of producing any of those germ ideas which fix themselves ineradicably in the minds of men and bear fruit in a later generation. Aside from his political genius Roosevelt did not have a commanding intellect. He saw just far enough ahead of the crowd to obtain great success during his lifetime, but not far enough to earn him the title of a great man. So little in advance of his day was he, that by 1914 popular opinion had caught up with him and by 1917 had greatly superseded him. He was obviously jealous of Mr. Wilson, whose arguments now had much more influence than his own. In fact he lost all sense of balance during the war, hoping against hope that somehow he might realize his militaristic idea. But popular opinion was no longer behind him. While he was bellowing away that Germany must be crushed, the country was preparing to make the world safe for democracy. He did not perceive it until too late and even then was incapable of understanding it.

We have mentioned Theodore Roosevelt's belief in a strong executive as security to efficient government and his understanding of the state's function as buffer between factions. The second is an excellent federal point of view, and Roosevelt's utilization of it is manifest. The former is not. A true federal executive is a mediator, or at most a conservative leader. His task is to appease conflicting elements justly and to execute projects when he is certain that the principles behind them have public or traditional approval. But no more. The executive should never be an extreme leader. Roosevelt was one, so fascinating that for a time the country followed him blindly, and instead of Roosevelt enacting the country's wishes, the country sustained Roosevelt's. But he was downed. And his fall was a mere matter of routine. He tried to boss Taft, whom he virtually elected as his successor; and when he couldn't do that he ran for a third term, bucking a stone wall which was too much for him. It was the first real defeat of his career, but an irrevocable one. This curt refusal of the nation to be bossed even by its own idol was a rare achievement. True to federal tradition, it denied, even as reward to a hero, any dynastic centralization of the presidency.

At the end of Roosevelt's administration the United States was more powerful than ever before; and what is more important, it was becoming conscious of its own force; a modern nation, thoroughly equipped with an immense fleet, international ambitions, and a competent and highly trained staff of government officials, with well-disciplined and obedient social classes. The country's amazing prosperity would lead one to believe that Roosevelt had accomplished his mission well, had not the emotional complement been lacking. But a nation does not attain the utmost plentitude of its existence until it is virtually in love with itself. The too material wisdom of Roosevelt left the people unsatisfied and their civilization incomplete.

Each great man appears in turn before the public, criticizing, complaining, advocating, exhorting; each with his exhibit, his remedy, his project, truth, or ideal. Each appeals to some desire or faith. A few touch some mute wish in the multitude, and the force of the individual, amplified through the many, is reflected back in gigantic proportions, transcending his own powers. Roosevelt's hour had waned. Another man appeared. A towering figure, intelligent, with that touch of hardness which men have who know and understand where they are bound for. Close to the people, yet far above them; sympathizing with them, yet incapable of mixing with them. More interested in minds than in man; less interested in other minds than in his own. Conscious of the limitations of the American Constitution, he would improve it by increasing the president's power—Roosevelt's method, and the practice of Jackson, Lincoln, and any strong president in a crisis. But unlike Roosevelt, his concepts were based upon solid pedestals of logic, reason, and historical experience.

Woodrow Wilson knew he was a leader long before he reached the presidency. He had learned to impose his will at Princeton, and had enough confidence in himself to insist upon having things his own way. As governor of New Jersey he humiliated the politicians who made him. He sought to govern in the people's interests by direct contact, disregarding their delegated representatives. He came to the presidency after a brief political experience, a liberal with a powerful will—precise, and methodical.

Wilson's theory of government was not in accord with American tradition. He did not approve of the tripartite balance of power. It appeared to him chimerical and unwieldy, equally unjust to the leader whom it oppressed and to the masses whom it confused. Federalism as applied to any one state did not appeal to him. With some unformulated reserves, he considered it not as a permanent form, but merely a "temporary phenomenon of politics," inclining "towards transmutation into a unitary state." Democracy in itself he accepted as an article of faith. I do not think it satisfied his mind; but given its present impregnable position, he realized the futility of combat upon such grounds and did not raise the question. He was judicious enough to make allowance for the limitations of the institution and to be guided accordingly. Government by the people appeared good to him only in so far as the people existed as a rational being, conscious and intelligent. The American people seemed to meet this requisite in a measure, but the American people alone. All others, he often declared, had more to lose than to gain by the premature adoption of democracy.

In actual practice Wilson's policies began as those of a democratic, more far-sighted Roosevelt with a comprehensive scheme in mind. He differed in method. He made no attempt to usurp legislative powers, but simply came before Congress in person to remind it of its duties and to remind his own party of their platform pledges. Then as discussion of some particular subject ensued throughout the country, he endeavored to give the various legislators his ideas as to how the general popular sentiments might best be materialized. The practice of the president appearing before Congress in person had been discontinued by Jefferson. Wilson, in renewing it, was attempting to secure more friendly coöperation between legislators and executive. In this respect his position was more like that of a Prime Minister in Europe, who is at once chief executive and leader of his party.

Three of Wilson's acts, all of them put through in 1913, his first year as president, do not only disclose his desire to curb excessive power; they also give evidence of a rare constructive vision. The Clayton Act may be passed over briefly. Trust-busting as inaugurated by Roosevelt under the Sherman Act of 1890 had gone the limit. But the interests had learned so many ways of getting around the act that more legislation was needed to cope with these evasions. In sum the Clayton Act represented what the government had learned in twelve years about handling over-ambitious business men. Of course, a Democratic administration meant a low tariff and Wilson proposed to eliminate all patronage. The interests set up a howl and collected great funds to maintain a lobby—a group of their representatives in Washington having access to various legislators—with the intention of obstructing the new bill. Sugar appealed to the nation. Wool predicted disaster. Cotton protested against undue haste. And the two wings of the Republican party prepared to get together. At the crucial moment Wilson made an exceedingly clever move. He publicly denounced "the extraordinary exertions being made by the lobby in Washington to gain recognition for certain alterations of the tariff bill." The Senate asked for an investigation, which resulted in revelations conclusively damning to big business. Needless to say, the president won. Attached to this tariff was the income tax enactment, recently validated by Constitutional amendment.

By far the most brilliant achievement of this year was the Federal Reserve Act. The old banking laws were not only out of date, they were a real menace to the whole country. The currency, instead of being regulated by the government, was controlled by a few bankers. Money flowed into the big centers (mainly into New York City), which was natural. But there it was thrown into speculative or local investments, and no provision was made for transferring the funds when and where they were really needed, nor for liquidating time assets in an emergency. The solution to this problem is a perfect example of the federal principle. Of course, a central bank, as in England, France, or Germany, could have been resorted to, but the inherent fear of such a huge organization under national patronage made it prohibitive. So a system of twelve reserve banks was evolved, each to operate in a given section of the country. These were to be bankers' banks whose stock was owned by national banks of the section—member banks. The member banks were obliged to keep on deposit with the Federal Reserve Bank a certain percentage of their own deposits, thus constituting a large emergency reserve. In return the reserve bank supplied liquid funds at short notice against government securities or bankers' acceptances. Moreover, it undertook to collect checks and drafts on all parts of the country at par and to transfer by telegraph large sums from one reserve center to another free of charge, thus neutralizing exchange over the whole country. A supervisory control over the twelve banks was entrusted to the Federal Reserve Board of eight: the Secretary of the Treasury, the Comptroller of the Currency, and six others appointed by the president for long terms. With this board, as can easily be seen, rests much responsibility for the financial soundness of the country. The fact that it successfully weathered the post-war years redounds greatly to its credit and demonstrates the suitability of governmental control over the nation's banking. Yet in 1913 bankers were violently opposed to it. The Bankers' Conference in August was very stubborn on this point and resolved to protest to the president. Carter Glass tells the story: "About three days thereafter, there came to Washington a committee of the greatest bankers in the land. We were to go up to the White House and convince the President that he was totally wrong and impractical in his denial of representation on the Federal Reserve Board to the banks. I headed the procession perfectly confident that we were going to win our case and put the President to confusion. But he heard those great bankers, heard them courteously and deferentially and amiably. And after they had finished he quietly turned to us, and with those jaws firmly set, said: 'Gentlemen, I challenge any one of you to name a government institution in this country or a government commission in any civilized country of the earth upon which private interests have representation.' There was a deep silence. Those great bankers were dumb. They did not undertake to answer him."

Underlying these conflicts there was something more than Rooseveltian opportunism. Wilson sought to liberate the individual from collective and irresponsible bodies. The animation which he lent to the presidential office was partly the result of his belief that the executive as an individual could stimulate the popular conscience where machines and corporations only stifled and blinded it. He had visions of a sort of idealogical Caesarism. No harshness; respect for the masses and for their needs; but more than that, respect and a preëminent regard for intelligence. He had no wish to destroy either the states or the upper classes; but his opposition to arbitrary barriers was inflexible. He wanted to see the people formed into one immense thinking and feeling mass, with the president as head and interpreter. He imposed no restrictions upon the will of this mass save to require that it respect intelligence and individual freedom. It is only fair to say that this Wilsonian democracy might be superior to federalism in many ways. But it requires raising the standard of intelligence to a high degree. It demands constant leadership and supreme wisdom such as even Wilson himself could not supply. It needs ambitionless and incorruptible politicians and legislators. Finally it presupposes an understanding, sympathetic, and appreciative public. If these dreams were to come true, it would make very little difference what sort of government we had.

While Wilson was planning for the welfare of his people, the war broke out. So instead of being able to devote himself to psychological training and social reform, Wilson was obliged to turn his thoughts to foreign policy, which had heretofore been conducted prudently and honestly. First of all he desired that the great catastrophe should not distract the attention of himself or his nation. This is the spirit which dictated the famous letter on moral neutrality. Unfortunately the war engulfed the whole world, and it became unescapable. It had to come up for consideration in American politics. It was here that Woodrow Wilson showed his greatness. He was not well prepared for diplomacy, so instead of attempting it he simply transferred his work in America to the world as a whole. He wished to create a world-wide conscience, considering foreign governments very much as he considered political machines at home. He desired to reach the peoples behind the governments, as for instance in his notes to Germany.

At this critical period in President Wilson's life, his most profound instincts came to the surface: his democratic religion, his autocratic methods, his respect for established aristocracies and dominating personalities, his tendency to seek the living beings behind the masks of institutions. His dream was to create a Europe where there had been only belligerents, a world where there had only been great powers. The fourteen points aimed merely to find a basis on which peoples could feel united, could think in common and become conscious of their common humanity. The League of Nations, in the mind of its creator, was not to be a tribunal, nor a series of offices, nor a judicial organism, nor a world power. Rather it should be a club where men would meet, to which they would be expected to bring their ideas in a spirit of good will, and which would have promoted a sentiment of material and moral partnership born of discussion, frankness, and fraternity. For him it was never a question of a rigid league supported by military and judiciary. On the contrary he envisaged a supple and adaptable instrument destined to be the means of persuasion and understanding between nations. His league was an arm, not against the people, but against their governments. Wilson sought, by creating a higher moral force, to restrain the modern state based on the interests of a rather small group of capitalists and politicians. His league was to be a sphere of action solely for great peoples and great leaders, who alone could make it of use.

The place which the United States was to occupy in this great project was an important one. To Wilson the American people alone seemed fully conscious of its personality and in possession of a well-developed aptitude for government. Thus the United States would guide the young nations, and with their good will behind it, would become the moral power which it deserved to be. America would impose its moral hegemony upon the world solely by mobilizing spiritual forces. The American, rich, peaceful, optimistic, religious, outside the agonizing territorial problems of Europe and Asia, would have a privileged rôle. The United States would become the aristocracy of this new organization. Like Jefferson, Wilson sought to give his people a new world. By the suppression of armies and by renewed economic activity he would open the door to world supremacy.

To succeed in such an enterprise Wilson needed divine gifts. He had to persuade the European governments to accept these strange ideas at a moment when they sought purely to liquidate a war which had taught them only too well the dangers of super-organizations. He had to persuade the American politicians, who hadn't the faintest idea what it was all about; and finally the American people had to accept this ambitious future which he was molding for them. With the backing of the people, Wilson could have prevailed against all other opposition; but without their example of generosity and their initiative, the rest was useless. In time Wilson might have succeeded. But destiny was against him. All the groups and machines which he had been fighting leagued together once again. Instead of wrangling with them, he decided to fight it out. Then came that tragic campaign in which he attempted, by rousing the people, to force a recalcitrant Congress to accept a League of Nations compact. When he was struck down at Wichita, Kansas, his cause was lost. His friends and colleagues were devoted, but they could not replace him. In Congress the league was but weakly and tactlessly defended. The discussion proceeded in an atmosphere of violence and injustice. Every weapon was turned against the president. The West was aroused against the league as an invention of the East. The Irish were assured that England was being given too great a part. The Italians were incited against it because Fiume was not given to Italy. The Germans were informed that the league sanctioned territorial losses. And finally all the politicians were told that the league would become a supergovernment and that it was already menacing their privileges. The result was as devastating as it was unfair. The generous Americans were hardly equal to their president's conception. It is strange indeed what so-called honest men will do in a crisis. Henry Cabot Lodge, Wilson's arch-enemy, was intelligently alive to the country's responsibility in 1916. He said: "I do not believe that when Washington warned us against entangling alliances he meant for one moment that we should not join with other civilized nations of the world if a method could be found to diminish war and encourage peace. It was a year ago that I made an argument on this theory: That if we were to promote international peace at the close of the present terrible war, if we were to restore international law as it must be restored, we must find some way in which the united forces of the nations could be put behind the cause of peace and law. I said then that my hearers might think that I was picturing a Utopia, but it is in the search for Utopias that great discoveries have been made. 'Not failure, but low aim, is crime.' "

Walter Lippmann cites another example of how political

motives often warp reasoning: At breakfast on the morning of September 29, 1919, some of the Senators read a
news dispatch in the Washington *Post* about the landing of
American marines on the Dalmatian coast. The newspaper
said:

FACTS NOW ESTABLISHED

The following important facts appear already established.
The orders to Rear Admiral Andrews commanding the Amer-
ican naval forces in the Adriatic, came from the British Ad-
miralty via the War Council and Rear Admiral Knapps in
London. The approval or disapproval of the American Navy
Department was not asked. . . .

WITHOUT DANIELS' KNOWLEDGE

Mr. Daniels was admittedly placed in a peculiar position
when cables reached here stating the forces over which he is
presumed to have exclusive control were carrying on what
amounted to naval warfare without his knowledge. It was fully
realized that the British Admiralty might desire to issue orders
to Rear Admiral Andrews to act on behalf of Britain and her
Allies, because the situation required sacrifice on the part of
some nation if D'Annunzio's followers were to be held in check.

It was further realized that under the new league of nations
plan foreigners would be in a position to direct American Naval
forces in emergencies with or without the consent of the American Navy Department. . . .

The first Senator to comment is Mr. Knox of Pennsylvania. Indignantly he demands an investigation. In Mr.
Brandegee of Connecticut, who spoke next, indignation has
already stimulated credulity. Where Mr. Knox indignantly
wishes to know if the report is true, Mr. Brandegee, a half
minute later, would like to know what would have happened
if marines had been killed. Mr. Knox, interested in the
question, forgets that he asked for an inquiry, and replies:

If American marines had been killed, it would be war. Debate proceeds. Mr. McCormick of Illinois reminds the Senate that the Wilson administration is prone to the waging of small unauthorized wars. Mr. Brandegee notes that the marines acted "under orders of a Supreme Council sitting somewhere," but he cannot recall who represents the United States on that body. This arouses the Democratic leader, Mr. Hitchcock of Nebraska. He defends the Supreme Council: it was acting under the war powers. Both sides now assume that the report is true, and the conclusions they draw are the conclusions of their partisanship. A few days later an official report showed that the marines were not landed by order of the British Government or of the Supreme Council. They had not been fighting Italians. They had been landed at the request of the Italian Government to protect Italians, and the American commander had been officially thanked by the Italian authorities. The marines were not at war with Italy. They had acted according to an established international practice which had nothing to do with the League of Nations.

The scene of action was the Adriatic. The picture of that scene in the Senators' heads at Washington was furnished, in this case probably with intent to deceive, by a man who cared nothing about the Adriatic, but much about defeating the League.

As the world is still getting over the effects of Wilson, an accurate balance sheet of his record is not possible. Many regrets for what might have been have received formulation. Mine is that his study of American history did not result in a truer appreciation of federalism and its contents. His greatest potential outlay, the League of Nations, interested him not as a means of settling conflicts through obligatory compromise, but as a way of imposing his own American hegemony or of establishing rule by intelligence.

That is obviously too much to expect. However, Wilson did get to a point where intelligence might have secured an equal footing with either wealth or numbers. He should not have expected more. On the other hand, Wilson's idealism stirred the peoples of Europe profoundly and gave a concrete form to the spiritual ambition which slumbered in the American nation. His people denied him but they could not forget that perception of their own moral dignity and pride which he had revealed and in which he placed so much confidence. One cannot understand modern America, ever mindful of realities yet eager to affirm its spiritual nobility, without taking into account the enterprise of Woodrow Wilson, the American crusader.

CHAPTER V

THE AMERICAN STATE

For various reasons it is inadvisable to trace the historical sequence of events since the downfall of Woodrow Wilson. The perspective is not yet broad enough; and besides, so far as can be judged today, nothing of great moment has occurred. Once the national conscience was eased, nearly every one was quite content to return to the routine of money-making and to let the nations of Europe repair their ruins as best they might. As this was the one topic upon which public sentiment approached anything like unanimity, the government could but acquiesce and withdraw as far as possible from international politics. The task of readjustment fell to the Republican Party, which on the whole, thanks to Coolidge, Mellon, and Hoover, has accomplished that thankless task very well; so well, in fact, that the Democrats have fared badly. Hopelessly divided among themselves, they have failed to see or to make their own an issue which is rapidly gaining momentum, although it has been their heritage since the time of Jefferson. Today it cannot be called states' rights, but it is closely akin to it. Sectional rights is a more exact term.

During fifteen out of the first twenty years of this century, the White House was occupied by exceptionally strong—almost imperialistic—men. This condition was flagrantly opposed to the first axiom of practical federalism, namely, antipathy towards centralization. Thus it is not surprising that when Wilson got into difficulties, the immense power of federal tradition should have opposed him.

The situation has been greatly aggravated by the onerous prohibition laws, so that the liberals of both parties (Governors Ritchie and Smith, Dr. Nicholas Murray Butler, the New York *World,* the Chicago *Tribune*) are virtually joining forces in a demand for less centralized control. A certain apathy towards centralization is already noticeable in public sentiment, but it will require a good deal more agitation before it is shaped into an issue.

The clash between sectional liberties and centralized legislation is the most persistent one which the United States has had to face in the past and will probably have to face in the future. It was the basis of the initial Federalist-Republican disputes. Andrew Jackson faced it. The great orators, Clay, Calhoun, and Webster, were vitally concerned with it. The slavery question was inextricably linked with it. And now, in spite of all that has been said, written, and done to alleviate it, the problem of sectional rights remains. But it would be misleading to imply that this conflict demanded an irrevocable settlement. On the contrary, it is far healthier that it should continue unsettled than that one side should gain permanent ascendancy. There are many things more deleterious to a nation than political squabbles and clashes among group interests. So long as the animus to fight can be directed into such channels, there need be little fear for the nation's prosperity. At the present time the pendulum has swung far in the direction of centralization. For it to swing back would be altogether proper.

Problems of less importance than sectional rights are continually cropping up to agitate the country for a year or so, and then to drop into oblivion. They sweep in waves, back and forth, up and down, through press and pulpit, club, office, and home. Sometimes they become issues which split Republicans and Democrats. Sometimes both parties take the same side. More often both carefully ignore them. In the end one faction may gain its objective, as in the Japanese immigration flurry, or the issue may just burn itself out, as the Ku Klux Klan episode seems to have done. It is an intricate task to discern what interaction of forces actually accomplishes this, as they are differently aligned in each specific case. Still they may generally be put into one of three classes.

1. The people at large. The great body of human beings which responds emotionally to ideas and personalities. This dense mass with its institutions, its jazz, its movies, its *Saturday Evening Post,* its comic strips—all common to Miami, Kansas City, and Seattle—forms the warp and woof of the country's unity. Violent indeed must be the shock to rend it.

2. The concurrent units. The groups of men who have power and who are ambitious; whose interests conflict with one another or with the country at large—business interests, newspaper groups, political or social sub-divisions, railroads, the Anti-Saloon League, the American Farm Bureau, organized labor, the National Chamber of Commerce, the League of Women Voters, and many others. These are nuclei upon whose harmonious interworking the nation's tranquillity largely depends.

3. The governmental machinery and those who run it.

The first two of these classes present a multiplicity of facets for observation which will be considered in subsequent chapters. The theoretical composition of governmental machinery would require a volume in itself. The reader who is not already sufficiently acquainted with the subject may refer, of course, to a number of text books.[1] But care must be taken not to estimate too highly the value of mere structure. This may well be compared to any arbitrary arrangement of hazards in an obstacle race. It is nevertheless of some utility

[1] E.g., W. B. Munro, *The Government of the United States.* Macmillan, 1925. And, of course, Tocqueville and Bryce can always be reread with profit.

to examine the various sectors of the governmental area and to estimate their success or failure as instruments in a federal system.

The conception of the chief executive in the United States is not readily attached to any theory. According to Article II, Sections 2 and 3, of the Constitution, his powers, except during hostilities, are principally recommendatory and administrative. His initiative in the matter of treaties and appointments is held in check by being made dependent upon Congressional approval, just as he in turn can restrain legislation by the veto. In making provisions for a president, the Constitutional Convention evidently thought it advisable to bridle the exuberance of incipient democracy with this stabilizer of old-world form. As George Washington was already there to fill the office, they probably thought of the office in terms of him, assuming that the electors would always seek an administrator of wisdom, dignity, and prudence.

Unfortunately the method of choosing a president—the party system—involves a totally different objective. It is of far more importance to the party that the man selected be a successful candidate than an able executive; more important that he conform to party tenets, if elected, than follow the counsels of competent advisers or his own judgment. On this score the party is adamant. If it decides that an obscure man is the best candidate because he has few enemies and will probably swing his own doubtful state into line, there is nothing to be done save hope that he has latent powers commensurate with the exigencies of the position. One would expect the choices made by such a democratic process to reflect pretty much the quality of the electors. And so they do, if due allowance is made for the fact that many of the superior men are not available and most of the inferior ones are ineligible. The following arbitrary

table may be of interest as giving a rough classification of
the presidents according to those personal qualities which
are generally considered necessary in a statesman—intellect,
force, comprehension, persuasiveness, adaptability, urban-
ity, etc.

Exceptionally gifted	Capable above average	Average		Inferior
Washington	J. Adams	W. H. Harrison	Grant	Tyler
Jefferson	Madison	Polk	Garfield	Johnson
J. Q. Adams	Monroe	Taylor	Arthur	
Jackson	Van Buren	Fillmore	B. Harrison	
Lincoln	Hayes	Pierce	McKinley	
Roosevelt	Cleveland	Buchanan	Taft	
Wilson			Harding	
25%	21.43%	46.43%		7.14%

If we omit that exceptional group, the Massachussetts and
Virginia dynasty, as not truly reflective of popular selection, we find:

$$18.18\% \qquad 13.64\% \qquad 59.09\% \qquad 9.09\%$$

This is about what we should expect; rather better than the
average hereditary dynasty, but rather worse than, say, the
last century of British Prime Ministers.

On the other hand, the collective record of the presidents
is better than one would anticipate from their individual
merits. Briefly the traits of practical federalism may be
summarized as: (1) mistrust of centralization; (2) dis-
inclination towards war; (3) tendency to compromise. The
first of these applies to the mutual check of executive and
legislative. Through an abridgment of speech, the president
is very often given sole credit for joint accomplishments
in which his rôle is slight, possibly one of mere acquiescence.
In addition he is usually credited with the achievements of
his cabinet officers. Conversely, in order not to impair the
dignity of the office, failures are, whenever possible, laid to
some lesser official.

The second point concerns foreign affairs. The fortunate situation of this country, coupled with the policy initiated by Washington and Jefferson, has reduced this division of government to a minimum and has given it a negative and standpat character. Thus the principal bugbear of statesmen, and the source of innumerable difficulties, is reduced to a minimum.

Lastly, the compromise. Here, practically, lies the president's greatest field. Internal dissensions are legion and have always been so. The chief executive is admirably situated to arbitrate most of them. Though he may displease factions of his own party, he will invariably gain immense popular approval by effecting the settlement of a knotty disagreement. Now a compromise is by no means the most difficult of achievements. Exceptional mental gifts are not required. In fact a president who has his own ideas to advocate is rather at a disadvantage (as with J. Q. Adams and Wilson). An ordinary amount of common sense and a dogged persistence are far more efficacious. Thus, in the long run the accomplishments of the executives are mainly an accumulation of settlements effected between warring factions. Half-steps, to be sure, but perhaps they are more certain than full steps forward plus full steps back.

In discussing so large a body as the Congress of the United States it is almost impossible to say anything which is not either self-evident or highly controversial. The eighteen clauses in Article I, Section 8, of the Constitution tersely enumerate its powers, the principal ones of which are:

1. To tax and borrow.
2. To regulate commerce.
3. To declare war, raise and support military forces.
4. To establish post offices.
5. To coin money.
6. To constitute inferior courts.

In addition there are a number of minor powers relative to naturalization, copyright, bankruptcy, and the government of the national capital; likewise the supplementary power of making all laws necessary for the proper exercise of its other powers.

The method of choosing the men who collectively hold these powers is also simple, although its adoption was a compromise, and perhaps the most notable one of the Constitutional Convention. For the people of each state, representation is equal in the upper house, and proportionate to population in the lower. Two senators are elected from each state, and today there is one representative for about every quarter million of inhabitants. A senator's term is six years and a representative's two.

It is perhaps needless to remark that Congress has not made the strictest interpretation of its powers as enumerated above. The first clause of Section 8 states, among other things, that "The Congress shall have power to . . . provide for the . . . general welfare of the United States." This amounts virtually to *carte blanche,* as almost anything may be twisted into a provision for general welfare. At any rate the passing of laws has become almost a mania, ranging from the federal government down to the most insignificant municipality. The number of laws nominally in force at the present time is estimated at about two million. It may well be asked what pressure is behind this avalanche, which is certainly not due to the personal preferences of Congressmen and is not dictated by the public at large. But the organized groups can probably account for 98 per cent. of our federal laws. Not that bribery is rampant, for apparently it is not; but the fear of not being reëlected is great. Any society which is well enough organized to be able to direct a bombardment of letters and telegrams at will is extraordinarily powerful. As there are many such societies, Congress finds itself obliged to pass a quantity of bills without much thought of their intrinsic value.

Most of the real work of Congress is done by its committees, whose task it is to examine the bills and sort, eliminate, or whip them into shape. The volume of bills is enormous—several thousand at each session—but about nineteen out of every twenty are killed in the committee rooms. The principal committees in the Senate are those on finance, appropriations, the judiciary, interstate commerce, and foreign relations. Of the sixty-odd committees in the House, the most important are those on ways and means, appropriations, rules, the judiciary, commerce, post offices, agriculture, immigration, banking and currency, military and naval affairs.

All in all, the American legislative system is far from perfect. Bertrand Russell once said that Americans should be thankful for the inefficiency of Congress, as its inability to get anywhere prevents it from making still more blunders. Yet if the system of delegated authority is to be retained at all, it may be modified to advantage. As it stands now, the Constitution does not hold Congress sufficiently in check. Moral questions, such as prohibition and child labor, on which there is a wide divergence of opinion, can be settled with greater fairness by the individual states and should be so settled. Congress has been the leading power in combating centralization everywhere except within itself. But today it has an inflated opinion of its own competence which is very difficult to dislodge. It would be too paradoxical to expect Congress to curtail its own powers. Another point deserving consideration is that of minority representation. All the voters whose candidates meet defeat are left voiceless. In other words nearly half the voters—sometimes over half—are without representation. As a result, on a close vote in Congress it may easily happen that the will of one quarter of the voters prevails. The new Constitution of

Germany provides for minority representation through a system for consolidating minorities. It is too soon to state that the increased accuracy in reflecting popular will outweighs the added unwieldiness of the legislative body. But the experiment is significant and merits close observation.

The American Congress, in its slightly gruff simplicity, possesses at least the advantage of coherence. Its greatest weakness is perhaps that collective vanity which so often places it at odds with the president. Due to a Constitutional brevity which makes little provision for difficulties, such a conflict virtually stultifies the nation's political life. Opposing factions can only glare at each other or indulge in sarcastic jibes. In tranquil times the nation as a whole frequently gains by this, since legislative inactivity often comes as a welcome respite to the citizens. The natural rivalry of official organs is again aggravated by the varying lengths of the terms of office. A president is elected for four years, a senator for six, a representative for two. For the best results these three powers should work together as a team, acquainted with each other's capabilities and prepared for coördinated effort. But somehow the voters seem to take a malicious pleasure at the mid-term elections in depriving the president of his best friends, his supporters and advisers. At times even the Congressional majority swings from one party to the other. Thus the Democrat, Wilson, was opposed at the end of his term by a Republican majority, and the conservative Republican, Coolidge, confronted by a Senate where Democrats and radicals preponderated. This is no longer a simple state of inertia, but an embittered rivalry whose effects are felt in all parts of the administration.

The theory of division in governmental power is not a little responsible for this, as Wilson clearly saw, but it has the august poise of age, since it goes back at least to Aristotle.

Nevertheless had not Montesquieu brilliantly developed it shortly before, it would hardly have gripped the minds of the framers of the Constitution so forcibly as it did. In particular, the rôle of the Supreme Court would probably have been differently conceived. But were it not for this peculiar conception of the Supreme Court, the Constitution would long since have been moldering in the archives —a musty document, of interest only to antiquarians. But the framers seem to have been cannily skeptical as to what fantastic uses their descendants might make of the freedom accorded by republican principles. For they were very careful to restrain the legislature by presidential veto and to imply that the Supreme Court should have power to invalidate laws which did not measure up to the constitutional yardstick. In other words, upon the Supreme Court was placed the heavy responsibility of arbitrating between the momentary interests of the living and a fixed code of conduct evolved by the most successful generation of their ancestors. Moreover, the arbiters were to be appointed for life by presidential choice, dependent only upon confirmation by the Senate and upon good behavior in office. This has resulted in there being comparatively few chief justices to weigh the nation's laws—only 10 up to 1925, as compared with 29 presidents. The list follows:

Jay	1789–95	Chase	1864–73
Rutledge	1795	Waite	1874–88
Ellsworth	1796–1800	Fuller	1888–1910
Marshall	1801–35	White	1910–21
Taney	1835–64	Taft	1921–

When so brief a document as the Constitution is applied to an immense domain, the coefficient of individual interpretation must necessarily be large. It is not unreasonable to infer that the character of the Supreme Court has been largely molded by its leaders, nor that these same men have had an effective influence upon the nation's development. Particularly significant are those five who spanned the period from 1801 to 1910—Chief Justices Marshall, Taney, Chase, Waite, and Fuller. The work of John Marshall receives today the appreciation due it. The solidifying effect which his decisions had upon the youthful nation is gratefully respected. Marshall was a federalist in the Hamiltonian sense—an advocate of strong centralization. However abhorrent this may be to the true federal doctrine, no candid thinker can deny that it has had its value. The distinction between state and national authority, as delineated by the Constitution, was in practice highly controversial. But Marshall unequivocally and consistently ascribed to the central government every power for which constitutional implication could be found. Coming at a period when state feelings, fired by Jeffersonian utterances, were high, his decisions were a great factor in awakening a sense of national homogeneity. "Marshall has cemented the Union," wrote John Quincy Adams, "which the crafty and quixotic democracy of Jefferson had a perpetual tendency to dissolve. Jefferson hated and feared him." On the other hand Marshall did not possess the personal qualities which make a great man's memory loved as well as revered. To him the universe could be explained in terms of constitutional clauses and points of law. To be sure he viewed things broadly and philosophically, and always sought the idea behind the written word. But still his thought was characterized by a rigidity and formality which was perhaps to be expected of one who thought that "the whole duty of government is to prevent crime and to preserve contracts."

Marshall's successor, Roger Brooke Taney, though not

quite so great a legist, is more sympathetic, particularly now that the bitter issue which involved his tragic downfall has lost its vehemence. An appointee of Jackson's, he was an excellent antidote to Marshall, whose ideals somewhat outlived their significance once the sense of nationality had been firmly established. Taney's principal achievement lay in stressing the importance of the police powers retained by the states. With him the question of human welfare was a determining factor in judicial problems. And he correctly observed that smaller legislative bodies were usually better qualified to take account of this in their decisions. Hence his doctrine of "the right of the State legislature to take such action as it saw fit, in the furtherance of the security, morality, and general welfare of the community, save only as it was prevented from exercising its discretion by the very specific restrictions in the written constitution." Such a doctrine is federalism of the most genuine sort, and Taney attempted to apply it in a truly federal spirit. Of course it was far more difficult to apply than Marshall's, since it required a fuller understanding of human requirements and of social institutions. Taney's perception of these elements was quite as keen as his predecessor's, or perhaps even keener— and the two chief justices might now possess equal eminence had not the disastrous Dred Scott decision put an indelible stain upon the name of the man who rendered it. In this case Taney overstepped the points at issue, in the hope of making a judicial settlement of the slavery question and thereby averting civil conflict. In other words, he tried to legalize what he thought to be the lesser evil in order to avoid the greater. But Taney had not reckoned with the temper of the people, which was heated to the point of rebellion and flatly refused to abide by a decision which, though perhaps constitutionally defensible, was humanly unjust. This ruined the Court's prestige for nearly two decades, and the last years of the chief justice were embittered by the scathing obloquy which he could not live down. Half a century hence, historians may draw an interesting parallel between Taney and Wilson.

Justices Chase, Waite, and Fuller, while they filled the chief magistrate's position well and honorably, were not of the same caliber as Marshall and Taney. The court seemed to lose the philosophic consistency which had previously characterized it. There was a greater number of closely divided decisions. And the decisions perhaps followed public opinion more often than they led it. Chase was particularly handicapped in office. Prior to his appointment he had had a busy public life. It galled him to withdraw any irons from the fire. His ambition to be president was well known. Moreover, as he had not practiced for twenty years, his law was decidedly rusty. This meant doubly hard work for him in preparation. Nor did he ever acquire that fluent command of his medium which is the prerequisite to a distinguished career. Nevertheless, his sturdy conservatism was not without merit. It did much to keep a power-mad government from casting federalism to the winds in the process of reconstruction. In view of Chase's previous radicalism, he is more to be praised for his accomplishments than censured for his lack of more brilliant qualities. In a post-war period blunt common sense is not the least of virtues.

It is difficult to define precisely the trend of decisions under Justice Waite. His court considered a multitude of cases arising from the greatly enhanced business life of the nation. The commerce clause and the police power (with the added complication of the Fourteenth Amendment) had to be construed so as to embrace the many complex relations between the corporation and the state. This seems to have been done with singular obscurity. For instance, some of the most important cases dealt with the power of states to

determine railroad rates. In 1877 the court favored the states
and declared that corporations engaged in public service
affecting the public interest, were subject to (state) legislative control as to rates. Then thirteen years later the court
brought the matter under national jurisdiction by maintaining that the reasonableness of rates was a question for ultimate judicial decision.

In the main the tendency of the Supreme Court during this
period was to increase the power of the national government.
But this was really not so much because the court had any
imperialistic notions as because the state divisions had lost
most of their popular significance. People were far more
interested in the deliberations of the national legislature than
in their state assemblies. The court had been so affected by
the sway of public opinion that it did little to stem the
natural drift of power towards centralization. Justice Fuller
tried to dignify this virtual confession of weakness into a
theory of "upholding the progressive and experimental, social and economic legislation of modern times."

As a whole the Supreme Court does more credit to its
philosophical antecedents than do most political innova-
tions. While it has not, in recent years, shown as much
courage as might be desired, and has not always upheld
constitutional ideals so well as it could, yet it has contrived
fairly well to keep those ideals in view and at least to compromise between them and various powers. We may perhaps
ask more than this of an individual, but not of an institution.
A judiciary bound by a few principles which are as immuta-
ble as humanly possible, is probably superior to one guided by
the shifting contours of the dunes of legislative vagary. In
ordinary practice the superiority may be negligible, yet it is
wise to provide the authority whereby, if in time of crisis a
great man is furnished by Providence, great achievements
may be accomplished within the limits of the Constitution.

Likewise the presidency is commendable, particularly in the great disparity between peace and war powers. It would be difficult to misuse the latter which, by sanctioning an overnight change to dictatorship, afford a democracy its sole opportunity of conducting an efficient war. On the other hand, the legislative assemblies, as mentioned before, have several philosophical defects. They do not provide accurate representation, and they are not conscious of their own limitations. Any future constitution makers would do wisely to consider a stricter maintenance of absolute federalism, to limit their legislature to certain specific, well-defined functions, and to beware of elastic clauses.

A nation pays dearly for a Napoleon, and the burden which he imposes is a heavy one. After more than a century France is still feeling the effects of his career. There is nothing of the kind in America. Here the nation builders established a guide but no limitations. And consequently time has respected their work and new generations have revered it. The Constitution contains ideas to delight the federalist, the monarchist, the aristocrat and the democrat. Its influence has been modest but its usefulness immense. For the real key to America, however, one must look to its people, their instincts, needs, and ideals.

CHAPTER VI

THE AMERICAN MASSES

In its great, thinly populated continent, with its supple and comprehensive Constitution, a nation which already possesses historical greatness though its past is still sparse and indefinite, the American people spreads out with greater freedom and fluidity than any other nation. It has room to develop all its instincts, its desires, its dreams, and to expand infinitely. There are no strict limits and but few constraints. It is modeled after its own inclinations and not according to forms imposed upon it from without. Hence one cannot understand this people nor clearly interpret its activities and institutions without first making an effort to comprehend the forces which animate and guide it. In France the monuments and works of art represent and explain the soul of the people, while in the United States those immense, sympathetic and avid crowds have not yet graven their names on any stone, nor entrusted any external object with the secret of their ideas. They still bear their ambitions within them; and within them one must go to understand and judge.

Few people have done this; and those who have ordinarily content themselves with a few vague high-sounding words. Democracy, equality, liberty, spirit of independence, brotherhood of humanity; all that and much more has been attributed to the American nation, surrounding its image with an ethereal, multicolored, but fallacious halo. Nevertheless, the voice of this people is loud enough and its movements sufficiently brutal, one might say, to make their meaning apparent. How is it possible to mistake that appetite for greatness betrayed in every gesture? How can one ignore that taste for the gigantic which •is obvious everywhere? Cities with five million inhabitants, buildings fifty stories high, fortunes running into the billions, that is what is seen and talked about in the United States. Immense figures gleam, resound, dance, and proclaim themselves. The greatness of things is always formulated in numbers. They say: a man worth ten million, an article of twenty thousand words, one hundred per cent. Americanism, etc. Means have been invented for mingling arithmetical calculations with all the actions and preoccupations of life. In a restaurant the menu indicates the exact number of calories you ought to absorb and the quantity of vitamines contained in each dish. At school, a system of mental and physiological tests permits you to know in exact figures the intellectual capacity and output of your son. Everything done by man is registered in figures, totaled and ceaselessly repeated in huge formulas. Statistics rule; physical, intellectual, and political life are all penetrated and dominated by numbers which represent an acute and perpetual concern with greatness. In many other lands, and particularly in that tiny Europe, figures are used abundantly, but in a different manner. In the old world they are used to analyze and control activity, never to stimulate it. America has truly invented vital and intoxicating figures. American crowds are not at all like those of the Orient, compact and indefinite masses in which individuality and unity are absorbed to give place to an animal or mystic collectivity. The American crowd is at once a powerful collective being and an assemblage of individuals, conscious of their numbers and individually stimulated thereby. Go to a football game or a boxing match, and you will find, in an immense arena full to the brim with carefully numbered seats, thousands of people who begin to yell and sing and dance because there are ten, twenty, fifty, or eighty thousand of them, because they know it and like it.

That instinct is ingrained and spontaneous in every American. He loves his country for its well-regulated immensity. He is proud of his people for their accurately reckoned masses, for their commerce and industry, for their extent and amazing activity which can be statistically proved. The minute, detached, or isolated does not interest him. Do not talk to him about politics, about the distant and paltry Philippines. These islands are retained half-heartedly, as a matter of prudence, but without pride or joy. Perfection of detail usually makes but slight impression upon him. The American tourist remembers Paris by the Eiffel Tower. But sizes which have never been calculated and which are not amenable to the criterion and precision of science leave him cold. Modern Russia, for instance, in spite of its magnitude finds little favor and no prestige in America. It may be great but men don't know it or feel it. Feeling not aroused by figures remains inert and calm. That is why so many evaluations are made in money. Money is a measure, the common denominator of diverse fields of activity which it binds together in an American unity. This is not the fetichism of money, but a passion to count and to calculate size exactly by means of figures.

These customs are in conformity with the essential tendencies of democracy, where numbers are both law and supreme wisdom, the measure of everything. Thus, spontaneously, the American practices and loves democracy. He accepts it as an appropriate framework; he upholds it and respects it without question, since it meets a personal need. It maintains unity, restrains those who wish to break away from the crowd or isolate themselves, just as it prevented the secession of the Southern states eighty years ago. In order to obviate the occasion or the pretext for division, it causes the sacrifice of ideas which were precious, and of sentiments which were a source of pride. It endeavors to expand a majority into unanimity. American citizens have come from the four corners of the globe, they belong to all races, have been trained in opposing, even hostile theories. But thanks to this instinct, there is nowhere to be found a more homogeneous crowd than that of the great American cities. Clothes, pleasures, attitudes, styles, opinions, momentary preoccupations, belong to all, and are adopted or rejected by all, under the same conditions and almost at the same instant.

It is hard to account for this state of mind; one becomes hopelessly entangled in attempting to explain it as the spontaneous product of a new soil or in attributing it to social factors (which, nevertheless, may have had some influence, as isolation in a vast and hostile wilderness made men more sensitive to the value of society and human collaboration). But whatever its causation, its existence is undeniable. Its influence is felt in all phases of the national life. It explains a great many phenomena and particularly those which seem most mysterious to Europeans. It seems to be on the increase daily—and has proved to be a guiding passion in hours of greatest consequence to American destiny. Perhaps then we should do well to trace its actions and repercussions through the life of the nation.

The first thing to strike a foreign visitor, and the one which leaves the sharpest yet simplest impression, is the extraordinary material unification of the United States. You can roll for five days between New York and San Francisco without perceiving the slightest change in civilization. There is no change or innovation in the appearance of houses, signboards, clothing, or automobiles. From one end of the land to the other the cities resemble one another, with huge buildings at the center, surrounded by little square boxes, either shops or residences, and in the suburbs myriads of cottages, each with its own open yard. The same customs prevail everywhere, new household products are brought out simultaneously in every corner of the nation. The play which has succeeded in New York in March will succeed in Boston in May and in San Francisco in September. Children of all classes indulge in sports. Their parents always possess automobiles. There are actually more than 15,000,000 cars in the land, one for every seven people. Bankers, clerks, professors, workmen, farmers, all have their machines; and often people who are quite poor, such as widows or day laborers, possess some kind of vehicle. Every family has something to carry it forth on Sunday with the baby swinging in a collapsible cradle hooked to the top. Lunch is taken; likewise, bathing suits and a phonograph, to permit indulgence in sport and the arts! The covered wagon returns at midnight, its occupants in a state of exhaustion after having rolled along all day at twenty miles an hour over dusty roads congested with millions of the same species. In the automobile the baby gets its outing, the children are taken to school, the young man courts his fiancée, or sows his wild oats, and eventually goes on his honeymoon. Again, it is the automobile which indicates the increasing prosperity of the couple as they are able from year to year to afford machines which are better equipped and are capable of greater mileage. It is the automobile which takes the old people on quiet drives to see the sun set over Niagara; and finally it is the silver motor hearse which carries them to cemeteries bordered with motor-laden highways. The automobile has become essential to the professional and family life of all classes; it typifies the diffusion of well-being, and it develops a sense of similarity and equality.

Such a curious condition, however, did not result without preliminary groping. Conscious of the immense resources of their national territory, Americans have for some time been aiming to establish an equality of wealth instead of the equality of poverty which seems to be the objective of most left-wing parties in Europe. Still, no decisive steps could be taken in that direction so long as the government was in conflict with the trusts whose object was to monopolize production and dominate sales. But despite the struggles and triumphs of Roosevelt, all that is now history. Stimulated by its predilection for greatness, by its desire for power and unity, fascinated by the huge figures which represent great organizations, the American people as a whole seem to have become reconciled to trusts and great industrial powers. Only recently, both the American Bar Association and the American Federation of Labor took pains to point out some of the advantages of monopolies and the defects of the Sherman and Clayton Antitrust acts. The present Secretary of the Treasury, Mr. Mellon, who is considered by many to be the most able public financier since Hamilton, is one of the wealthiest bankers in the new world. In 1924 his fortune was estimated at about $150,000,000. Of course his appointment was attacked (in particular by the New York *World*), but the attacks were not effective, and even the conservative and prudent Coolidge did not hesitate to retain him in the Cabinet.

One of the most popular men in America, one whose words and actions are constantly being cited, is Mr. Ford, whose fortune is conservatively estimated at $500,000,000 and who is probably the richest man in the world. It is remarkable to note that the multitude—and even the very poor—admire him much more than they envy him. In particular, they are grateful to him for bringing the pleasures of motoring within the means of every one. In reducing

the price of cars below three hundred dollars,[1] when workmen are currently paid fifty dollars a week, he transformed
a luxury into an object of common utility. Where spaces
are great and transportation is one of the chief obstacles to
social life, this transformation has been of incalculable significance. Ford is considered a philanthropist of such prestige, and his local salesmen are so brilliant, that should he
present himself as presidential candidate, his chance of
success would be far from negligible.

Ford would never have succeeded in producing so low-
priced a car were it not for the habits of the American
public and his own original methods. Had the new world
purchasers been like those of the old, they would never have
been attracted to an object while surrounded by millions of
others like it. Ford could never have sold his car in such
myriads as to make the venture profitable. No other example
demonstrates so strikingly the American love of uniformity and numbers. At the same time the great industrialist
owes a large measure of his success to his own creative
genius. The efficiency of his stupendous plants has become
legendary. Work is systematized and controlled with rigor-
ous severity. Auxiliary industries have been included in his
enterprise so as to simplify construction and facilitate the
supplying of materials. He has his own flax plantations,
forests, railroads, and even a newspaper (*The Dearborn
Independent,* where he attacks in turn the Jews, the financiers, and the vices of humanity). His factories are admirably managed, his workers royally paid, and his agents
kept incessantly on the alert. This great organization assures
Ford a formidable predominance in the market. He has
created what is now called in America a super-trust; a
term applied to a centralized group of industries, kindred

[1] Second-hand Fords which will still run can be purchased for thirty
dollars.

though diverse. The trust is no longer simple, but extremely varied and complex. The United States Steel Corporation operates a dozen different industries contributory to the manufacture of steel and steel products. The Ford Motor Company makes automobiles; it also runs sawmills, coal and iron mines, a fleet of ships, a brick-works; finally it has established veritable towns for its employees, down to the shops and the church. The United Drug Company, which began as a sales organization for chemical and pharmaceutical products, now manufactures them in enormous quantities and in addition produces candy, rubber goods, and writing paper. The first man to work out this theory of group industries was probably Andrew Carnegie, who, as early as 1897, was developing iron mines in Virginia and quarries in Pennsylvania while running foundries of all sorts. The Steel Corporation, with its 152 factories in operation (1925) and its twenty-five railways, gives an idea of the magnitude and complexity of these super-trusts which are so much admired. This tendency towards concentration is to be seen in all domains of industry and material life. Recently there has been much talk of fusing various railways. The Nickel-Plate project of the Van Sweringens would have represented a capital of $1,500,000,000 and 140,000 miles of track. While that consolidation was under discussion the newspapers spoke of it with enthusiasm, admiration, and pride. Distant indeed seems the time when Roosevelt's crusade against the great magnates of finance and industry was upheld by public opinion. The liking for size and the need of economic unity have brought about the acceptance of principles which were but recently considered odious. A journalist writing in the New York *Times* said, "It is these super-trusts which have made possible this great economic miracle: augmented profits, reduced prices, and increased wages. Take the reports of the Ford factories and arrange

the figures in three parallel columns. They will prove that
paradoxical statement: the price of cars has been reduced
every year, while salaries were increased, and still Mr. Ford
pays a greater income tax than any one, Mr. Rockefeller
not excepted. The super-trust as administrated by Mr. Ford
raises many questions which we thought settled. It intimates
to the statesman that there is perhaps some good in big
business. Without resorting to monopoly, big business, well
coördinated, can obtain reduced prices, increased general
prosperity, and progressive elimination of extremes. It suggests to the union laborer that if his employer will continue
to increase wages voluntarily and improve working conditions, the union should find less negative and less violent
reasons for existence. It demonstrates to the industrialist
that the ancient and respected principles of paying the worker
as little as possible and extracting as much as possible from
the consumer are absurd in the face of modern methods."
Similar language is to be found in many other papers of all
regions. But more curious and more characteristic still is
the fact that the government takes the same stand and that
Mr. Coolidge may bow to the captains of industry without
jeopardizing his popularity. The photograph of Coolidge
talking amicably with Firestone, Edison and Ford was
widely published in the American press. That picture, taken
by one of the President's friends and destined to be utilized
by his adherents, indicates the high degree of consideration
which the great constructive industrialists have acquired.
Moreover, the Webb-Pomerene Act legalized and encouraged the formation of these trusts, provided their activity
was directed to foreign trade.

In the face of these powerful and vast organizations, local
authority and provincial differences are beginning to disap-
pear. These companies need much room to live; unless they
can develop constantly, their existence is jeopardized. What

does a board of aldermen represent in a city where Mr. Ford has a factory? How much weight does a state senator or even a governor carry when confronted by Mr. Rockefeller, Mr. Ford, or Mr. Morgan? The latter wield real power which can be mobilized at a moment's notice. The power of the former is theoretical, regulated and controlled by all sorts of complicated laws. The ambition and acquisitiveness of American industrialists tend constantly to unify the nation, to render it more powerful and to create a more extensive market for its products. The little industries which are local in character are gradually being absorbed. Soon there will exist nothing but a few Pan-American giants. Effective resistance to this tendency is rendered infinitely difficult by the fact that the great consolidations have brought with them prosperity and comfortable living conditions. Even the union leaders find an advantage in having the workers massed in great groups where they are easier to handle; and the great enterprises are capable of both more brutality and more generosity than the small corporations of earlier days. All this is resulting in the suppression of economic differentiation among the various sections of the country. The big industries move their factories from one end of the land to the other, in accordance with their need of raw material, power, labor, or transportation. Thus many of the textile plants have left New England, where high wages are becoming onerous, for Virginia and the Carolinas. Cities vie with each other in trying to attract industries; some, such as Baltimore, whose praises I have heard sung by many industrialists, even resort to methods of diplomacy and refined propaganda. All parts of the Union are equal in the eyes of the American citizen. No boundary stops him, no ties bind him to one district. Local patriotism is now but a fiction. A man who started life in New York will not hesitate to finish it in San Francisco if he is offered a better salary there. He feels himself steeped in a homogeneous medium, and is quite oblivious to that sensation of being uprooted so painful to the Frenchman who moves suddenly from Lille to Bordeaux, or from Lyons to Tours. No acclimatization is necessary; the same objects are found everywhere. The passion for size, stimulated by the trusts, has destroyed everything which might distinguish material existence in one state from that in another.

This has also tended to suppress the notion of class and social differences. The material world has been so well unified that one and all live among the same objects, act similarly, and seek pleasure in the same occupations. Autos, sports, movies belong to every one. In poorer quarters the movie costs ten or fifteen cents; in more well-to-do districts, admission is rarely dearer than fifty cents or a dollar. There is no city dwelling without running water, electricity, and at least one bath. The well-paid factory worker, enjoying a good deal of leisure and many low-priced mechanical objects manufactured in quantities, has lost nothing by this revolution. Those most seriously affected are the small industrialists and tradesmen—the bourgeois class which was established in the eighteenth century and rose to independence in the nineteenth. It is being crushed between the working class and the magnates. One by one its prerogatives have disappeared, until now its members are largely salaried employees in the great enterprises which brought on the ruin of its own prosperity. Such a condition might have given rise to much bitterness. Some is indeed perceptible in Massachusetts and Virginia, but for the most part it is mere resignation. In truth national prosperity has been so rapid and formidable that, even to the dismembered bourgeoisie, the situation was far from intolerable. It lost its authority, but not its well-being. Where the lower classes gained, it lost, in prestige but not in caste.

The principle of mass production has been pushed so far, and under the ministry of Mr. Hoover it continues to be applied so methodically to all domains, that the individual can do little else than accept what is offered him. Even if he is wealthy, there is no alternative but to wear the same clothing and frequent the same places as the crowds. He must use the same make of automobile, painted like all the others, whereas a European would at least add a thread of brilliant color or some other mark of distinction to make him feel that it was his and was adapted to his own tastes and personality. Then, possessing something unique and individual, he would feel proud. But the American with his Ford at $295 or his Cadillac at $2,500 is in complete harmony with his neighbors with whom he jokes and votes and joins in forming the most powerful crowd, the most compact nation, in the world.

Great is the wisdom and rare the good fortune in thus avoiding the differences in material condition which have been for most peoples the reefs upon which brotherhood has foundered. But that is not all. Democracies are famous for their quarrels, jealousies, and cabals, in a word for all their dreary political upheavals. These cannot be avoided without betraying the very heart of that system which demands of each citizen perpetual vigilance and constant participation in national affairs. Such a conception is not without grandeur, but it is not easily reconciled with the passion for unity which animates the American nation. This became evident as, under the increasing burden of years, the growing republic had to face graver responsibilities and more complex and agonizing problems. Finally, the Civil War threw a tragic light on the danger and taught the politicians a costly but unforgettable lesson. Henceforth political parties, in dread of overwhelming responsibilities and animated by an admirable sense of the nation's best

interests, developed along lines quite distinct from those of
French and English factions. Whereas French parties multiplied rapidly, and in England the conflict between Conservatives and Liberals (or Radicals) gradually became the
center of national life, parties in the United States have
been intermittent, quickly made or unmade, and have soon
telescoped into the one, the winner, as moral union was always reëstablished in its favor. But in Europe men instinctively formed groups which were violent, distinct, and
compact, and became subdivided in turn, giving rise to disputes among the factions. With no particular effort the
Americans always inclined towards a single program, and
the spirit of rivalry figured only in concrete problems or in
the selection of individuals.

This tendency to avoid theoretical discussion, this desire
for agreement, and this endeavor to succeed through merit,
skill, and energy, rather than through ideas, seem today
the most permanent rules of American politics. The instinct
of competition and conflict is not suppressed, but it is
transposed to a domain quite unfamiliar to the European.
Discussion is more personal, more concrete, and less prolonged. Success is easy for the man with courage, audacity
and perseverance. But control by the masses over the lines
of national politics is rendered exceedingly difficult. Authority is confined almost exclusively to the persons in high
offices and to the organizations which placed them there. It
was Washington's dream that the electors should choose
from among the candidates the one best qualified for office
and should then give him free rein to do as he saw best
for the country. Without parties there would be no intrigues,
no violence, no demagogy, he thought; the best men would
rule as they saw fit.

Times have not changed so greatly as to leave no vestige
of Washington's conception. Two parties have indeed been

formed, but not at the expense of those instincts which animated Americans in former days. In their conflicts they have retained an amazing similarity of ideals. Rare, indeed, is the European who can explain the distinction between Democrat and Republican in the United States; and most Americans, while feeling the difference, are incapable of analyzing it in logical and intellectual terms. Neither by their names nor by their platforms are the two parties concisely differentiated.

When I was at Harvard in 1919 an important newspaper organized a competition, the object being to compose the best possible program for each party. The students went to work at it, and I noted with curiosity that the most successful were those who succeeded in making the essays fundamentally identical, parallel on all points, and divergent only in tone, allusions and criticisms. And I noted that the politicians at the two party conventions followed precisely the same method. The positive element was vague and platitudinous. Only by nuances and restrictions could one tell that there were two organizations in conflict. Each let it be understood that it held the keys to prosperity and that victory for its adversary would spell disaster. But the two conceptions of prosperity were exactly alike. Moreover, the party not in power conceived of no more imaginative method of attaining its ends than suggesting that a new personnel would improve the government. Burning questions like prohibition were left obscure or were nullified by contradictory promises. But the Republican platform was the more skillfully drawn up, and it contained an invention, a first-class novelty, a happy catchword which delighted the crowds without hampering their leaders in the slightest. It announced the return to normalcy. "Back to normalcy" was posted everywhere, on trains, trolleys, factories, telegraph poles, even in the heavens on banners attached to kite strings.

Another formula was employed with almost equal success. It proclaimed that henceforth the "best minds" would be called upon to guide the country. In November, 1919, every one talked seriously of normalcy and the best minds, but today even very many Republicans will admit that it was only part of the game. Among the best minds eventually selected were Mr. Fall and Mr. Daugherty.

I will not permit myself to pass judgment, as I know too well the value of words and their creative faculty. But a foreigner, in studying preëlection programs, and platforms, has the impression of reading a set of good resolutions, such as we had to write when studying the catechism; they are well done and prudent, but are not finite documents capable of guiding a nation and of convincing uncertain minds. One would be astonished that men separated by such weak distinctions could conflict so violently, were it not for the immense accumulation of power and wealth which the American government represents.

In all this there is little truly deserving of censure. The spirit of competition is natural to all men; it is good since it eliminates the weaklings and tests the strong. Americans like party politics for that very reason. The great machines try out men and give success and power to the most competent. But politicians are classified in accordance with results gained within the party, rather than by local or national reputation, for a strong personality is often outdistanced by a man almost unknown who has the machine behind him.

Such was the case in 1920 when the nation would manifestly have preferred the candidacy of Mr. Hoover, whose philanthropic rôle was universally admired. But the Republican party chose Mr. Harding, and the nation accepted with docility. His name and record were almost unknown; his personality was esteemed, although soft and weak. Nevertheless, thanks to the smooth functioning of the machine, he was placed at the head of the most powerful nation in the world at a time when difficulties were legion. Thus the more prudent and conservative the parties have become in ideas, the better they have strengthened their organization. It is this which now seems to legitimize and guarantee their existence.

Americans instinctively simplified their politics as much as they could. But they have not been able to attain such unity on this score as in economic and material fields. The states have been reduced to one federal unit, while political groups have been consolidated under two names. From an intellectual point of view one has the right to say there are no parties at all in America, at least according to the French sense and understanding of the term. There is no organization endowed with the task of elaborating, realizing, and following out an original program, intellectually defined, and considered as a purpose. The sole aims worthy of mention are national prosperity and individual success within constitutional limits. All else depends upon momentary circumstances. Even the desire for isolation or the tariff are conditional dogmas, always available as formulas but frequently neglected or negligible in a practical sense.

There is nothing in America comparable to the French parties, each of which is armed with its own universal theory; nor to the English, whose duties, limits, and scope have been firmly established by tradition. The parties are two in number, since the country refuses to tolerate anything more complicated or to permit free rein to individual ambition along political lines. The two rival teams are animated with the desire to get or retain the upper hand. But beyond a very small group, people are quite uninterested in politics most of the time. The Northeast is the Republican stronghold, and the Southeast that of the Democrats, but even here fidelity is not absolute. The parties exist as popular organizations solely during the brief election periods and become conscious entities only in the rare instances where a problem arises demanding a concise and immediate solution. The League of Nations dispute of 1919 offers a good example. The parties, despite platforms of perplexing obscurity, were constrained to take contrasting attitudes (at least in appearance). Each then assumed a conscious and living personality for several months, though grudgingly and only because of the pressure of circumstances. Those who knew American politics were much alarmed by this and prophesied evil results for both victor and vanquished. The real politicians felt obliged to offer suggestive, if not precise, explanations of the solutions which they were to propose to a world problem; yet they thought that the parties would compromise themselves by so doing and would be treading on dangerous ground. Would it not jeopardize American unity to speak clearly and distinctly about these terrifying problems? Would it not disrupt that formless mass of people vibrating in two sections? But since 1919 all important questions have been carefully excluded from the electoral campaigns. The League of Nations is meticulously draped and set in a corner. The interallied debts, although a burning topic and one on which it would be interesting to learn the true opinion of American citizens, is scrupulously avoided; likewise the Japanese and Mexican questions.

Finite programs, precise and radical solutions, are to the party much what the flower is to the cactus. The cactus blossoms once in twenty years. Its flower is very pretty; it is large, red, and lustrous, but it kills the plant. So the parties propose formal solutions but rarely, and only as a last resort. They know that complete success will destroy them, that failure will undermine their prestige for some time to come, and that whatever the outcome, the nation will not pardon them for having involved it in so dangerous a quarrel. The careful gardener watches his cactus and nips the flowers in bud. The good political tactician juggles with problems, turns them about or cultivates them, but he avoids being compromised or suppressing them completely. The eighteenth-century Federalist party disappeared after it had persuaded every one of the necessity for a federal union. Its own success destroyed its utility and its existence.

However, parties cannot do without catchwords, since they must appeal to the popular imagination. They need mottoes, metaphors, and to a certain extent, doctrines. Therein lies their real problem. How is it possible to find formulas striking enough to interest the whole people and sufficiently pliant not to impede the government's action? The great party conventions which meet every four years, six months prior to the elections, devote most of their time and energy to this task. As these are the most solemn conclaves which the party ever has, it is evident that weighty documents do not cut much figure in American politics.

Appealing to the majority, seeking to attract, and requiring their support, not for a principle but for a team, the party must eliminate from its solemn declarations anything which might alienate a class or a region. Failure is certain to follow the espousal of regional or social prejudices, at least when confronted with an adversary who is sitting tight. The electoral fidelity of the South to the Democrats is one of the principal sources of that party's weakness. The two political machines are constantly sponsoring a more comprehensive union and uniformity, both social and geographic. No power, however slight, must be placed between them

and any group of voters. This renders their approach to any
question vague and general.

Between election periods the attempt is made to increase
the number of citizens who will vote the straight party ticket
regardless of local rivalries and distractions. The straight
Republican or Democrat, blindly disciplined, votes neither
for ideas nor for persons, but for the party. A goodly number of these exist, since the parties maintain in every ward,
in each precinct, representatives whose special duty it is to
keep in contact with all persons sufficiently disinterested or
tractable to be sure voters. Thus they retain a large clientele
of street sweepers, postmen, customs inspectors, policemen,
municipal employees, etc. These worthies are attracted and
held by the spoils system, which has been adopted everywhere and which consists in filling all the jobs from the
ranks of the victorious party. It furnishes a vital interest
to elections, and assures each party a nucleus of devoted followers unswayed by vain ideology or personal seduction.
Who would attack this ancient custom? It goes back to
the eighteenth century forbears, to the virtuous Jefferson,
who seems to have been the first to see its national utility
and to practice it. To maintain their local agents, the parties
require substantial budgets which can only be met by commerce and industry, in particular the big trusts which are
vitally interested in fostering national unity and in reducing local problems to insignificance. To achieve this completely is out of the question, but the tendency is apparent.

The parties take scrupulous care not to inveigh against
any class or any class doctrines. After all, both rich and
poor are essential to them, the former being needed to supply
the wherewithal to purchase or attract the votes of the latter.
A committee would be insane if it neglected either of them.
They are the two raw products on which political commerce
is founded. The parties are simply brokers between manu-

facturer (the people which produces votes or majorities) and the purchaser (the wealthy who need majorities to govern within the law). To propose that either party break with maker or buyer is absurd. Yet a number of naïve or overly scheming politicians have suggested that the Republicans should become conservative and the Democrats radical. The elections which are now auctioned off to a majority and acquired by the team making the most attractive offer or promising the greatest degree of prosperity, would become dangerous and obscure transactions in which the masses, instead of competing in the friendly and businesslike spirit of the merchant who desires to win while keeping his market intact, would attempt to do each other reciprocal harm, and would remain in violent opposition. This would be a crime against American unity and plasticity. But up to the present it seems to have been avoided, nor is the menace imminent. It was talked of for several months in 1922, yet that seemed enough to convince every one of the danger residing in such a malevolent innovation. So the two parties flourish, each harboring conservatives, liberals, opportunists, and radicals. Certain Republicans entertain the theories of extreme socialism; others are almost monarchists. There was a greater distance between Mr. LaFollette and Mr. Lodge than between M. Marin and M. Caminal, or Mr. Baldwin and Mr. Macdonald. But they worked side by side, tacitly accepting the principle that parties must first repress all class feeling, must destroy it in the bud, and constantly impose uniformity. The Republicans have well merited the appellation of the "Grand Old Party."

The material, social, and political aspects of the United States have all been so regulated as to bring the citizens into one great compact brotherhood, intoxicated by its own strength, its happiness, and its good will. But in the modern world that is perhaps not so difficult; while on the other

hand it is a most unwieldy and almost impossible task to
procure true moral, spiritual, and intellectual union in a
nation, because of the incongruous elements which compose it, the complex and contradictory traditions of which
it is formed, and the multiplicity of individual interests
which clash within it. The United States is the only great
nation of modern times which has succeeded in attaining that
intimate and intense unity which all desire. In the early days
it was far from easy to evolve a national idea which would
be acceptable to all citizens. Many American families have
sprung from the races of Western Europe (Latin, Anglo-
Saxon, Germanic), or from the Slav; still others came from
Africa, some are Semitic, and finally there are the Japanese,
Chinese, and Indians. Certain families settled in the new
world in the seventeenth century and have, so to speak,
ripened there. Others came during the Revolutionary period
and received the imprint of that epoch. But by far the greatest number belong to the nineteenth century, when they fled
from the political quarrels and economic crises of Europe.
Each one of these groups had its own conception of Americanism.

Even before the formation of the Union, when the Puritan colonists of the North traded their furs and cod while
the free-thinking settlers of the South sold tobacco to Europe, there already existed a simple, clear-cut, though rudimentary patriotism. People wanted to be let alone. They
clung tenaciously to their land, to their traditional social life,
to the English tongue, the Protestant religion and English
customs. They worried little about other things. They hated
invaders of their soil: Indians and French, Spanish and
Dutch. They hated any one who did not speak their language or pray as they did. Moreover, they killed various
and sundry of these enemies upon favorable occasions and
thus fulfilled their duty. That was called "British Loyalty."

The settlers did not think very highly of the king who re-
sided in London, nor of his bishops, courtiers, ministers,
frivolous and useless writers. Still they wanted to retain the
good old English language, English cooking, and English
liberty. The spirit of brotherhood figured little in their
attitude. Their interests were simple, individual, and few
(quite unlike, I believe, those of French Canada, which
was kept more closely in hand by the mother country).
A rapacious attachment to the soil and to English traditions,
complemented by a hatred of everything foreign, was strong
and quite sufficient.

Under the influence of philosophy and prosperity this state
of mind was gradually altered. During the eighteenth century men spoke more and more of philanthropy and co-
operation. The wars undertaken collectively against the
French gave the colonists a semblance of unity and inspired
mutual esteem. Still, American patriotism did not enter its
second phase and assume its incomparable luster until after
1770. Then suddenly it became a shining example to the
world and a most illustrious monument dedicated to the
new spirit. In the name of liberty people were beaten, tarred
and feathered if they remained loyal to the King of England.
Under the aegis of fraternity their property was confis-
cated. Finally the great wave of love which was to produce
the French Revolution began to exhale foreign, heavy, and
intoxicating perfumes. The Declaration of Independence was
the decalogue of that new law which expounded new formulas of philosophic patriotism.

Thenceforth Americans were conscious of their unity
and of their distinctive patriotic ideals. The native land was
no longer merely another soil for English customs, but an
ideal being, a people, which voted, deliberated, and willed,
all with equal infallibility. What it decided was law and
truth. Patriotism meant not only the defense of one's house,

church, granaries, and purse, but likewise the championing of that collective being and its personal dignity. In truth, this democratic state was a sort of absolute mystic entity, beyond religion and morals. One of the most admired philosophers of the time, Abbé Raynal, wrote, "The state is not made for religion but religion for the state; when it has pronounced itself the church has nothing further to say."

American patriotism became a thing immense. There were American patriots in Boston or Philadelphia, of course; but they were also to be found at the court of Louis XVI where the insurgents' colors were hoisted, in certain monasteries where monks and nuns prayed for the Bostonians, in the armies of all nations where men raised the standard of liberty, in schools and theaters where Franklin was madly acclaimed. Moreover, it must not be forgotten that at first, manufacturers and merchants were very keen American patriots and bore witness to the fact by sending merchandise to the new world. But as the speculation turned out badly for most of these venturesome exporters, who were paid in depreciating currency, their enthusiasm quickly waned.

The immense prestige of American patriotism is one of the most curious phenomena of the period 1770-1790. Lafayette paraded all over Europe in his uniform as an American general and even visited the King of Prussia so attired. Condorcet was writing little essays to prove the premonitory character of events in America and particularly of the force which raised a whole people in defense of land and liberty. America was both a country and a church. Rome for the Catholics, Geneva for the Protestants, Mecca for the Mahometans, and Philadelphia for the patriots. Many tears were shed over the exploits of these "New Cincinnati." Franklin, the inspiration and guide of the great movement, was worshiped rather than loved, and kings hastened to do him homage. Voltaire never attained such heights.

This sun shone for twenty years. Then Franklin died (in 1790) and the French Revolution occupied the horizon in place of the American. Paul Revere and John Paul Jones gave place to Lafayette and Danton. In the speeches of the early revolutionary days, we find this theme constantly recurring. The Americans were the first to heed the call of philosophy, but we will go further and succeed better than they. Fauchet, in particular, never tired of developing this idea, so full of enticing promises. And so indeed it did happen—one of those rare cases where the revolutionary leaders actually realized their original projects. The American Revolution was outstripped in six months; by the end of two years it was rarely mentioned; later people spoke of it as reactionary and it was not well thought of.

This brought on a crisis in American patriotism. Between 1770 and 1790 it had not been a purely domestic phenomenon, as are most contemporary sentiments of similar nature; it possessed international significance, like Russian patriotism of today, though it was even more universal. The Americans, it is true, had emotions of their own, but they were supported by all the generous minds of the time and were stimulated by the exhortations, praise, and philosophical advice of the whole world. Poems, treatises, essays, speeches, books, even money, were all heaped lavishly upon them. It was substantial assistance, but at the same time it imbued the country with an exaltation which was somewhat dangerous to social tranquillity, as witness several uprisings of debtors who were anxious to repudiate their obligations and tax-payers over-conscious of their civic rights.

The wealthiest and most influential Americans, finding that this volatile patriotism had played its part and was becoming dangerous, sought to curb it, and to that end utilized a constitution, English in character, discreetly verging upon constitutional monarchy. Washington was among those who willingly left to the France of Danton and Robespierre the rôle of Messiah-nation—which was too gaudy and hazardous in his eyes—and guided the United States back to the road which they had only just left. This almost amounted to a second revolution. The populace, accustomed to excitement and theatrical demonstrations, was at first bewildered and made some protest. Then it calmed down, thanks to Jefferson and his fine phrases. The Constitution was the law and the prophets, but it did not hinder the keeping of slaves, it did not foster closer collaboration with republics than with empires, it did not prevent material prosperity and territorial aggrandizement—thus retaining those despicable advantages which had been brought into disrepute by the philosophers.

In this third phase of American patriotism, the great democratic formulas are still heard but they have lost all power to offend. Wealth and the wealthy are no longer frowned upon. The immense acquisition of Louisiana created an empire richer and more solid than Napoleon's. The United States was no longer the heart of the world, nor was it much interested in its own heartbeats. Yet consolation was readily found in a territorial and utilitarian patriotism similar to the proverb: where we are comfortable, there is our fatherland. The free spaces of America gave many millions a material and moral prosperity which they could have found nowhere else. That alone sufficed to create in simple, straightforward folk a loyalty much akin to patriotism.

While such a sentiment was quite enough to hold together the hard-working Westerners, it did little to stimulate a sense of nationalism in the East. Consequently American patriotism suffered a distinct set-back in that region during the period 1800-1818. The critical moment was the second war with England, when certain factions of the Northeast contemplated secession. While the project was not realized, it resulted in a regional inertia during the conflict which to our eyes seems almost criminal. But through the efforts of two eminent men, spirit was at length revived. The conservative J. Q. Adams and the Democrat Monroe (whose political career had been, theoretically, that of a radical) collaborated in producing the doctrine to which the latter gave his name. In order to permeate the whole nation with that thrill of conquest which so stirred the pioneers and bound them in flesh and sentiment to the new soil, the government assumed the rôle of protector of the new world. With great boldness Monroe extended the meaning of American patriotism to possession and defense of a continent. Thenceforth the peoples of Europe were forbidden to establish colonies or to attempt to gain sovereignty over any part of the Americas not already in their possession.

In fine the Monroe Doctrine was a first mortgage on the new world. Despite its vagueness, or perhaps because of it, this document supplied food to the waning sense of patriotism and nourished it for many years to come. It well replaced the revolutionary flame which time had enfeebled and circumstances had dimmed in the opulent republic. However, the coming decades were to prove that American loyalty had not yet found its balance, that it was still intimately associated with sectional prosperity. When the South felt too keenly the conflict between its interests and those of the North, it did not hesitate to disrupt the Union and defend its new Confederation with every atom of its force: blood, money, happiness, and the future of the coming generations. No European people of the nineteenth century was touched by such a crisis of national conscience nor had its patriotic bonds so perilously enfeebled.

But the evil brought its own remedy. The anti-patriotism of the South inspired an equally ardent patriotism in the North and permitted the West—the veritable savior of the union—to display its strength and zeal. Once again the United States owed its salvation to the generosity and physical greatness of its people. The most humble and rustic citizens, those least inclined to idealism, maintained the principle of nationality, for they had perceived it in its most tangible form. Their numbers brought the decisive odds to the armies of Lincoln. While that attachment to the land was largely material, it is wrong to consider it as materialistic. On the contrary, if its roots were deep in the soil, its desires were turned spiritually to a noble though incoherent future.

Here must be noted a trait of American patriotism which differentiates it from all others and endows it with an original character: its tendency to avoid strict limits and to seek a constantly enlarging scope. The Frenchman knows his dominion and stays there; other European peoples may extend their ambitions, but they are always defined and explained. The American never limits the extent of his sentiments nor restrains the enthusiasm of his attachments. The Monroe Doctrine envisaged the defense of the weaker nations in the new world against European cupidity. With time it was expanded into a theory of Pan-America which implied that the fortunate occupants of so rich a domain should be united and should collaborate in one comprehensive American ideal.

Since 1881 Pan-Americanism has been an important factor in the preoccupations of the United States government. Moreover, it attracted the people. In the Pan-American Congresses the United States took pains to play the rôle of big brother, clear-sighted, strong and reserved. As the public followed its leaders, Pan-Americanism became one of the most significant forms of patriotism. It corresponds to *Gesta dei per Francos,* to the theory of "France, the eldest daughter of the Church." One might state it as:

American unity through the instrument of the United States. From 1880 to 1915 it was a sort of crusade, the highest and vastest conception of the nation, the boldest incarnation of its national spirit.

But even more stupendous projects were near at hand to solicit the attention of American idealism. The war inspired first a loathing and then a frenzy whose influence will be felt many years hence. Developing from a simple and healthy love of the soil and the community, American patriotism was about to become a patriotism of all mankind, about to create a universal nation which the generalizing mind of a professor, the enthusiasm of a few, and the inordinate ambition of a young people to whom circumstances had suddenly revealed their power, sought to impose upon other nations stunned and weakened by a long ordeal. Such was the League of Nations as conceived by Mr. Wilson and his adherents.

They saw in this a veritable apotheosis of American patriotism. Not alone were the two Americas united; the entire human race was reconciled and returned to its ancient brotherhood under the aegis of an American ideal and the protection of American force. This truly magnificent hope was all but realized. Had the peace treaty been signed in a few weeks, without territorial clauses or complex economics (both quite futile, judged Mr. Wilson, when considering so great a project), and had not its sponsor been stricken in mid-campaign, the American people would surely have become patron of the League and would have thus attained the highest, loftiest pinnacle of moral greatness conceivably attributable to any nation. The enterprise was suddenly arrested, and a brutal reaction seized the masses, not because of the exaggerated amplitude of the project, but due to the difficulties which Mr. Wilson and his colleagues encountered in Europe and which prevented them from giving a sufficiently American character to the peace of 1919. The ruin of the Democrats and the downfall of their president-prophet resulted primarily from the slow and exasperating negotiations at Versailles and the irritation which they caused among the various ethnic groups in the United States. During the interminable months of discussion in 1919-1920, American patriotism cooled. War feeling was rapidly dissipated, particularly since the proportion of casualties to population was very small. A re-reading of the newspapers in the principal cities between October, 1918, and 1921 confirms this view. The world had been thought plastic, readily adaptable to an American ideal, and as such it attracted passionate interest. But from the moment that the European nations began to stress their original qualities, their distinctive organisms, and to appear less tractable in regard to unity as conceived in America, they lost their appeal to the imagination and declined as a source of interest. If they could not accept a sane and docile participation in a centralized universe, governed along American lines, they were unsavory and odious.

The last days of Mr. Wilson presented a sorrowful picture. Denied by many, his work seemed at times destined to oblivion. But it would be erroneous to hold such an opinion now. The League of Nations, henceforth a European organ, is unpopular in the United States. Little hope is entertained for universal reconciliation under American protection—certainly not as a goal near at hand nor as a political program. Nevertheless in all walks of life there are to be found citizens who have retained Wilsonian patriotism to the exclusion of almost any other kind. Professors, bankers, missionaries, elderly ladies, social workers; in sum a great many serious-minded people still regard it as the ultimate vocation, the normal, logical, and inevitable tendency of the nation's activity. This young and composite people, in their opinion, is destined to endow the world with a sense of its own unity, to teach it how to attain mutual understanding and agreement throughout all its parts. This Pax Americana is to be even vaster, solider, and more moral than the Pax Romana of history.

We have tried to outline briefly, but as accurately as possible, the principal forms which the patriotic instinct has assumed in the four centuries of its existence. To be exact it must be added that all these forms still exist concomitantly in varying degrees in the United States of today. The original conception of the landed Anglo-Saxon is still perceptible in some regions (particularly in the Northeast) and in some classes (the wealthy and well-to-do of purely British origin). In general it remains in the background, although the war brought it to the fore. Since then the Washington Conference and the naval pact with Britain have given it much stimulus. Mr. Page's letters form a memorable example of this instinct. His devotion to England was as great as his love for America, or rather they were one and the same.

Revolutionary patriotism, in the style of 1776, may be observed in several classes and is voiced by such organs as the *New Republic*. The editors of that weekly are worthy and legitimate successors to Tom Paine. Their doctrines are those of the so-called radicals—urban laborers, farmers of the Northwest, some professors and students (largely of Jewish extraction) and a number of women of the world.

On the other hand the majority, the great happy masses living in the Central regions, have never forsaken the conceptions of Washington and Jefferson. They are attached to the land, which is generous, boundless, and inexhaustible. The Iowans sing, "Iowa, Iowa, that's where the tall corn grows." To the Middle-Westerners their territory is "God's own country." Being in the geographical center, they consider themselves the backbone of the nation. At times sentimental vagaries from the East or West will sway them, but their natural inclination is to look upon the United States as a vast, abundant granary, the fortuitous union between a strong race and a fertile soil.

The ambitious patriotism which connects the two Western continents is primarily rooted in the urban regions of the East. It is dear to the merchants and industrialists, in fact to all those who seek an export market or a rich and constant supply of raw products such as Chilean nitrates. A number of newspapers are among the perennial advocates of this doctrine, and governmental diplomacy is favorably disposed.

At times one individual may be inspired by these sentiments simultaneously or successively. During the intervention in Europe all but the Pan-American variety were keenly alive. The old Anglo-Saxon loyalty and the revolutionary enthusiasm were commingled with the devotion to the soil and the vision of a world transformed by the aid of America. Today the attitude is much as it was in 1914 except for the new element of Wilsonism. The four instincts do not seriously conflict; often they work together. In 1923 President Harding allowed British sailors to march in the Fourth of July parade. Americans do not hesitate to associate opposites. Intellectually, as well as emotionally, they feel an irresistible demand for cohesion.

It may seem astonishing under these conditions that they have never found a general formula to reconcile and coordinate their various types of patriotism. No specific idea links together these divergent types of social self-love. The messages of presidents and statesmen, and even their documents, are amazingly vague of their kind. Nowhere else can such obscure and prudent phraseology be found in official utterances. Even in rejecting the League of Nations they affirm a desire to collaborate with the rest of the world. While playing a lone hand in China they insist upon solidarity among the white race. At the very moment when Congress passes harsh measures against Japan, the executive proclaims in most courteous terms a reign of good will in the Pacific.

American patriotism has always revolted against logic, and has done so successfully. The aims of French, Italian, and German opinion are always clearly discernible; in those countries one knows what party is behind each movement. But in America one must be prepared to see the whole people champion some undertaking, purpose, or crusade, which had seemed utterly chimerical to most of the people the night before. There are four or five solutions to the problem of a national vocation floating in the air, and one never knows which will be the first to land. They are dreams, but they may be very quickly and very energetically converted into action.

In Europe, and particularly among the Latins, there is a belief that if instincts remain nebulous and are given no intellectualistic framework or rules of procedure, they lose their strength and are gradually dissipated. While this observation may be accurate for the Mediterranean basin, it applies less to the Nordics, from the English to the Scandinavians, and it becomes wholly fallacious in the United States. Here an idea is most often the final form of a feeling which has exhausted its other possibilities and has come to the limit of its evolution, the borderline of its efficacy.

But in this sphere also the American seeks coördination and unity. His psychology parallels his social orientation and enables him to face without embarrassment a paradoxical situation whereby several conceptions of patriotism may flourish simultaneously and the different categories of citizens may choose whichever appeals most, while they are all maintained in such a way as to avoid too precise, too strict, or too intellectual a definition. In a word, no one kind is permitted to menace or proscribe the others. This is achieved by confining them all to the realm of sentiment, keeping them duty-bound to a sort of gigantic and serene misunderstanding which conceals their divergent aims.

An idea, a sentiment, a movement, may, if well launched, penetrate this entire human body within a few hours and carry it away without ever encountering effective resistance. This happened with the war from the very moment it was declared. The Americans call these irresistible national movements landslides. A landslide swept out Mr. Wilson and brought in Mr. Harding. Most national events are accompanied or caused by such dense waves of opinion.

Such a force is at once a power and a danger to its possessor. The Americans have a deep hatred for no one. They are sincerely peace-loving, and are primarily occupied with their own magnificent areas. No restless ambitions or evil intentions with regard to their neighbors are visible. Reason and wisdom appear supreme. Nevertheless the United States is a disquieting factor by virtue of the extent and violence of its reactions, because of its self-confidence and its assurance of sincerity. Many nations are more brutal; few are more prompt to act, and few act with less reflection. Any one who has lived in the great American cities cannot help liking their crowds. At the same time he must own that there is nowhere a more volatile conglomeration. General individual prosperity guarantees peace. But the animal need of a great exaltation from time to time, without reflection or heed, must always alarm the foreigner. For nothing can withstand those tidal waves.

CHAPTER VII

AMERICAN INSTITUTIONS

It is quite apparent that the juggling of human masses into equilibrium and unity would be impossible did not the people readily lend themselves to it; did not institutions prepare individuals, social and ethnic classes to understand and accept one another. But Americans have instinctively and spontaneously directed their entire educational system along these lines. In sixteen out of forty-eight states there are laws giving the right to vote only to those who possess a certain degree of education. It would seem that sooner or later this may become an accepted principle throughout the Union. Education enjoys an appeal in the new world as wide as its conception is different from that of Europe. It aims to be easy, agreeable, universal, and selective, in sharp contrast with the French competitive system. Everything which embitters the life of a French student—general competitive examinations, baccalaureates, competitive examinations for Saint Cyr, the École Normale and the École Polytechnique—is spared the American. He is instructed, but with the intention of making him a good citizen and eventually a gentleman, if his means permit. He is expected to be happy, and to this end education is adapted to the subjects instead of the subjects being adapted to education, as in France. Consequently there are an immense body of students and a great number of professors. The professional career is a popular one, since it may lead to anything, even to the presidency. American education charms its disciples. Politicians expect much of it as a means of welding into one people the hundred and ten million individuals of all colors, races, nationalities, religions, and civilizations. It must Americanize the negroes, Japanese, Slavs and Latins and enable the Anglo-Saxons to live among such incongruous but essential elements. Since the days of Rome educators have never had so ambitious a task, so important a rôle, or so enviable a situation. In the original conception of the federation the central government took no part in education, although Washington, J. Q. Adams, and others did have ideas about such matters. Education was the concern of the state, the municipality, the church, and the individual. Even with the extensive development of centralization, the field of public instruction has never been brought within the scope of Congress or the president. There is a Bureau of Education at Washington, but its purpose is to gather information, publish statistics, and act in a consultant or advisory capacity. It has no power to impose its views upon the states, the universities, or the churches. Education is accordingly free and unhampered. To be sure there is some demand for a federal organization or control, but it has not yet appealed to the masses, who find the present condition satisfactory. The state laws make education compulsory with children at least up to the age of fourteen. In the West there is a tendency to organize state schools, but in general the expenses for primary education are divided about as follows:

> State .... 17 per cent.
> County .... 21 per cent.
> Township .... 62 per cent.

A good many children go to sectarian or private schools. It was estimated in 1920 that of 18 million students, two million attended private institutions.

Consequently education has none of that rigidity which

characterizes it in France. Americans have many reasons for looking upon the European treatment of children as barbarous. For them childhood and adolescence are the best moments of life. They possess a religious respect for childhood, a naïve but sympathetic admiration. As for youth, it is adored; it shines everywhere throughout the land, the joy and pride of all. Regardless of social or racial quality the teens of the young American are glorious, and all agree that they should be so. Education must therefore be made easy, agreeable, and useful; no harsh rules if they can be avoided. In the sunny classrooms where boys and girls work together, teachers endeavor to render learning as little burdensome as humanly possible.

The schools are bursting with children; there are so many in the cities that often they have to be divided into squads which attend classes in turn. New York has 735,000 day students in the city proper; Chicago has 305,000; Philadelphia, 200,000; Boston, 103,000. These primary and grammar schools correspond generally to the French primary instruction. Then comes the high school, not very different from the European lycée, liceo, etc. It is ordinarily dependent upon the township. As in the grammar schools the two sexes are mixed, particularly in the West and Central regions. In the East it is different. The boys of the well-to-do bourgeoisie and upper classes are sent to private schools situated in the country and called preparatory schools. The most fashionable of these are in New England (Connecticut, Massachusetts, and New Hampshire). One might name at random Groton, the American Eton; St. George's, almost its equal; Phillips Exeter, more modest, more serious and full of charm; Phillips Andover, known for the excellent students it has produced. Life in these private institutions is delightful. Instructed by comparatively young masters neither too erudite nor crabbed, the boys learn the pleasure of being together, of being healthy and strong, and of being respected. They get the taste of success and defeat in their sports and clubs. Their moral discipline is strengthened, and instruction is in general fairly good. These boarding schools for boys (from 12 to 17) bear no resemblance to the veritable prisons familiar to the old world: clean rooms, simply decorated, a profusion of bathrooms and showers, flower beds and lawns about the dormitories, musical instruments. During the evenings, the instructors often gather in their rooms those of the boys who wish to talk with them. Nowhere else in the world have I seen so much happiness and candor. By his prep school friendships the youth's character is irrevocably molded. Groups are formed which endure as long as life. To the young American his school friendships are more significant than his marriage. They have greater influence over his fortune and happiness, or else they are more dangerous. There are similar schools for girls, quite as charming and quite as useful.

Then comes higher education. To the foreigner it presents an inextricable chaos. Universities and colleges are everywhere, with every conceivable form, system, program, and dimension, and ranging from Columbia with 35,000 students to Highland College in Kansas with but 40. In all there are about 450,000 students in the higher institutions of learning. While it is possible to compare American and European education in the primary and secondary grades, in spite of vital differences (intellectual and encyclopedic culture versus utility), there the similarity ends.

To picture adequately the great American universities, let us select three illustrious examples: Harvard, the oldest in the new world, and typically a private institution, attended by the upper classes and by the intellectuals; Columbia, the largest on either continent, the most ambitious and perhaps the best managed; and then the University of California, a

state organization, young, superb, and enormous, and imbued with a spirit of conquest which represents all that is
finest in the Western territory. Harvard, with 7,000 students,
possesses, according to official statistics, a capital of $52,-
000,000. Columbia, with its 35,000 students, has an official
wealth of $41,000,000, although to be exact a good many
more millions should be added to this figure, since a number
of schools, though nominally separate, are under the direction of Columbia. The University of California can boast of
but $8,000,000 in capital, but each year a substantial budget
is allocated to it by the state. Harvard maintains a staff of
1,000 professors; Columbia, 1,200; California, 1,300. All
three are headed by men of the very first rank, whose merits
it would be superfluous to enumerate here, as Europe knows
them almost as well as America: Mr. Lowell, historian and
complete man of the world; Mr. Butler, whose words and
accomplishments have so often been appreciated in France;
Mr. Campbell, one of the greatest astronomers of today, but
recently made president of California.

Here the resemblance ceases. In other respects the three
universities are clearly different. Columbia, in the heart of
New York, is far removed from serene Harvard, whose
ancient trees and brick walls protect it from the encroachments of the town and give it that aspect of concentration
and polish peculiar to things apart from mundane activity.
Harvard, with its old buildings, its drooping elms, its river
where the youthful oarsmen exercise, with its naïve life
of joyous melancholy, Harvard is ever New England, even
though it has become a universal center of wisdom and
erudition. Royce, William James, Santayana and Henry
Adams all taught there. Harvard is the citadel of liberalism. When a strike of the Boston police attracted world-
wide attention and stirred the whole United States with indignation, a Harvard professor defended the strikers pub-

licly against the authority of Governor Calvin Coolidge. This man who attacked the principle of authority was overwhelmingly criticized on all sides and abandoned by every one except his superiors, who declared, "Every man at Harvard is free to speak his opinion." This professor, an English Jew, intelligent but radical, socialistic, and critical, was neither dismissed nor molested. In all things such has been the attitude at Harvard. No formal rules against the admission of veritable hordes of Jews, negroes, or Asiatics. No severe rules over the students. They live two or three together. Meals are served in university dining rooms, but the students may eat in their clubs or in public restaurants. They may choose their own courses of study, within a wide range; and apart from attending lectures and passing examinations they have no obligations. Vacations are long: a week at Christmas and Easter, three months during the summer. Sports are well organized. Most of the young men at Harvard are preparing for their Bachelor's degree. But in recent years, thanks to the stimulus of former President Eliot and Dean Haskins, there has been a large number of men studying for the higher degrees of Master and Doctor. The schools of law and medicine are among the best in the land, while the history department is without a peer. To those who have lived there, Harvard evokes enduring images of peace, beauty, and nobility.

The splendid library open to all for thirteen hours each day; the stadium with its 70,000 seats, crowded with excited masses of youth during the autumn football games; the spring evenings—that sudden New England spring where summer heat arrives before the snow has melted; all this unblemished life, so full of naïve contrasts, devoid of fear and bitterness, has a charm which I dare not try to express, lest I be called a fanatic.

Columbia is a world. Perched upon the hills at the northwest of Manhattan, its monuments of brick and marble stand close by the mighty Hudson. Columbia is tireless; its indefatigable and inexhaustible population is at work night and day, winter and summer, without repose or respite. It has been called a factory. But what factory can boast of such an output? Columbia, open to all, hospitable, intelligent and strong, is the typical institution of learning in the new world. It has relatively few baccalaureate students, but a vast number of courses for those preparing for professional careers, journalism and business. At Harvard all the men live about the campus. Columbia's dormitories house only a minority. In spite of its racial liberalism, Harvard still has a predominant strain of New England stock, whose tall, slender, powerful, yet supple form is everywhere reproduced, even in the architecture. On the other hand, Columbia is Babylon; all races and civilizations throng there. In August they are teaching Chinese and Abyssinian; in December, magi and prophets from India stroll across 116th Street. Columbia offers evening courses for those who are employed during the day but wish to continue their education. It has summer sessions—the most popular on the continent—for professors and teachers who wish to utilize their vacations for self-improvement. Its school of journalism is one of the very best; its courses in pedagogy are renowned.

California, situated in a fairyland at the foot of eucalyptus-covered hills on the edge of the plain encircling the Golden Gate, is a city of white marble. Scattered about an immense marble tower are irregular buildings, which gleam in the sunlight and are surrounded by a profusion of flowers growing at all seasons. California is more like Columbia than Harvard. There are few dormitories; undergraduates are in the minority. The university applies its zeal and care to an infinite number of young folk of all social categories. California is a public university where tuition is even lower

than at Columbia, where life is more democratic, where the
sexes are even more intermingled, and where Western liberty
is everywhere apparent. A handsome, strong race attends
its courses, tall young fellows developed by sunlight, heat and
fresh air who form a sharp contrast to the almost European
crowds of New York. They are not less ambitious intellectually, but their attitude is different. They are more attracted
to practical life, to the conquest of places and things. Finally, California possesses a thoroughly democratic organization, whereas Columbia is monarchic. At Columbia all
important decisions are made by the president, although
the body of professors acts in an advisory capacity. At
Berkeley the professors of each division meet to decide upon
programs and the use of the funds allocated to their department. The president serves as coördinator, a kind of minister of state for the university. The whole organization
includes a board of trustees which takes care of financial
matters, the state government which subsidizes it and imposes its own policy, and the groups of professors which
regulate all matters of detail. It is highly complicated, and
imposes upon the president duties as delicate as they are
important. On one hand he must deal with the state
government, which is highly susceptible to popular pressure;
on the other are the trustees, among whom are some of the
wealthiest, most influential men in the nation. And finally,
there is the faculty which, taken as a whole, is democratic
in the extreme, almost to the point of radicalism. In the
field of education the University of California presents a
spectacle as unique as it is magnificent. A European wonders
that such an enormous machine can maintain itself under
democratic conditions. Upon learning that the heads of
all departments are elected annually by their colleagues and
that a sort of perpetual electoral campaign is going on in
every one of these beautiful buildings, a foreigner must in-

evitably conclude that intellectual work suffers as a consequence. However, such does not seem to be the case. President Campbell and Vice-President Hart coördinate the various institutions with great skill, and the exceptional ability of the faculty assures equilibrium in all departments.

Each in its way well adapted to economic and social conditions, Harvard, Columbia, and California are all equally eager to procure an authentic (and not a theoretical) liberty for their students and faculties. Even the administrative machinery does not lose sight of this. The student may decide where he wants to live and what he wants to study, taking at least four courses a year (for instance, music, Chinese, philosophy, and English). Each professor signs a personal contract with the administration, a contract strictly confidential, revocable in case of non-execution by either party. He knows that the success of his courses or of whatever books he may publish will have a direct and immediate bearing upon his situation, will bring him more authority, more prestige, and more money.

In these three universities, as well as in all others in the United States, the real center of the student's life is along lines of social activity; sports afford the greatest pleasure, study is the most imperious duty, but social achievements alone make a success of the student's career. In these immense universities the students have a life of their own: clubs, newspapers, religious, charitable, political, and sociological organizations. It is in these clubs and meetings that the leaders stand out, making an impression upon the others, winning approval and respect. The student knows well that his reputation will depend upon what he accomplishes along such lines rather than upon scholastic attainments, provided that the latter are not too disgraceful. The sons of bourgeois intellectuals at Harvard, and of wealthy farmers at California, and of all classes and conditions at Columbia, are, taken as a group, capitalists and political leaders in the making. Thus a contrast arises: whereas everything in the professor's life leads him to cherish his individual liberty, the entire attention of the student is devoted to the standards of society. His greatest interest is in conforming to the type approved by university and country and in not being a dissenter. He must show college spirit and be a good mixer. When the young men leave college after four happy years, they are thoroughly prepared to collaborate in the great work of unification which represents the supreme effort of the North American continent.

Everything which then surrounds them tends towards this end: economic structure, political organization, and finally the press, which is of vital importance. At first sight the press in America strikes one as the most penetrating and most violent in the world. To know what America thinks one turns to the newspapers and magazines, which reign supreme. Whether as cause or result, the daily papers represent the closest approximation of public opinion. They are a more powerful factor than education, which influences but the first twenty years of a lifetime. They are the most effective and most constant element in the formation of ideas, opinions and feelings.

The American press is sovereign. It is concerned with everything, penetrates everywhere, speaks freely, and sets the fashions. It was almost the first luxury which the poor ambitious New England towns permitted themselves. As early as the middle of the eighteenth century each and every Anglo-Saxon community of importance had its newspaper. By 1770 the principal cities had four or even five. Since then, this figure has attained fabulous proportions. There is not a town today which does not boast of at least one sheet; not a group, industry, or interest without its own newspaper, magazine or bulletin, from baseball players to undertakers. There are magazines devoted to the theater, movies, vaudeville, poetry, cowboy tales, true stories, strange confessions. Each university has its paper. At Harvard there are at least four of them, all edited by the students and devoted entirely to student interests. There are more than 2,000 newspapers in the United States which all told sell about 30,000,000 copies a day (1925). Every one reads the paper, or rather several papers, and almost every one with any ambition has in some way or other a hand in a publication. Consequently every conceivable custom or topic gets into print. Compared with the American sheets, European dailies seem monotonous and devoid of the picturesque. It is not that the old world is lacking in lawsuits, scandals or crimes, but that the papers give them less space. In America they reflect everything faithfully. Everything that happens finds an immediate echo. If one has a son, gets married, goes to Europe, becomes a Freemason, gives a tea, goes to a class reunion or buys an automobile, the newspapers will know it and print it. At times they will get details wrong, but they would rather publish many inaccuracies than neglect a single truth or probability. In 1780 many American papers announced that the Pope had given the whole American continent to the King of France. Every year between 1780 and 1790 the report was published that France was about to attempt the recovery of Louisiana, without there ever having been the slightest foundation for the statement. Today, the newspapers inform us that living dinosaurs have been found near a Patagonian lake; that a hen in Corpus Christi (Texas) fainted after having hatched a nest of alligator eggs; that some worthy people of New York formed a society to protect the religious rites of animals. Sciences, letters, politics, learning, travel, society, genealogy, geology, paleontology, optics, theology, all find their way into the American papers. They tell you how to

go to heaven, and publish Biblical texts for daily meditation. The press is constantly in search of new food to satisfy
the curiosity, or rather the voracious incuriosity, of the people. It makes a public triumph of Einstein and Mme. Curie.
A little later it devotes its generous attention to the discoveries of Lord Carnarvon and thereby launches an Egyp-
tian craze. Every new enterprise must have the support of
the press, whether it be a publishing house, a grocery store,
or a social career. If it mentions such and such a shop or
such and such tea, success is assured; but if it remains silent,
all your wisdom will never bridge the gap. It is the newspapers, in the small towns as well as in New York, which
make and assure a reputation in politics, literature, society,
or religion. In a word the power of the press in America is
what is most feared and most respected. The displeasure of
the government or of a class may harm you, but what is that
compared with the newspapers which, without effort, can
transform your life into disgrace or triumph?

This remarkable strength of the press is attributable to its
peculiar character. In the eighteenth century when the first
papers were founded and sought to build up a reading public, they deliberately chose the economic field. The early
French papers were intellectual and social organs. The great
French press of the eighteenth century was a powerful instrument in politics, literature, and philosophy. The *Gazette
de France, Mercure de France, Journal des Savants,* contained carefully prepared articles, erudite and destined for
an élite quite apart from material preoccupations. Even
those with utilitarian pretensions were principally occupied
with theoretical discussions. French journalism of the
eighteenth century was intellectual; American journalism of
the same period was primarily concerned with the material
development of each community. Often the papers were published on market day. The merchants and farmers bought

them, discussed the various items of news between trades, and took the papers home to their families. Even in 1750 the section devoted to literature was meager. But there were plenty of official notices, since each paper sought to be the organ of the governor, the assembly, and the municipality. Likewise there were notices announcing the arrival of cargoes of slaves, handkerchiefs, rum, books from the old world or the Antilles. Such was the character of more than half the items. Then came notices of escaped slaves and faithless wives. "Stop the Satire" reads the heading of one column in a New England paper of 1770. And the warning was explained and clarified by a cut of the devil with his trident. In proper season stallions and bulls were advertised for the benefit of the farmers, and were naïvely pictured as ready for service. The vivacity, zeal and capacity for work depicted in these eighteenth-century journals reveal the country's spirit and development more strikingly than any other source. The only papers in France comparable to these were the *Annonces de Paris* and the *Journal de Paris,* but they made a specialty of notices and advertising. But the American papers one and all gave most of their space and attention to matter of this description: little theory, few useless quarrels. When disputes did arise—and they were not infrequent—they were concerned with subjects of actual and immediate interest. Reality and facts were abundant, but little else; no articles, no editorials, a few letters from readers on topics of interest to the farmers or city dwellers. News items were selected from the sheets which arrived on the ships and coaches. After Franklin had improved the postal service, there was a more regular exchange of news between the colonies. The collection of papers which Thomas used in editing his gazette at the end of the eighteenth century has been preserved and offers a curious example of the way in which public journals were then made up: a mis-

cellaneous assortment of news items selected without rhyme
or reason, notices, readers' letters, official announcements,
a few local items, rare bits of literature, once in a while a
poem—if one dare grace with that name the contemporary
pieces of satiric doggerel.

To all intents and purposes the press was free. In theory
it was subject to neither bans nor restrictions. Nevertheless there were stringent limitations on its independence. If
its attitude on any topic was distasteful to the populace, the
office would in all probability be mobbed and pillaged. If
it incurred official displeasure, the privileges of the post
would be withdrawn or the fee raised exorbitantly. Having
neither official standing nor subsidy, a newspaper was ruined
if it lost the support of the public. Nor were its patrons always prompt in paying for their subscriptions. Often the
editors would remind them after a plentiful harvest or a
good fishing-season that thin air alone afforded meager sus-
tenance. The press wanted to be looked upon as a business
—a business with facts as merchandise. It had no pretensions to original qualities of mind nor to literature. It was
merely a catalogue of daily life.

It has retained this character down to the present day.
The New York *Times,* one of the best edited among the
great papers of the new world, is a typical example. Each
one of its departments, even those devoted to intellectual
life, is a chronicle of facts, a summary of events, without
commentary or discursive observations: political occurrences,
local and social happenings, intellectual notes (largely devoted to books), occasional documentary discussions of the
great problems of the day, one single page of editorials
modestly concealed in the middle section, brief and inten-
tionally objective sidelights on what is happening—nothing
more. Such is the most renowned newspaper of the United
States. On Sunday there is an illustrated section, again con-

cerned with facts: portraits of people who have gained notoriety during the week, scenes or events of a historical
nature; no imaginative or artistic pretensions. The aim is to
present every occurrence in the form of a well-told story.

The American newspaper has no counterpart in Europe.
Its pages are larger than those of any old world daily and
there are often as many as forty of them—all for two or
three cents. Two-thirds of the space is devoted to advertisements which flourish in such amazing abundance that the
foreigner is overwhelmed: placards, drawings, boxes, catch-
phrases of varying descriptions.

Sensational news items are given headlines on the front
page. Editorials, theatrical, musical and literary notes appear in the middle or rear sections. At least two pages are
devoted to sports, and two more to finance and the stock
market. Of the remaining pages usually two-thirds of each
one is devoted to display advertising and the other third to
news. Then finally there are four or five sheets given over
entirely to classified advertisements. Scattered here and there
are comic strips or cartoons, which are of signal importance,
since few readers pass them by. They contain the truly original, imaginative side of American journalism—a feature
unknown in other countries. These strips and cartoons, which
are not ordinarily satirical drawings but variations on the
great themes of life, typify all that is individual in the
American conception of existence. They may be ugly, but
nevertheless must teem with life and with a fascinating
sense of humor. Nothing indecent or cruel, but simplicity,
gayety, and freedom. Together with the movies they bear
witness to the Americans' love of visualization. Intellectually
and philosophically they are without merit, save for a primitive and quite spontaneous philosophy which some of them
possess. At the least they attract and retain for a few moments the reader's attention.

The American newspaper, because of its size alone, can never hope to make money from subscriptions or newsstand sales. Advertising is the profitable field; but that is truly a gold mine. The annual balance sheet of the New York *Times* shows gross receipts of $18,000,000 with a net profit of $4,000,000. This organized advertising enables the papers to live in independence and self-respect. All other factors—news, columns, cartoons—are but bait to tempt readers and to assure a wide circulation which will in turn attract advertising. In the universities where journalism is taught, there are courses and professorships devoted exclusively to advertising. At the Columbia School of Journalism, publicity is considered of particular importance. An editor with a talent for composing good advertising copy is sure to prosper. Similar fortune awaits the successful advertising salesman. There are thousands of young people of both sexes who devote their time to these subtle sciences. As a matter of fact, publicity is much more carefully done in America than in Europe. Catch-phrases are sought after which not only strike the imagination but also hold it and point out the qualities of the article. There is already an extensive literary store of this nature. Several distinct formulas are currently employed. One seeks precision, endeavors to set forth the value of the commodity by a succinct analysis. Another designs to fascinate by a persistent catch-phrase, such as the Chesterfield "They satisfy," illustrated by the handsome youth whose face beams with joy as he smokes. A third method consists in surprising, mystifying, or arousing curiosity. In California recently, one could encounter this strange inscription, against a white or yellow background: "Ask our cousin in Oakland, he knows." To understand this one had to know that Ford calls all his agents his cousins, and that he had one in Oakland. Thus in a roundabout way he suggested the superior value of his cars. Most American signboards and cards are more specific than this; they quote figures and examples. Nevertheless there has recently been a tendency—not always successful, perhaps—to adopt psychological formulas of no little complexity. To conform to their teaching I will give a few figures as an indication of the magnitude which publicity has obtained in the United States. The Chicago *Daily News* published the following statistics relative to its advertising service for the first eight months of 1923, 9,676, 876 lines divided as follows: 3,900,000 lines for department stores, 1,-500,000 for clothing, 615,000 for household furnishings, 500,000 for food products, 426,000 for automobiles, 108,-000 for bibelots, 42,000 for radio, 80,000 for books, 77,000 for real estate, 65,000 for educational institutions, 49,000 for churches, 17,000 for opticians, etc. This will afford some idea of the part that advertising plays in an American newspaper and of the variety of its clientele. However, the figures cited above must not be taken in a relative sense. As a rule each newspaper specializes in some particular branch of advertising. The department stores do not always take up half the space, nor the churches one hundredth part of it. One paper may specialize in automobiles and another in real estate. The Chicago *Daily News* is instructive as it accomplishes fairly well the difficult task of developing all branches thoroughly. Incidentally there are few cities which outrank Chicago in the matter of advertising. A good publicity department is of primary importance to each newspaper since it alone can transform a disastrous financial loss into a profit. The advertising rates depend largely upon the paper's circulation. Therein lies the fortune of the New York *Times* with its 350,000 copies daily, and of the *Saturday Evening Post* with its weekly sale of 2,500,000.

The advertising in this last publication is famous, and although space is very expensive it is much in demand. With a fine sense of both the moral and commercial value of good faith, the editors adopted the policy of never publishing fallacious advertisements nor those relating to products of other than proven merit. The journals which accept the publicity material of patent medicines or other doubtful articles expose themselves to the scorn of their more discriminating competitors and of a large section of the public. Indeed, today the reader's judgment of a publication is in a large measure based upon the quality of its advertising.

The press is an important wheel in the economic machinery of the United States. It is affected by every industrial crisis, as commercial prosperity is reflected in the increased volume of display publicity. As a matter of fact the press is organized along industrial lines. The newspaper of the free-lance journalist or of the small group is fast disappearing before the rising tide of publishing trusts which extend their ramifications far and wide. A few sheets have endeavored to conserve their originality and individual character, but the task seems futile. One of the most famous of these, the New York *Evening Post,* succumbed in 1923. In the hands of Edwin Gay it was a typically free, intelligent, and intrepid paper. It has now passed into the hands of C. H. K. Curtis of Philadelphia, proprietor of a powerful press group comprising the *Saturday Evening Post,* the *Ladies' Home Journal,* the Philadelphia *Ledger* and a host of smaller publications. The press magnates are gradually placing an embargo on all the individual organs. The most famous of these groups are the Hearst and Scripps-Howard. At a recent date the former possessed eight morning, twelve evening, and thirteen Sunday papers, distributed in fourteen cities and read by three million people. This group owes its success to the genius of Mr. Hearst, an able journalist and astute tactician. His papers are found at all points of strategic importance: New York, Boston, Chicago, San Fran-

cisco, Los Angeles, Seattle, Fort Worth, Washington, Detroit, Oakland, Milwaukee, Rochester, Syracuse, Atlanta.
In the industrial regions of the East, Middle West and on
the West coast the Hearst syndicate is strongly entrenched,
but it is weak in the South and agricultural districts. On
the other hand, Scripps-Howard with its twenty-seven
papers is impregnable in the South. It has organs in Cleveland, Akron, Columbus, Cincinnati, Terre Haute, Evans-
ville, Toledo, Youngstown, Memphis, Knoxville, Norfolk,
Houston, Dallas, Fort Worth, El Paso, Covington, Denver,
San Diego, San Francisco, Washington, Indianapolis, Sac-
ramento, Des Moines, Oklahoma, Baltimore, Albuquerque,
Pittsburgh. In 1923 it acquired the Pittsburgh *Press* under
curious circumstances. The price was $6,000,000 in all, and
$1,000,000 in cash. The purchase was made during the
absence of Mr. Scripps, who was voyaging on his yacht.
On his return he ratified this enormous transaction which
had been put through by his secretary. There are at least four
other groups possessing a minimum of six papers each:
Schaeffer in the Middle West; Perry and R. Lloyd Jones in
the South; the Booth company in the Northwest; and the
Lee syndicate in Iowa.

The organization of these press-groups is far from uniform. Each proprietor has his own ideas. Mr. Hearst, for
instance, has a predominant hand in every detail of his
papers from the editorial section to the comic strips. On
the other hand Mr. Scripps is liberal and leaves his editors
full latitude within certain limits. The Hearst group is highly
centralized and Mr. Hearst reigns as dictator. The Scripps
group is quite the contrary. Its treasury department is in
Cincinnati, its commercial office in Cleveland, its publicity is
directed from New York, the editorial division finds Washington most convenient, and finally the general headquarters
is on board Mr. Scripps' yacht. This group is naturally

Democratic and championed Mr. Wilson ardently. But except on questions of foreign policy and those of primary national importance, each Scripps editor may choose his own policy. Mr. Hearst, on the other hand, maneuvers his forces like a regiment. In all these groups, the foreign, political and economic news, comic sections and photographs are supplied from headquarters. All else is the work of the individual editors.

In comparison with the immense number of newspapers which exist in the United States, the few which we have enumerated would appear insignificant were it not for the fact that they possess the greatest numbers of readers and thereby the most influence, and were not the process of unification constantly in operation. Besides his daily papers Mr. Hearst owns three news bureaus (International News Service, Cosmopolitan News Service for the evening papers, and Universal Service for the morning); four syndicates for the distribution of photographs and movie films (International Film Corporation, International Newsreel Corporation, Pathé News, Cosmopolitan Film Corporation); five syndicates devoted to special articles, drawings, etc. (King Feature Syndicate, Premier Syndicate, International Feature Syndicate, Newspaper Service, New York American Features). Many features in American papers are syndicated over a vast area. After Mr. Hearst has used his material in his own papers, for instance, his subsidiary companies sell it to others; news to some, special articles to others, and photographs to a great number of Sunday editions. Thus his empire is made to extend far beyond the group of papers which he actually controls. Moreover, he and his wife are strongly entrenched in the magazine world, where they own nine publications: *Good Housekeeping, Hearst's International, Cosmopolitan, Motor, Motor Boating, Harper's Bazaar, Orchard and Farm,* in America; *Good*

Housekeeping and *Nash's Magazine* in England. Such is the kingdom of an American prince in the twentieth century, a kingdom which even the bravest monarch might dread. These vast groups extend their tentacles over the whole world. Scripps-Howard through the United Press Association has invaded Canada and England, where it has news bureaus. The Chicago *Tribune* sells its cable dispatches to at least thirty-five dailies, including the New York *Times*, the San Francisco *Chronicle*, the Toronto *Globe*, the Vancouver *Sun*, the London *Daily Telegraph*, the Glasgow *Daily Record*, the *Danziger Zeitung*, the *Morgen Post* in Berlin, the *Neue Freie Presse* in Vienna, and the Paris *Matin*. Such is the resonance of a news item in the *Tribune*, and such is the power of its owner, McCormick, and of the nation behind it.

This colossal organization affords the journalist a free, worth-while, and interesting kind of life; and it also entails a species of servitude. The newspaper is henceforth an economic organ in which no originality is permitted. It resembles soaps, railroads, and toothpaste; it must be the same every day to assure its circulation and to meet the expectations of the masses, its indispensable clients. Boldness of thought is banished. A narrow social conformity is required, together with a naïve tendency to flatter and indulge the tastes of the many. The editor has forsaken leadership to become a servant. And of course, in such huge organizations, if he is astute, close-mouthed, and endowed with more practical imagination than intellectual genius, more verbal talent than cerebral power, he will be quite happy in this atmosphere of intense production. He will develop; he will earn a large salary and will gain the respect of groups which would never have noticed him had he not been in such close contact with economic life.

An institution like the Associated Press—founded by the principal members of the American press to keep them posted

on what is going on in different parts of the world—illus-
trates the qualities of the system. Every reporter of the
Associated Press is a man of the world, well paid, exempt
from attack, whose situation is one of much prestige and
importance in international affairs. So long as he stays in
the realm of facts, he may express all he deems just and
prudent. But should he attempt to support theories or enter
into a controversy of ideas, his position would at once be
gravely compromised. He endeavors to see and hear as much
as possible and to condense what he reports into moving,
vivid, penetrating, readily grasped paragraphs, but without generalizing or forming theoretical attachments. There
exist several other less important news bureaus, such as the
United Press, already mentioned.

The American press is omnipotent; it knows everything,
but it is short-sighted. Facts are massed upon facts with
no attempt to connect them or to draw general conclusions.
From behind his fifty journals the magnate bombards the
public with facts in order to suggest the idea which he
scrupulously conceals. The idea to which he owes his position and fortune is American unity. This concrete national
homogeneity sells his papers, his news, his articles and his
jokes to the many millions. All his energy is bent upon safe-
guarding and promoting the social sense which gives him
power and makes him censor of customs and witness of
deeds and acts.

The organization of the press has exerted a great moral
influence upon the country. Thanks to it, literature, which
ordinarily maintains differences and upholds individual contrasts, has been led to see things on a large scale, to solicit
the many rather than the few. In France a literary success
is generally a scandal. A great welcome is given the book
which stands apart, through either the striking character
of its vices or the surprising qualities of its virtues (as

in a recent novel of Bernanos, *Sous le Soleil de Satan*). In America the literary success is the best seller, proving that quantity is uppermost in the minds of most authors as well as all publishers. One best seller builds a reputation and a fortune. Mass support is indispensable. Consequently the forms which flourish are those best adapted to crowd tastes, notably the novel and the biography. Nearly all best sellers are novels, or biographies in romantic style. The *Ariel* of M. Maurois is among these. *The Constant Nymph* and *Gentlemen Prefer Blondes* are also striking examples. Usually such a book is not far removed from the masses, but just enough above them to stimulate. Except in humorous works the basis is a compound of imagination and realism. The novel is bathed in reality. It represents a possible, readily conceivable and ingenious variation of the real. Such are the elemental rules of the game, but there is still another factor of considerable importance. It is quite apparent that most American novels are modeled after standard English types. The whole conformist literature is easily linked with Anglo-Saxon tradition. The English language, so instrumental in molding the collective mentality of America, brought with it the whole literature of Great Britain, and thanks to the American sense of unity, the literature is now as firmly entrenched as the language.

Although rich in good authors and in poets of originality and genius, the United States as a people has no adequate perception of its own distinctive literary tradition. Among its truly national authors are Emerson, Cooper, Poe, whose influence on French poetry after 1860 was so essential, and Whitman, who thrilled several generations of Europeans. But the country which produced and nurtured these men —or allowed them to starve—sent them out into the world and let them depart without regret. English literature prevails in the schools, where Poe the eccentric receives little

attention and Whitman is often banned because he "wrote
badly" and mentioned subjects customarily avoided. American literature is sometimes taught, but the study of English
literature is compulsory. In truth, the latter has the overwhelming advantage of forming a long, continuous chain.
To an American, his native literature is merely a series of
names, more or less interesting but without relation to one
another. See, for example, *The Cambridge History of American Literature.*

The great and individual American writers, whom Europe
received enthusiastically, or rather carried in triumph, pay
the penalty in their own country for their too exacting individuality—the very thing which brings them applause in the
old world. The American nation, in its full social development and solidification, may praise such men as pioneers, but
it must reject them as conditional or uncompromising
citizens. The literature which it accepts is not based on
local or indigenous feeling, but on Anglo-Saxon tradition.
This English despotism is completed by a turn of the American mind, which though richly endowed in many respects,
has little aptitude or natural taste for psychological analysis
and introspection. The American likes ideas and sentiments,
but he does not care to dissect them into finite, intellectual-
ized states of consciousness. He does it badly, in all probability because of a sense of repugnance or indecency. One is
at a loss whether to call this a remnant of puritanism—a
reluctance to confess, even to oneself—or a result of contact with nature, or another manifestation of that omnipres-
ent dislike for anything fluid, unbounded, indefinite. American writers, aside from those with poetical inspiration,
are in a tragic position. There is no vast body endowed with
both national characteristics and an intellectual method to
aid them in knowing, understanding, and assimilating their
country. Again, the exigencies of international literature

(Académie Française, Nobel Prize, etc.), in particular since the advent of "science" and "progress," oblige the author to "clarify the depths of the soul" and "interpret phases of consciousness." The American who seeks a universal reputation and an imposing situation in his own land is obliged to seek the support of the English novel.

The products of this Anglo-American art are often worthy of esteem, but rarely interesting, although one must make exceptions for Mrs. Wharton's talent in style and presentation, J. J. Chapman's splendidly clear diction, and a few others. But even the best of these writers are hampered by a duality of purpose which is probably unconscious with them: without relinquishing the English traditions, they want to write for the American masses, which attract them, interest them, and provide their food and their veritable impulse to produce. The thought of the crowd obsesses this orthodox group, which makes no attempt to ignore it nor to do other than please it, directly or by chance. In order to survive, these authors must turn out large quantities at regular intervals, with no variety in method. They are in general less concerned with what they write than with the effect it will produce. If the great public loses interest, both profit and raison d'être are gone.

The intent to write for keenly alive masses is not objectionable in itself; it obliges authors to write well and simply, and to find good stories. It keeps them in contact with a productive and ambitious people. When it leads to stories like those of Jack London, nothing more can be demanded. More curious still is the periodical press in which this literature flourishes. On a Thursday evening, whether in New York, Chicago, or San Francisco, one may find at least ten copies of the *Saturday Evening Post* in every subway car or trolley. In the suburban trains they are even more abundant. The goal has been attained. Magazine literature is sold like a food product. Its circulation and the demand for it are identical with the market for shaving cream and carpet sweepers. It pleases. Why should it not, with such pretty girls, virtuous youths, and amusing anecdotes? But though written expressly for a given milieu, it has the outstanding defect of not knowing, or of systematically avoiding the fecund, creative, and profound qualities of that milieu. It supplements the work of the schools in Anglicizing and unifying the masses of people which it pretends to satisfy. In a land where the Anglo-Saxon is the most admired social type, it is not hard to play upon vanity in such matters.

Thus the *Saturday Evening Post* gets along, and very nicely. Its reading matter is absorbing though soporific. And yet it is but one of a great many such, and is not the most curious. There are others which tell tales about all classes of society, such as *True Stories* (mostly fictitious, of course), *True Confessions* (idem), etc. These publications lack the respectability of the *Saturday Evening Post,* but they make up for this in pungency.

One might easily believe that this constant flood had inundated the entire continent. But a number of writers, burning with indignation—as befits a writer—at this cheap imitation, this vile courting of popular favor, have reacted violently. In opposition to the Anglo-Saxon school, which is mildly imaginative, sentimental, romantic, conservative, and reserved, they have produced a literature of turbulence. It is daring, realistic or naturalistic, it is frankly outspoken on all subjects, and generally selects the most indelicate ones to elaborate with great detail. This "young" or radical group, as the current vocabulary terms it in contrast to Anglo-Saxonism and unity, is on the whole composed of authors influenced by German and Scandinavian tendencies or by French realism and naturalism. Among their numbers are some excellent critics. They are seeking the reality of modern America with courage and complete awareness, though often with a touch of brutality. Public opinion, which was violently hostile at first, is now showing them some marks of favor.

The most eminent representative of this group is Mr. Sinclair Lewis, whose fat novels, *Main Street, Babbitt, Arrowsmith, Elmer Gantry,* have aroused the most bitter polemics. As a writer Mr. Lewis is not lacking in power. His presentation of social problems under striking aspects is done with rare skill. He sees physical and moral conditions intensely and portrays them without reticence. Although heavy, his psychological art is thoroughly honest. In a word he conforms to the formula of European naturalism in an endeavor to extract the essentials of American character from the stifling tendency of Anglo-Saxon art. Unfortunately, his novels are dull; so slow, so long, so true (so exaggeratedly true) and so enamored of problems. In his endeavor to represent the individual oppressed by the masses and to glorify the struggle for freedom, this man is incapable of character portrayal. His perception of nature is entirely physical, material; his thinking, when it functions at all, is oppressive and unpliant. And he fails to give a sense of life; the instincts of the intelligence, all those furtive, evasive, latent, profound and subtle nuances which differentiate persons whose intellectual development is not great, escape him entirely. Mr. Lewis is not negligible, but neither is he a master, nor a liberator of the ego. Indeed, in this group (where the Jewish element is of much importance and in which I would include such talented authors as Waldo Frank, so well known in Europe, H. L. Mencken, etc.) the dual and essential shortcoming is a neglect of personality itself, except in so far as it is a factor in social conflict. These men have been carried away by the social obsession which prevails in the new world, where crowds are dense and magnificent and where economic and social theories are seized upon with pious frenzy. They endeavor to lead the people in a direction which is not Anglo-Saxon, but they are always speaking to the multitude, and of the multitude. Consequently, they seem to have much in common with their bitter enemies, the "bourgeois" writers. Both classes unite in stressing social development and the collective life. Neither has ever taken the detached and abstract position which characterizes the great European authors, particularly the French—Maurras, Valéry, Gide; men who flourish in a world of ideas and personal forms, whose work is built upon a solid intellectual framework and attracts the individual and solitary being. American authors are curiously plastic, constantly impelled to retain contact with the masses, whether in open conflict or in the depths of its backwaters. American literature resembles that light, intangible phosphorescence, without shape of its own, which the ocean swell lifts to its crests, molding and unmolding ceaselessly.

The same is true of the other arts, at least of those which make their appeal to the individual or which are based on the development of personality. They do not prosper. But there are three which have attained an unequaled degree of splendor and originality; the status of American taste is revealed in the triumph of large-scale architecture, the popularity and originality of music, and the vitality and beauty of the motion picture.

American architecture cannot be viewed with indifference. One may hate an American city; and by that I mean hate New York, for despite the observations of certain people to the contrary, every city is New York in so far as it is American and not a reproduction of Renaissance or Gothic, of Babylon, Palmyra, or Luna Park. One may certainly hate it or detest it, since the only alternative is to love it ardently, to admire and adore it with all one's faculties. New York dominates. Thanks to it I have been able to understand Rome, which previously seemed a vain illusion of archaeological dreamers, and whose ruins appeared like shabby traitors to its past. New York, like every great metropolis, overwhelms us with its incongruous magnificence, its power and voluptuousness. Buildings fifty stories high, covered with marble, shining in the sunlight, sparkling and clear cut, fantastic cathedrals of pink and red stone glistening against a sky of harsh blue. At the lower end of Manhattan a cluster of towers advances menacingly towards the sea with banners flapping, and smoke and steam scattering before the humid breeze. Further to the north more skyscrapers stand out, pointed, square, bristling or terraced, and below them are thousands of tiny boxes surmounted by round cabins, the houses with their water tanks. Straight lines everywhere, horizontal and vertical, which affirm the will to simplify, to act directly, to make room for millions of people. New York is dirty; there are newspapers everywhere, even on the tops of the buildings, when the wind blows. There are no lawns, no trees, no peace or respite; a city of rectangles, harsh and brilliant, the center of an intense life which it sends out in all directions. Buildings lift it towards the sky and radios broadcast it; monumental railway stations launch it forth along their trunk lines into the interior; docks and wharves direct it towards distant regions to which the great ships anchored in the Hudson will carry it. New York is wretched and opulent, with its countless tiny brick houses squatting beneath the marble palaces which house banks and industrial offices. But New York is the only city in the world rich enough in money, vitality, and men to build itself anew in the last twenty years, the only city sufficiently wealthy to be modern. One may hate it, but think what admirable materials have been utilized in it; the finest marbles, the handsomest stuccos and building stone! What daring in the vertical lines, precise and accentuated, which rise from the chaos at their feet to astound and enchant! And along with the appealing quality of the material there is a sense of great fearlessness. One is stunned at the sight of these upright masses; this weighty substance has indeed found its master, yet in defeat it retains a ponderous and casual majesty. Is it beautiful? Some say that it is, others deny it. They declare that these buildings have no proportions or that they are out of proportion. By European standards this may appear exact, but not when measured by America. New York is constructed to the scale of the United States, as Athens was built for the Greek Republic, and Paris for the Kingdom of France. The very thing which I admire most in New York is its adaptation to the continent. In this sense, its architecture is intellectually reasonable, logical and beautiful. Skyscrapers are the dwellings of the super-trusts; they are Eiffel Tower cathedrals which shelter Mr. Rockefeller, the Emperor of Petroleum, or Mr. Morgan, the Czar of Gold. Since they extend their dominion over so much brute matter, these accumulations are legitimate trophies, similar to the pyramids of skulls which the Great Mogul erected before his cities in commemoration of his conquests.

Some say that New York crushes them—and not without reason; the individual is overwhelmed by these great buildings. This is not an architecture for men, like the Parthenon or the châteaux of the Loire and Versailles. It is an architecture for human masses. Such buildings do not shelter or isolate men as do those of Europe. They gather and shuffle them. Often more than five thousand persons are united under one roof. The Woolworth Building, over one-eighth of a mile high, and the Equitable, whose estimated value is over $30,000,000, are worthy of the land where senators are elected by 500,000 voters, a governor by several millions, and where the president can unite 16,000,000 citizens on election day. The New York skyscrapers are the most striking manifestation of the triumph of numbers. One cannot understand or like them without first having tasted and enjoyed the thrill of counting or adding up enormous totals and of living in a gigantic, compact, and brilliant world. American architecture has the inconvenience (or the advantage) of symbolizing the divergency in attitude between the European who on his arrival is so astonished at finding a life so analogous to that of the old world, and the American, settled in his way of life and his point of view and forgetful that there may be others. Thus the Woolworth Building is one of the most frequent and fruitless subjects of discussion in New York. Such a debate can prove nothing, for the skyscrapers are but picturesque manifestations of a profound and universal, although reticent tendency. They are an indirect result which explains nothing.

In the other arts it is easy to find similar conditions. Music, for instance, is much more popular, more fully appreciated, and better understood than painting. The concert halls are always well attended. Music schools have had an exceptional development. Wealthy women devote their time and money to musical patronage. In all the colleges and in many business and social organizations, groups are formed for choral singing which attracts big audiences. In a word, music bids fair to become a national art. Its public is thoroughly cultured and familiar with the latest developments. The best European artists spend much of their time in touring America, visiting cities great and small where they reap a harvest of enthusiasm, glory, and wealth. It is not the same with painting, whose public is still very limited. While American concerts equal or outclass those of Europe, the art exhibits can hardly be compared with the French or English in point of interest or popularity. Music, rhythm, movement, the persuasive and emotional which vaguely absorb both mind and senses, and carry away the hearer along with a whole auditorium made into a unit, provide an ecstasy which melts all individuality; music is thus able to give collective pleasure and arouse social sympathy. The appeal of painting, on the contrary, is through the isolated, distinct, intellectual picture, which the individual confronts for a moment in an endeavor to understand and appreciate its beauty through personal effort; painting and pictures stimulate the individual with a more analytical type of satisfaction.

Of all the arts, music has been the particular choice of America. A predilection for dancing has perhaps had something to do with this preference. At any rate, the two tendencies have combined to create a popular music. Ragtime, blues, Charlestons, negro melodies have flooded the world. They are perhaps what Europe accepts and best understands of America. With their brutal, warm sonorities, accentuated and precise, they have conquered the youth of every nation. No other music can so overwhelm a gathering of people or transform an assembly of young folk from critical and observant pairs into a sincere, unconscious, and spontaneous crowd. One may find here an echo of negro hordes venting their joyousness in dancing around an image; or one may explain it as the systematic intoxication of a nation which is overly agitated and eager to forget; but at all events one must admire its efficiency. Here again Americans have found the means of becoming a human mass, conscious of a living unity and joyous uniformity.

The visual arts, despite their intellectual character, have not been abandoned. National genius has been able to give them a form which embodies the peculiarly American predilections. Painting may receive little honor, and even signboards may be mediocre, but the movies are adored. Under the stimulus of popular encouragement, this industry and its technique have attained a degree of perfection unrivaled in any other country. Charlie Chaplin, Douglas Fairbanks, Mary Pickford, Harold Lloyd are the Hugos and Alexandre Dumas of the cinema. Thanks to this new medium the Americans have been able to develop a sort of visual concert. No motionless figures, strictly delineated and fixed by one intelligence for appreciation by another, but mobile gestures, animated with instinctive rhythm and with the resonance of a symphony. The movie, which bathes the crowd in shadows and relaxes the nerves of the individual, brings a forgetting of personal cares through surging movements ever accelerated. The moving picture in America owes (or perhaps owed) its supremacy to a clear conception of the one essential truth that the cinema is primarily an art of gesture and not of expression, nor acting, nor tableaux vivants, nor sentiments, nor ideas, which should claim as little of the screen as possible. Chaplin and Fairbanks understood this and exemplified it admirably until the day when a pitiless Europe, through an absurd misunderstanding, persuaded them that they were thinkers and broke their spinal columns. The movie actor is a clown and a hypnotist, whose movements soothe and fascinate. His entire art resides in the beauty, novelty and naturalness of his gestures. If he falls back upon sentimental emotion, or philosophic theory, or melodrama, he breaks the rules. Sentiments and ideas can never be entirely eliminated, since absolute purity is hardly possible to so complex an art, but they should remain general and discreet. Such was the condition in America when the greatest films were produced, that is to say before they felt the effect of the German influence, so full of bad taste, so distorted by the theater. Such productions thrilled and soothed a delighted public.

The visible world which people loved so much, and which other arts had failed to stress, became a true source of joy. It mingled with the crowds. It adapted itself to them. It enriched their collective sensitiveness and became an essential element, a vital stimulant to that great common torpor which we call the social life of a people.

The arts in America have never abandoned the task which national instinct laid upon them. What they have lost in liberty they have gained in liveliness. They strengthen unity and stimulate collective energy, earning a reward of favor and prosperity. Despite a few conflicts, more apparent than real, artists and crowds are in accord. No irreparable misunderstanding separates them; no divergent principles bring them into opposition.

It has been much more difficult to adapt the demands of various religions to American social life; and for a time, it seemed questionable whether harmony would ever be attained. The eighteenth-century churches were without a doubt the principal obstacle to union or even confederation among the colonies. Each colony had its faith and ordinarily was intractable in regard to others. Virginia, Carolina, and New York were Anglican; Maryland, Catholic, then Anglican; Pennsylvania, Quaker; Massachusetts and most of New England, strictly Calvinist. Boston persecuted the Quakers; Salem tortured witches; Catholics and Protestants were up in arms against each other in Maryland. Dissenters and Catholics alike were maltreated in Massachusetts, and as a whole all the colonies rejected Catholicism. Virginia saw the arrest of Presbyterian ministers, while in New England, strict and liberal Calvinists argued and squabbled for the upper hand.

But after 1750 it became apparent that to preserve their influence the sects would have to undergo a change of spirit and show some inclination to coöperate. The European emigrants who were arriving in hordes, and whose presence was vastly necessary, belonged to all imaginable denominations: Mennonites, Shakers, German Lutherans, Dutch Reformed, French Huguenots, Irish Catholics, Genevan Calvinists, primitive and missionary Baptists, Methodists, etc. The sects multiplied and the differences between them became more subtle, while the people, engrossed in exploring, conquering, and developing a continent, were still further exiled from Europe, the source of all these cults, whose universities, seminaries, libraries, alone could maintain the exact boundaries between the divergent organizations and religious doctrines. The greater the number of sects, the more insignificant became the sense of their differences. Moreover, there was one group which worked actively to enfeeble these differences and render them obsolete. I mean by this the Freemasons, who were active and powerful as early as 1740. Their doctrine was one of great piety, deistical, but hostile to all dogma. Its endeavor to direct religion towards a cult of humanity and charity was remarkably well defined and exemplified by Franklin, their principal leader and greatest apostle. He even wrote a book of prayers, invocations, and exercises which reduced religion to a zealous and tolerant deism. Above all, faith should be a bond between men and should on no pretext separate them. Definition, theology, and dogma should be relegated to the background and an attempt made to work in concord along charitable and social lines. The significance of this movement is readily appreciated when one recollects that Washington, Jefferson, Gouverneur Morris, Madison, Monroe, in fact almost the whole Virginian aristocracy, including all the great Revolutionary leaders, maintained this point of view. It did indeed encounter long and bitter resistance, particularly from New England where the clergy was well entrenched and more intellectual than in other parts of the country, and where it was perceived that the religion whose idea of divinity was vague, empty, and inconsistent, might have its inconvenient side. Religious history in the United States during the nineteenth century is marked by a protracted struggle between these two currents; one which desired to preserve the churches with their precise, concrete and abstract doctrines, and the other whose wish was to maintain, develop, and enlarge them, at the same time casting aside all questions of dogma. For the latter group, religion was before all a communion of men who were resolved to unite in doing good and to eliminate all influences which might separate them. Consequently, the overly strict or zealous search for truth was gradually proscribed, being replaced by the tendency to moralize for oneself and one's neighbors, all for the common welfare.

This movement went so far in the nineteenth century that the various sects, alarmed by their thinning ranks, joined in a movement which seemed for a time to presage a definite fusion of all denominations. They attempted an ambitious collaboration, the Inter-Church World Movement, which, after formulating a vast program and collecting huge sums of money, frittered itself away in financial disputes, and left nothing but a poignant memory and some regrets. However, the dream has not been entirely abandoned, and when in June, 1925, the reformed churches of Canada entered into a federation for their collective benefit, American newspapers loudly sang their praise. *The Christian Century*, a liberal church magazine published in Chicago, hailed the event as follows: "Inscribe Wednesday, June 10, 1925, as a new and monumental date in the annals of ecclesiastical history. On that day was seen, for the first time since the Reformation, the accomplishment of a gigantic reconciliation and reunion of Churches hitherto distinct. Nearly ten thousand parishes scattered over Canada from the

Atlantic to the Pacific ceased in a day to be groups of Methodists, Baptists, Presbyterians, or Congregationalists, in order to become members of the United Church of Canada. They brought with them all the spiritual treasure, ideals, and experience inherited from original traditions, but they left behind, as empty and worn out forms, their individual organizations and their names." It is obviously the wish of *The Christian Century* that this fine example might be emulated in America. And certain attempts are being made towards this end. For instance, in many towns there are Union Services, religious celebrations open to all members of all Christian sects; but as yet results of general importance have not been attained.

There are, as a matter of fact, two great forces inimical to such a fusion: Catholicism represents what one might term the right wing of this opposition, and the scientific spirit is the left. Catholicism is very strong in the United States and is in full development. In 1923 there were more than 18,000,000 Catholics in the United States. In the decade between 1909 and 1919 they constructed 3,258 churches. In addition they organized the Knights of Columbus, an anti-Masonic institution, attracted a great many Protestants, and opened schools, colleges, and even universities in many parts of the nation. While the Protestant sects have inclined towards greater and greater intellectual, dogmatic, and liturgical simplification, Catholicism, in maintaining its dogmas and ceremonies, has gained immense prestige. Doubtless a good many Catholic immigrants—Italians, Germans, and Slavs—allowed themselves to be converted to Methodism or Congregationalism as an act of Americanization; but these defections were largely compensated for by the immigrants who remained faithful and the Anglo-Saxons who have forsaken organizations which seemed weak and sluggish. Catholicism has thus reached an isolated and privileged situation, not without causing a good deal of anxiety to the Protestants. Not content with maintaining its dogmatic ground alone, the Catholic Church adapted to its own ends certain methods of its rivals. At Chicago in 1926 it organized a Eucharistic Congress in which many cardinals and bishops participated along with a vast number of the faithful, counted by tens of thousands. Such a manifestation was a striking answer to the popular affirmation that to attract the masses it was necessary to be accommodating in matters of dogma and liturgy. This Eucharistic Congress made a profound impression on American opinion.

Opinion had indeed already been much upset by an absorbing incident, which I do not place on a level with the preceding, but which also contributed to the anxiety of the directors of American Protestantism. This was the Dayton trial. From this trial it became evident that at the extreme left of Protestantism, at the very boundary of Christianity, there had developed a sort of sect without precise organization, banded together by an ardent and positive link, a scientific dogmatism which could not admit that the findings of science should be doubted or rejected. At Dayton, Tennessee, where Protestantism is still very much alive, a young school teacher was being tried for having taught the theory of evolution and having explained to his pupils that they were descended from apes. The parents of the students were much incensed and the teacher was certain to be condemned, as the law of the state explicitly forbade the teaching of evolution. The trial developed into an oratorical contest between Darrow, who attacked the Bible outright, and the Commoner, Bryan. The latter became so heated in his defense of religion, talked so much, made such a rumpus, and ate so inordinately, that he died. This scandalous and unfortunate trial, where both sides presented but a caricature of what they sought to defend, revealed to the public the difficulties with which American Christianity had to contend. The reformed churches sincerely desired to effect a compromise by which their dogmas should be set apart as subjects of discussion to be avoided. But they could not tolerate in their midst a hostile system of precise and readily intelligible theories which one day would form a barrier between them and their congregations. It became apparent that they had among them a corps of social engineers, formerly called pastors, or ministers, and a militant clergy composed of apostles and directors of conscience, hitherto thought to be merely professors.

To avoid this danger the Protestant sects saw two courses open to them: either to accept the new dogmas as a part of religion and teach them along with the old, which is the procedure of modernists like Fosdick, who do not hesitate to preach evolution; or to condemn them outright and attack them by popular and direct arguments utilizing all emotional resources. Such has been the method of Rev. Z. Colin O'Farrell, of Butte, Montana. I have seen a photograph of him in the pulpit, holding a gorilla in his arms, while a projector floods him and the ape with a light which is only slightly less brilliant than his inflammatory sermons. Thus he proved that man and monkey are quite different. Most pastors are not so direct in their methods, but all teach a strict interpretation of Bible and Gospels. Such are the fundamentalists; they are less intellectual and not so fashionable as the modernists, but they are powerful and well organized, and possess many means of propaganda. In 1923 it was estimated that the fundamentalists had become masters of a fourth of the churches in the East, half of those in the Middle West, and three-fourths of those in the South and far West. Their teaching is impressive and is primarily addressed to the masses. They announce that

Christ will return to earth accompanied by all the terrors prophesied in the Gospel. About them are grouped a flock of ecclesiastics, who, whether holding this belief formally or not, are ready to combat the modernist spirit and the influence of science. Among these crusaders are Bishop Manning of New York, Billy Sunday, Dr. Arcturus Zodiac Conrad, etc.

The modernists, who are in the majority among the bourgeois classes and have the support of a great many professors, are well entrenched in the East. Sometimes their methods are sensational, such as those employed by Dr. Guthrie at St. Marks-in-the-Bouwerie in New York. Dr. Guthrie has not hesitated to bring into his church on Sunday barefooted dancers in filmy robes, who dance prayers in the pious dusk to the music of the organ, while he offers an elucidation from the flag-draped pulpit. Taken as a whole, the modernist school prides itself on being more intellectual than the fundamentalists, more scrupulous—or at least more discerning—in their choice of means. They claim to render faith interesting and attractive even to those thoroughly imbued with the modern spirit.

It would seem that religious life in America is clearly divided into two camps. But closer scrutiny of conditions seems to indicate that such is not the case. Even this bitter and stormy quarrel has not eliminated the desire for unity. The fundamentalists of all sects work together, as do the modernists. Thus at the very moment when the fundamentalists are defending the literal sense of the Bible and endeavoring to restore dogmas to their original purity, they present an example of collaboration and tolerance which proves that they, like their adversaries, have not given up hope of an eventual reconciliation. These divergent opinions have not led to any serious rupture. The Episcopalian fundamental·ist will confer with his friends the Baptist fundamentalists, on the choice of arguments for converting the modernists of their respective sects. Then he will join in congress with his modernist brethren to discuss the temporal and spiritual management of all their churches and to work out campaigns of propaganda for launching among other sects. This unity is complex but it exists.

Such conditions have naturally impaired the prestige of the Protestant churches. In 1920 it was estimated that 58,-000,000 Americans belonged to no church at all. In the more sparsely settled regions of Oklahoma, Wyoming, Arizona, Nevada and Oregon, impiety was especially prevalent. This appears strange indeed in a land where religion once played so important a part. Naturally enough the zealous clergy has been working to revive religious faith and to restore it to its former high estate. Their principal method has been to bring a systematic influence to bear upon the habits and well-being of the people. In a country where poverty is, relatively speaking, reduced to a minimum, it would not be possible to attract and retain public sympathy through works of charity. Something better than that must be found. The more remote material and moral needs of the people must be disclosed and served. The American churches have set to work at this social enterprise, which restores a certain degree of unity and enables them to assume a moralizing rôle even though this is not their traditional mission. The greatest success in this field has fallen to the Y.M.C.A.; branches of this organization are to be found in every city and town of any size, generally under the benevolent protection and patronage of the Protestant churches of the community. Open to all, the Y. M. C. A., with its club rooms, lounging rooms, restaurant, billiard tables, and often a gymnasium and swimming pool, takes a prominent place in the life of the young American without fortune and renders true service. There, between a roughhouse and a swim, or between the fried potatoes and the apple pie, a discreet and grave man offers sage advice, moral, almost religious counsel, in a low voice, and slips a pious little volume into your pocket. On your bed table you will find a Bible with a list of verses to read if you have lost your money, or are fatigued, if your wife is sick, or a friend has played a trick on you. (Bibles are also found in all hotel rooms, placed there by the Gideons.) These Y. M. C. A.'s have been a real aid and comfort; they still are, and they encounter no opposition. This is not the case, however, with the other project of the American churches, the prohibition amendment, which was put through in a moment of enthusiasm. The various churches (Catholic excepted) collaborated to support the Anti-Saloon League, which, thanks in some measure to the subsidies of Mr. Rockefeller and other capitalists, persuaded Congress to prohibit the sale of alcoholic beverages. Thus the churches had the satisfaction of annihilating the source of drunkenness, so prevalent in the land which produced and consumed a great deal of whiskey, and of reducing other vices which find their stimulus and occasion, if not their genesis, in alcohol. They had the additional satisfaction of placing the Catholic Church in a delicate situation, since alcoholic wine is used in the celebration of Mass and the Catholic priests had never joined the campaign. Finally they counted upon the support of a preponderant majority of women and of many important industrialists. The latter had indeed accurately figured that if the workers stopped spending money in cafés and saloons, they would buy so many more automobiles, safety razors, and phonographs. Then of course, the pharmaceutical and drug companies which supply the myriads of drug stores with soft drinks, were ardently in favor of prohibition. Thus Mr. Rockefeller, king of oil, Mr. Gary, king of steel, Mr. Ford, king of automobiles, Mr. Liggett, king of purgatives, and all the churches of America were harmoniously united. What could the unorganized opposition do save rest upon its own deceptive self-confidence? The paradoxical act was advocated with drum and flag; and while thousands of young men were still in service, it was voted, ratified, and attached to the Constitution. A fine example of extreme unification, is it not? Henceforth every American, regardless of age, sex, occupation, and taste, must quench his thirst with water or milk, although with the privilege, by way of celebration, of drinking orangeade, sarsaparilla, Coca Cola, or perhaps ginger ale put up in flasks to resemble champagne bottles. Such was the most recent and triumphal crusade of the reformed churches of America. I should more properly say "such is," for by one of those curious, and perhaps natural phenomena, the law became an object of attack as soon as applied. And the more scrupulously it was applied, the more intolerable it appeared. In endeavoring to have it respected, the government rendered it odious. In trying to be tolerant, the authorities were obliged to sit by while the law was flagrantly violated. Drinking became a favorite pastime with the youth of both sexes, since to its intrinsic pleasure were added the charm of disobedience and smuggling, the excitement of danger and the thrill of mocking their elders, not to mention the appeal of inebriation. Saloons disappeared from the street corners, it is true, but only to reappear in clubs, drawing rooms, and college dormitories. Surprised at the moment it considered the battle at an end, the Anti-Saloon League acted imprudently. Its funds were misused and its superintendent in New York was jailed for fraudulent accounting. This alienated Mr. Rockefeller, whose morality is exacting. Finally public opinion, ever inconstant, became disgusted with a law so costly to enforce. Although it would be difficult to abrogate this Constitutional amendment, it can be violated with increasing ease. In spite of everything,

alcohol filters in from Canada, Mexico, and through all the
ports. The churches appreciate that their task is an ungrate-
ful one. Rebels are cropping up in their own ranks, and
they are much concerned. Perhaps the project was too ambitious.

To the European observer the religious confusion in the
United States seems to have been enhanced by the prohibition amendment. The effort to impose a morality from
without, to give society a rôle which belonged to the individual conscience, is grandiose, but also dangerous. Indeed
it is well in line with what we have tried to emphasize in
this chapter. And we should have preferred, for the sake
of our generalization, that on this score also the instinct
for unity, the desire to establish one social type, should bend
all else before it. But in this instance the habit of conformity
embodied in the churches and utilized by them overshot its
mark and may be severely upset by a reaction.

It is probable that prohibition contributes to general
prosperity in the United States. It is certainly useful in a
land accustomed to very strong drinks. It protects the home,
it helps the worker, its economic rôle is salutary, it tends to
cleanse politics, it protects the race. Perhaps a foreigner who
knew nothing of the United States before and during the
war is not in a position to make comparisons. But the moral
evil resulting from prohibition is incontestable. The discredit which it brings upon the churches is serious; the
taste for disobeying the law which it engenders in the
younger generation is baneful; and most of all perhaps, the
policy of transforming the state into a tribunal of customs,
moral virtues, and individual preferences is contrary to all
the demands of modern man. In this respect American
democracy has pushed its tendencies to a point where it joins
with Russian Communism. It is true that religion, whether
understood or not, is the greatest stimulant to our passions,

as was demonstrated by M. de Chateaubriand on his return from America. But what power has the religious instinct retained in the United States? Abandoned by intelligence, denying its most dynamic ideas, it gropes about in all directions. There are Christian Science, a sort of religion of will, New Thought, a religion of the body beatified, a number of ethical groups, Seventh Day Adventists, American Buddhists, Bahaists, Christadelphians, the Church of God and the Saints of Christ, the Church of the Living God, the Church of the New Jerusalem, the Disciples of Christ, the Free Christian Church of Zion, etc. Hardly a week goes by without a gathering of some mystic or religious society in one of the big New York hotels. Two years ago a minister might have said, "At the Hotel McAlpin there will be a lecture on divine metaphysics, followed by an auditory treatment. At the Biltmore, the 'Hidden Giant,' the subconscious, will be discussed; also a course on 'Concentration and Prosperity.' " At the Hotel Ansonia I listened to a sermon on the "Religion of the Solar Plexus" which was quite new to me.

However, too much significance must not be attached to the picturesque and anecdotic side of these cults. It is only too easy to laugh at them. Their real interest is more profound, and reveals the vitality of religious instincts in the new world, their rich and undiscerning ebullience. They reveal the sympathetic quality of a people which is endeavoring to draw all its surroundings into its life, efforts, and exaltation. What they lose in precision they gain in extension.

Vast and dense, dominated by a desire, or rather a passion, for unity, in which it sees its principal claim to greatness, unity in its material, political, and spiritual life, unity in intellectual pursuits and religion—the American people is the most powerful force in the world today. Its alert sensitiveness, stimulated by its newspapers and by its need for activity, the speed and formidable intensity of its reactions, make it both admirable and dangerous. No human group is less calculating, it is true, nor more generous, for no other group has sacrificed so much in the interests of unity, nor been so thorough in renouncing all intellectual programs and subtle combinations which might involve unity in dilemmas and complex maneuvers. This people, so preoccupied with its greatness, has voluntarily remained simple and unaffected, while developing immense energies and unconscious ambitions. It is both proud and mistrustful of itself. It has confidence in neither its fleets, its army, nor its diplomats, who it thinks were duped by the Europeans. But it is sure of its destiny and of its masses. And those vibrant masses are always available.

With its profoundly religious instincts, its healthy animal spirits, the American people is one of the most fascinating and redoubtable forces on earth. Directed by prudent and far-seeing men, it is sure of a glorious future. But with blind and nervous guidance, it would go quickly and terribly astray. America has built and welded together an imposing block of humanity. But has it created men to utilize this? What has become of the individual?

CHAPTER VIII

THE AMERICAN INDIVIDUAL

Despite the intense efforts of these millions of people, despite the enormous amount of work which they perform, despite laws, regulations, and social restrictions which often appear irksome and shocking, the most general impression of the United States is one of vivacity and happiness. There are few obvious signs of poverty; few recriminations are heard. Every one seems to make it a point of honor to adapt himself to circumstances or to appear to do so. A kind of vague yet energetic hopefulness flickers about the younger faces, while older ones express a mixture of satisfaction and strain which is less sympathetic, but none the less encouraging. Thus one comes to the conclusion that a compromise has been struck between the masses and the individual which guarantees the latter a sufficiency of personal development in the heart of this absorbing and inexorable social life. The sensation of crowds, which is oppressive elsewhere, is here attractive and stimulating. The nation is exhilarated by its own mass; the individual enjoys it and does not lose himself.

There are indeed marks of distinction and a sort of hierarchy in this homogeneous people. Individuals are not entirely amalgamated, nor buried under its mass. Even in this holy land of democracy, certain persons have acquired a kind of nobility, while others represent a bourgeoisie or sub-altern class. Question them, and some day you will be told, "In looking for an American do not mistake your man. There are many inferior types among us—Latins, Slavs,

Africans, Asiatics—who never become an integral part of our essentially Anglo-Saxon civilization." You so often hear the expressions, "to Americanize" and "Americanization," that you eventually come to look upon them as a doctrine or the symptom of a general condition. There are many degrees of citizenship, graded according to birth or race, all more or less thoroughly American. It has been thus for many years, but in the last three decades these distinctions have become accentuated and have assumed a more important aspect in the national life.

The Anglo-Saxon [1] American is the legitimate or voluntary descendant of the Puritans. From them he received his stature, his strength, and that handsome refinement and simplicity which bespeak the traditions of an ancient civilization. The long sojourn of his ancestors in the wilderness seems to have strengthened his muscles and soothed his nerves, imparting calm and serenity to both physique and features. His carriage bears evidence of a free and glorious destiny; and even among the humblest of his kind, one notices a natural pride and distinction. In an Anglo-Saxon family of Wisconsin farmers, where poverty had prevailed for at least three generations, I was struck by the way the children hastened to wash their hands after touching the cattle, as though impelled by an irresistible disgust. The parents declared, moreover, that they had never been meant to till the soil and would never succeed at it. Despite the repulsive odors of the pig-sty near the house, and despite utter poverty, they were still aristocrats with a refinement which fate might humble but could never vanquish. The European who visits New England is thoroughly and agreeably surprised to come in contact with a people of exacting politeness, who are somewhat stiff and overly fastidious, perhaps, but

---

[1] In the term Anglo-Saxon, we have included Scotch and northern Irish as well as English.

on the whole have much more nobility than is to be found in the good-fellowship of the French peasant or the suave manners of the French townsfolk. With such spontaneous distinction, such truly representative beauty of trait and gesture, and such a brilliantly clear complexion, the Anglo-Saxon American has good reason to be proud and to seek to preserve his race. His moral qualities are likewise distinctive and precise. He is ordinarily endowed with a keen sensitiveness to the beauties of form and matter. No other race shows so strong a liking for fine clothes, jewelry, furs, gorgeous fruits and flowers, or is so eager to embellish its surroundings with precious materials, gold, silver, and marble. This sense of physical beauty is developed to a degree which astounds the European. The young American frankly gives much time and thought to the matter of dressing well. He realizes that a smart appearance is helpful in business, an attitude which his superiors encourage. This is in contrast to crabbed Europe, where the less a man thinks of his personal appearance, the more value is attached to his work. As for the women, their luxury in clothes, perfumes, and ornaments exceeds anything hitherto known and supports many a French commercial house. Even among the artists, choice of fine materials is a predominant consideration, whether it be to cultivate a rich, elegant, and supple literary style, or to utilize all the resources of the painter's technique.

This tendency is associated with another which is apparently antagonistic to it, though the two may be easily reconciled. I refer to the instinctive habit of repressing, resisting, and concealing impressions. The Puritan considered everything in the external world as a temptation to be looked upon with distrust. His descendants are bathed in an atmosphere of material elegance and beauty which delights them without their ever permitting it to have any essential effect upon them. The American is at once sensitive and impermeable. An impression must be profound indeed to penetrate to the recesses of the individual. Ordinarily it remains completely outside, or at best on the surface. The interior is reserved for action, will, and serenity. But when impressions do touch the depths of the individual, they acquire an extraordinary value, an admirable richness, and an exceptional resonance. This explains why Whitman and Anderson at their best are such amazing poets. A zone of silence envelops the feelings of the Anglo-Saxon in the new world, isolating him in a state of calm and meditation which may produce either a brute or an original artist.

Ordinarily the interior faculties are devoted to action, which is considered the source of all sanctifying graces and the justification of lesser virtues. The need for action, which the early settler acquired from solitude and hardship, still pervades the soul of his descendant. Is it climate or tradition? One dare not say. But its effects are obvious. An English bricklayer transplanted to America will in a very short time increase his capacity enormously. Carpenters, mechanics, clerks, work at a speed which would shock the European workman to whom time and materials are things to be handled with caution and moderation. From the hodcarrier to the captain of industry, all seem possessed by the same demon of activity.

Work never frightens the American; it fatigues him, exhausts him, but in return it gives him a delightful sense of contentment. Idleness to him is a disease. No healthy man of good family can tolerate it. The idea of work is so deeply embedded as to make any sort of habitual idleness inconceivable. It has prevented more than one American from understanding the intellectual and artistic life of Europe. The atmosphere of every city is so impregnated with action that one must go a long way to escape it. Perhaps this partially accounts for the seasonal migrations to France and Italy.

In contrast to the stress laid upon action, sentiment holds a curious position in the American personality. A sentiment which chances to obtain a foothold often becomes an irresistible flood carrying everything before it. But unlike French or German sentiment, it passes rapidly. Immediately after the assault, the personality closes in upon it and covers up every trace of it. If it has not led to some glorious achievement, it leaves an unpleasant memory. If successful it may be recalled with pride and satisfaction, but it is seldom discussed. If it has been the instrument of trickery, the outcome is doubly humiliating and irritating, like the regrets of the occasional drinker who has broken things while inebriated. This disposition is too little understood by Europeans, who have come to look upon violent explosions of sentiment as an American pastime. Nothing is further from the truth. Sentimental crises are a necessary outlet; and though magnified and exaggerated by the peculiar social institutions of the country, they leave the individual with memories of glory and romance, or perhaps with suspicions.

The Anglo-Saxon American finds certain forms of intelligence attractive. He wants ideas to serve as instruments of action, as stimuli to his muscles or his will, as parts of a systematic structure. He appreciates the imaginative aspect of reason and intelligence, and consequently he likes all great syntheses. But if the intelligence turns to examine the human being, to dissect and analyze, he becomes fearful and revolts. The psychological and analytical French theater of the seventeenth century never has found favor in the United States. Such dry, blunt introspection seemed indecent and unjust. The old Puritans refused to confess. Their descendants experience a similar repugnance towards any analysis of their motives and intentions. Nearly every American writer begins his literary career with a story of his life, a

novel in which imagination and description hold a predominant place. The young Frenchman's instinct is quite
the opposite. Compare, for example, *The Apple of the Eye*
of Glenway Wescott with René Crevel's *Mon Corps et Moi*.
Through pride, the need for action, love of the future, doubt
as to the present, and a hatred for confession, the American personality remains reticent and repels self-analysis.
What it gains in grandeur it loses in lucidity. The gain is
largely one of freedom. The Frenchman, who never takes a
step without measuring, defining, and judging it, is quite incapable of doing anything without the accompanying sense
that his act is good, middling, or bad. Thus he has promptly
provided his own reward or punishment, and he feels obliged to maintain a rigid and consistent attitude, be it virtuous or blameworthy. In America, thanks to the obscurity
which surrounds a man's innermost nature, the realm of
transgression is much less sharply defined. Ordinarily a
moral judgment enters only with the overt act. I saw an instance of this recently along the shores of Lake Michigan
where, during the long summer evenings, there were hundreds of closed automobiles occupied by various kinds of
lovers—some of them young married couples, some engaged
or on their honeymoon, others flirts or boys and girls between
the ages of fifteen and seventeen, in their first cars, having
their first amorous experiences. Practically, these escapades
led to no evil results, nor did they leave the participants
with embarrassing recollections. The thoughts remained
pure, whether by being absent or prudently repressed—and
at any rate they were so disciplined as not to induce transgression, or at least an act of transgression.

Thus while the various races of the world have, in recent decades, taken pleasure in exaggerating their vices and
passions by the refined use of analytical thought, the Americans—at least the Anglo-Saxon Americans—have remained

mentally chaste. They do not, in the words of a great French poet, permit

> An adulterous intelligence
> To exercise a body it has understood.

Though in the midst of excessive prosperity and subject to the most acute excitations of the senses, this race has been able to preserve a spontaneous morality which many Europeans would call hypocritical, but which I find delightful in its pride and self-assurance. It is easy for the American to pass from a childhood as happy as that of the ancient Greeks to a maturity as reasonable as that of his Puritan ancestors. But woe to one whose mind is sullied and who sins in thought or actuality. Paradoxical though it may seem, a sexual indiscretion appears to stain the young American much more deeply than the young European.[2]

The Anglo-Saxon American is Christian in religious spirit, morals, behavior, and natural chastity. He is unconsciously half pagan in his taste for luxury, his refined hygiene, his physical pleasures, and his splendid bodily development. He is an aristocrat who conceives of a high ideal for his country, which he would like to see in the position of a benevolent world despot, though not at the expense of conservative social conditions and domestic equilibrium. He has a sense of proportion which is often curiously united to strongly original artistic tendencies. Nearly all great writers of the old school were Anglo-Saxons—Poe, Emerson, Whitman, Irving, Cooper, Mark Twain. Of similar descent are the young men of talent today—Anderson, Cummings, Wescott, Eliot, Fitzgerald, etc.

[2] Note this curious difference: a young American is not particularly ashamed to be seen intoxicated, whereas this would mortify the young Frenchman. On the contrary the latter takes a certain pride in showing off his mistress, a person whom the former would scrupulously conceal.

In comparison with the Anglo-Saxons, the Scandinavians and Germans seem violent and excessive. They have been veritably intoxicated by this new world, to which the Anglo-Saxons adapted themselves quietly and with grave, profound, and becoming exaltation. They dream of emancipation, sexuality, naturalism, radicalism, socialism, bold projects of all kinds. Moreover, their influence is great. The Central states, with the great cities of Chicago, Minneapolis, St. Louis and many powerful universities, form the bulwark of Germanic strength. The German masses are largely stupid and unpolished, and frequently despised. The Scandinavians, though often competent enough to rival the Anglo-Saxons, are chiefly occupied with farming. They have settled in great numbers in the agricultural districts of the Western and North Central states. Of the eight and one half million Swedes in the world, two million are to be found in the United States. The Scandinavians are thoroughly emancipated. Religion occupies little of their attention except as a target.

Between 1914 and 1917 there was a continual struggle, at first veiled and then open, between the Teutonic and Anglo-Saxon elements. The seriousness of this can hardly be exaggerated. These two groups had always esteemed and sympathized with each other. They had found collaboration easy, and in the mosaic of races which covers the United States, they might have been expected to be the first to 'reach a permanent mutual understanding. But the first months of the war ruined any such possibilities and involved the two most respected ethnic families of the new world in a civil strife, the traces of which are still evident in the North Central states: Illinois, Wisconsin, Iowa, and particularly Minnesota. During 1915-16 many hundreds of young Americans came from here to join the French ambulance corps as a manifestation of hostility to their Germanic environment.

The darker-skinned Europeans (the Italians and the Greeks, competitors in small commercial undertakings, such as boot-black stands, barber shops, fruit stores, cheap restaurants) are still far from realizing an American culture at all recognizable as national. They rarely receive a liberal education or advance to the bourgeois professions. To some extent they imitate the Anglo-Saxons. But politically they are opposed, often displaying an anti-European tendency and a vague but vehement nationalism which is frequently stimulated by hatred or jealousy of France and Britain.

The Irish have their religion as a centralizing influence, for which they demand—and generally obtain—a large degree of freedom. They make good citizens, with ideals which are on the whole very similar to those of the Anglo-Saxon, perhaps more moral and less pagan. But hatred of England and a rare aptitude for politics often make of them a pivot of resistance against Anglo-Saxon civilization. Governor Smith owes his extraordinary success both to his great personal ability and to his skill in grouping all other races around the Irish in opposition to the Anglo-Saxon bourgeoisie of New York State. The Irish hold a curious position. As a class they are despised by the Anglo-Saxons. But individually, thanks to their charm, imagination, and a certain capacity for work, they frequently attain situations of prominence. There are many of them at the bar, in the government and in clerical positions of all sorts. And of course they constitute a vast majority of the Catholic clergy.

In contrast to the Irish, the French Canadians, as an ethnic group, are held in esteem. But it is rare for one of them to rise above his level. They form compact and isolated groups in certain industrial centers, Detroit and Fall River in particular. They are excellent workmen, but always remain workmen.

Immediately after the war, eastern and southeastern Europe was in a pitiable condition. Swayed by the Russian upheaval, the other Slavic dominions eddied and swirled like dead leaves. Even many of the Latins came perilously near to the whirlpool caused by the destruction of the Czar's empire. Like the rats which flee from a foundering ship, these unfortunates, including hordes of Jews who had settled with them, embarked for the new world. They arrived by hundreds of thousands, and might have come by millions, had not their new hosts taken alarm. The upper circles feared for Anglo-Saxon supremacy, while opinion among the lower working-classes revolted against such an influx of ignorant laborers who were ready to work for a pittance and to accept exploitation with docility. Political groups were dismayed at the thought of a wave of socialism or communism. And the government viewed with concern the discontent of the old citizens and the demagogic exigencies of the new-comers.

The Slavs and the mixed races of the Balkan peninsula are placed at a great disadvantage by their languages, customs and traditions. They have none of the habits of cleanliness, moral instincts, nor social tendencies which characterize the Anglo-Saxons and Germans. Congregated in mining and industrial centers, they are employed as day laborers, bricklayers, etc.

Last come the yellow and black races. They are below even the most abject of the whites. The Chinese run laundries and cheap restaurants. The negroes are hardly capable even of that. They are day laborers, menials of inferior grade, porters, etc. The Pullman company employs thousands of mulattoes of the most varied assortment of shades, ranging from an inky black to a half-breed revealed only by lips and hands. But they are all "colored."

The blacks, after a hasty and ill-prepared emancipation, had been gradually reduced to a state of semi-subjugation by the Southern whites. Their voting privileges were nullified and they were limited to menial occupations, thanks largely to their laziness, low mental development, and incapacity for organization. But in 1917 the blacks were enlisted along with the whites and sent to Europe to make the world safe for democracy. Some fought well; all conceived a sense of pride and equality which had hitherto been foreign to them. Why should they not, after the way they were treated in France, where for the first time in three centuries they were permitted to patronize the same restaurants as the whites, to attend the same theaters, and to enjoy pleasures which they had believed entirely reserved for their white brethren?

Such things, striking the young blacks at an impressionable age, under circumstances which made the effect permanent, paved the way for a grave misunderstanding. Returning home prepared to live as they had lived in France, to enter New York theaters as they had entered those of Paris, they were harshly rebuffed. In the South particularly, where memories of slavery are still vivid and where the whites maintain a rigid discipline, this return was pitiful, almost tragic. After having saved the world, after having been thrilled by the most terrifying events the age has known, by the most frenzied ovations, and by the catchwords of the most arrant optimism, they came back to their former rank as pariahs. These negro conquerors would not accept such humiliation without resentment. A general exodus towards the North began. Fleeing the South where the cotton fields and the oppression of the whites confined them to work which was arduous and poorly paid, they drifted to New York, Chicago, Cleveland, Detroit, where they found more remunerative jobs in the factories, could see good movies, were given the right to vote and an illusion of equality. By changing their environment and coming to regions where slavery had never been known, they acquired a certain respectability which they took pains to cultivate. The Urban League of Detroit (an association of educated negroes devoted to the amelioration of their race) recently published the following recommendations: "Avoid noisy talk, vulgar and obscene language when in trolley cars, streets, or other public places. Remember that it harms us all as a race. Do not walk in the street wearing your aprons, night caps, underwear, or slippers. Wear street clothes when going out. Try always to dress neatly, but do not be a dude or wear gaudy clothing. It is as disagreeable and harmful as soiled garments. Do not sit on your door step, in the square, or in the public gardens and remove your shoes and carry them in your hand. Do not wear overalls on Sunday. . . ." Thanks to this advice, even though, from what I have seen, it is not always scrupulously followed, the negroes in the North have gained some consideration. Moreover, the Northern industries need them. With the supply of labor greatly curtailed by new immigration restrictions, the blacks find employment readily. They are well paid and happy, even though an unsuitable climate lowers their birth rate and reduces longevity.

The greatest disadvantage arising from the migration has been the sentiment of hostility towards the negro created in regions hitherto favorably inclined. Every district which has received a substantial contingent of blacks or mulattoes, has at once assumed the point of view of the Southern whites. In Chicago there have been homicidal riots, with negroes pursued and shot down in the streets in cold blood. In the more densely populated sections of New York, the negro is regarded with suspicion and jealousy. It is feared that he will be the cause of reduced wages. In fact the problem is no longer local, it has become national in scope and is to be counted among the most delicate phases of post-war conditions. There is a complete lack of understanding between the races. Still it would hardly be accurate to predict catastrophic results. The proportion of negroes is not large, their mortality rate is very high, and their power is insignificant. But at the same time it is undeniable that a nation must find a perpetual source of trouble and worry in the attempt to accept formally, on the basis of civic equality, a race which can never be assimilated into the majority, nor create for itself an independent situation, nor withdraw into an isolated and peaceful domain of its own.

As a matter of fact, America has developed the blacks in a remarkable manner. They have perhaps derived more from the new world than any other ethnic group, though more in the way of stimulation and pleasure than of durable benefits. Their political education has been negligible. They have never learned to utilize their own numbers, nor to take advantage of divisions among the whites. Their vote, save in a few Northern states, is of no consequence. Science is an unknown field to them. Even in their colleges scientific attainment is not distinguished by either quality or quantity. And finally, in neither the liberal professions nor the manual crafts has the negro's success been at all comparable to that of other races. He remains negligent, with little aptitude for intensive work. But the negro has found an inspiration in the feverish life and countless lights of the great cities, in the theaters, movies, and dance halls. This is his true dominion. The skill of the darky in inventing and elaborating all sorts of amusements is truly astounding. He is stupid in daily life and inert during the afternoons, but in the small hours of the morning, with dress clothes and drum sticks, he becomes a veritable magician, good-natured but formidable. He adds much to the local color of the United States, particularly to the popular arts, which really delight every one. On the whole the negroes are well liked and tolerated as naughty children, amusing and good for nothing. They are not despised, since no one takes them seriously. In the great conflict of races, they may be a distraction or a hindrance, but little else.

In this hierarchy we have made no mention of the Jews. Indeed, it is their desire not to figure as a race, but to be associated with whatever ethnic group they may be in contact with. Often they are successful. Thus the English or German Jew is higher in the social scale than the Polish or Bulgarian Jew, who is often more despised than the negro, and more feared. But since the war the Jews have been forced to coalesce despite themselves. Driven from other milieux, they have had to create one for themselves. But as they suffer from such a necessity, they protest against it and attempt in devious ways to escape it. They feel only too well that to acknowledge themselves Jews is to place themselves at the bottom of the ladder—between the Levantines and the blacks.

Great jealousy and competition exists among the ethnic classes. There are rivalries in politics, religion, art, intellectual and economic life. Moreover, each race has its own place in the social scale. America is fortunate in having no castes, nor even such firmly crystallized classes as there are in France, but it has the troublesome privilege of possessing a sort of racial hierarchy which is both irritating and stimulating to its citizens. Indeed, the distinctions are not easy to maintain, and on the border lines the conflict is often bitter. This is particularly the case with the less fortunate Anglo-Saxons, whose means do not permit a standard of living superior to that of the more prosperous Latins and Slavs. Once an Anglo-Saxon has fallen from his privileged position, he encounters much difficulty in regaining it.

The present Ku Klux Klan is largely composed of such men.

After the Southern whites had recaptured the power so gravely jeopardized by the emancipation of the negroes and by all which that act entailed, the original Ku Klux Klan lost its utility and gradually dropped out of existence. By 1918 it had been long since dissolved. Still it was talked of, and Griffith's great film, "The Birth of a Nation," brought a vivid and favorable picture of it to public attention. About this time its name and insignia were adopted by a new association, which was also secret, but was of much greater scope than the original one. Its organizations extended over the Central and Eastern states and directed their activities against a variety of real or pretended un-American elements—against Jews and Catholics, against the yellow and black races, against Italians, Slavs, and Greeks. It patronized morality and good conduct, and assisted in the enforcement of prohibition. It is known to have tarred and feathered a farmer who was suspected by his wife of being on too friendly terms with a servant. It often swings the election in local politics. The Klan also seems to have caused the destruction by fire of a number of Catholic churches, although this has never been conclusively proved. Again in Oregon it sponsored a law, directed primarily against the Catholic schools, to oblige all children to attend the public schools. This law was passed, but was eventually declared unconstitutional by the Supreme Court of the United States. In a word, while the central object of its activity has been maintenance of Anglo-Saxon supremacy, it has occupied itself with many details far removed from the crux of the question.

The principal doctrine of the Klan might be called Nordism. In order to find adequate support, it has appealed not to a strict Anglo-Saxon supremacy but to a general theory of the supremacy of the Nordic races. These ideas, derived perhaps from Gobineau, but more probably from the works of Houston Stewart Chamberlain, have met with much favor in America, not only in the Klan but with the public at large, which has taken keen interest in the disputes. Many volumes have been circulated insisting upon the dangers threatening the European races. I might mention in particular *The Rising Tide of Color,* by Lothrop Stoddard. Such grand and nebulous ideas have easily attracted the attention of a people which never tires of discussing social and ethnic questions. Consequently, even outside its own circles, the Ku Klux Klan finds much sympathetic tolerance. Besides, it is most intimidating.

Recently I had occasion to notice and study the activities of the Klan in a large university of the Middle West where social conflicts were flourishing. One of my students was of Italian origin, a lively and interesting boy, though little cultured, whom I pitied as he had lost an arm. Thinking he might have been wounded in the war, one day I questioned him. He did not answer immediately, but a week later invited me to lunch and told his story.

"My brothers and I—eight of us—left Palermo ten years ago to come to America. As soon as we could speak English, we decided to have our own business and set up a restaurant in one of the industrial towns of southern Illinois where there is a large Italian population. We made a big success as the restaurant was well situated and we worked hard and economized. In order to avoid disturbing the Ku Klux Klan and the Anglo-Saxons, we turned Methodist. We went to church regularly and sang hymns with the others. They watched us a little suspiciously, but the minister was a good fellow. I had some trouble as I gave lessons in English to other Italians, which made the American teachers jealous. But on the whole things went well. One day there came to town a Southern preacher and apostle who advertised a lecture on the 'True America.' I went to it with two of my brothers. As soon as I entered the hall I saw it was going to be hot. People scowled at us and called us dagoes. But we stayed on. Pretty soon the lecturer came in and began telling all sorts of stories about how this land had been discovered, conquered, and colonized by the Anglo-Saxons; how they had made it habitable and prosperous. But he warned them that if they didn't look out the fruits of their labors would be stolen by the coarse and greedy dagoes. After the lecture questions were asked. I asked if Christopher Columbus was a dago or an Anglo-Saxon, and they threw us out of the hall. But they did us no further injury, as we were armed. The next day being Sunday we went to church as usual. A group of about thirty men who were gathered around the door refused to let us in. That night they set fire to our restaurant and there was considerable shooting. It was then I lost my arm.

"Now we are here, all eight of us. If you ever have any trouble with these lunatics, let me know. My brothers and I have good revolvers and we know how to use them."

I thanked him, but was never in need of his services as I was not treated as a dago. The French are somewhat apart.

The little towns of the Middle West are quite frequently the scene of such ferocious conflicts. In the poorer quarters of Chicago hardly a day passes without shooting. Thus the Klan and its allies have a large field of action, corresponding to one tendency of public opinion. And though they do present their cause under a crude aspect, they are at least to the point. Encouraged by success, the Klan has endeavored to assume a more important rôle while at the same time divesting itself of its rather childish and ridiculous ceremonial. It recently launched a vehement, though fruitless campaign against the participation of the United States in the World Court. A grand dragon of the Klan wired Senators Fess and Willis that the proposal to send American representatives to the World Court should be rejected, and that he spoke "in the name of 250,000 Protestant men and women of Ohio." Thus in the final analysis the conflicting races carry their plaints to the government, which is considered the natural arbiter and the only one capable of allaying ethnic quarrels or at least of finding a compromise acceptable to the majority.

The Anglo-Saxons have been remarkably tenacious in maintaining their supremacy against all comers for three centuries. But in addition to their racial tenacity the Anglo-Saxons have had the good fortune to produce nearly all the personalities which were great and forceful enough to guide the destinies of the nation. Except for Gallatin, a Swiss, Jay, a descendant of French Huguenots, and Roosevelt, of Dutch ancestry (all of whom were thoroughly penetrated with Anglo-Saxon traditions), American history offers notably few great men of other races. But despite their illustrious members, and despite their tenacity, the Anglo-Saxons would most probably have lost their ascendancy were it not for other more subtle qualities which almost defy expression. They have given proof of a patience and calmness impregnable to all shocks and ruptures. The example of Washington and Franklin in accepting and stubbornly defending a constitution with which neither was satisfied, is a case in point. The Anglo-Saxons owe their exceptional prestige to an instinctive attitude which permits of constant flexibility, never preferring the gesture to the results, and always willing to accept the benefits of a compromise rather than sacrifice all to an idea. They have always appeared in the rôle of arbiters and have been accepted as such. In this way they have consistently escaped violent conflicts with rival groups which might have weakened or even ended their hegemony. Had the Southerners been more faithful to these tenets, they would have spared themselves many hardships. The victory of their Northern cousins was due less to armies and principles than to patience and the ability to carry on under adversity. The leaders of the nation have derived inestimable benefit from this tolerant, charitable and haughty attitude which is composed of involuntary reticence, slow-mindedness, reflective prudence, and a vague sense of danger. These factors account in great measure for the social and ethnic stability of the country— and also for its tardy and fruitful entrance into the war and its present economic supremacy.

The Anglo-Saxon Americans have not allowed their development to be hampered by any strict codes or formally accepted characteristics. They have adapted themselves to the widely differing regions of America and accordingly formed racial groups which are quite distinct. The Northeast has conserved the Puritan type, haughty and strong. The Southerner is less rigid and less robust. The Anglo-Saxons of the Mississippi basin, by virtue of contact with Germans and Scandinavians, are more open and impulsive, more self-confident and also more vulgar. They realize this and mention it frequently, as it gives them a sense of superiority. The routine-loving East is looked down upon, but the far West, which an abundant Nature has endowed with more leisure, luxury and ease, evokes a vague feeling of jealousy. Each of these groups is so thoroughly alive to its own qualities as to constitute, if not a new series of states, at least a sectionalism well defined by natural barriers, cultural differences, and conflicting interests. The Middle West considers itself the true center of the United States both geographically and morally. Its metropolis, Chicago, dreams of dethroning New York, the capital of the traditionally

Puritan East (though itself very far removed from Puritanism). As a way of becoming economically independent of New York, Chicagoans talk of an immense canal route from the Great Lakes through the St. Lawrence to the ocean. For some time this imposing project has been advocated by the Middle West and violently attacked by the East. The latter realizes only too well that such a scheme would spell the decline and ruin of the Northeast, the Hudson River basin, and Manhattan. Chicago would become the center not only of the United States but of the whole North American continent, with Montreal as its port. Under such conditions French Canada could hardly maintain its economic autonomy. Consequently the plan encounters serious objections, on the one hand from conservative Americans, and on the other from Canadians who are anxious to maintain their independence. The Anglo-Saxon of the South, while not greedy, is still much interested in obtaining his own economic emancipation through the hitherto rather neglected development of his natural resources. And above all, the Californians and the others of the far West consider themselves the élite of the nation. The Eastern Yankee lets them all talk, but in strengthening his banks and universities, in increasing his cultural advantages and broadening his relations with Europe, he takes certain precautionary measures. The others will not speedily overtake him. It is probable that this keen though peaceful rivalry will continue for many years, enabling the Anglo-Saxons to manifest their varied aptitudes and rich vitality. This federal and imperial race will continue to rule with taciturn prudence and resourceful dignity.

It has already found an admirable method for placating and satisfying the pride of the subaltern races. It takes pains to demonstrate that equality reigns in America and that every one may aspire to the loftiest position, though the hypothesis is not quite true. The United States is contrasted with the rest of the world, which is represented as unclean, impure, and unfit for self-government or democratic institutions. Their attitude is, in substance, "Let us agree among ourselves and have pity on the others." Even an unfettered and generous mind like Wilson's could not refrain from comparing the wisdom of the United States with the political immaturity of other nations. The daily repetition of these sentiments by the press goes far towards solving domestic racial problems. But it certainly does not improve relations between the old world and the new. Not that there is any probability of armed conquest or even of immediate economic exploitation. But it leads Americans to adopt a tone of condescension which, however kindly, is not always polite; and it fosters an autocratic viewpoint on international problems. A number of writers in the United States have recognized this.[3] But they have caused hardly a ripple in public opinion. As sincere and appreciative observers of the American people, we admire their complacency and watch them with curiosity, without anger and without illusions.

[3] See the article by Miss Repplier in the *Atlantic Monthly* for December, 1926.

CHAPTER IX

AMERICA AND THE OLD WORLD

In the new world, Europe and Asia are often pictured as the ruins of once great civilizations where declining races are fighting a last battle against the elements and one another before going under. The American gives them a pitying look and thanks a kindly Providence for his own more auspicious fate. This point of view must be stressed, since it is either unknown or ignored in Europe. The Americans whom one meets in the capitals of the old world are comparatively well read and cultured. They appreciate the charm of countries grown old and the pleasures of an intellectual life. Quite a number of them have settled in Europe. They are wealthy, generous and well disposed towards their adopted homes, but their number cannot possibly exceed ten or twenty thousand. The hundred and ten million Americans at home, on the contrary, are thankful for a rich, fertile and prosperous country, for the Atlantic Ocean which separates them from tumultuous Europe, and for the Pacific, which protects them from the yellow hordes. The American, in an immense continent which became comfortably settled, developed and regulated in three centuries, is genuinely grateful for the attitude of aloofness so well inculcated by Washington, for its corollary, the Monroe Doctrine, and for the utterances and acts of Polk, Seward, Blaine, and Olney in furthering the same policy. Moreover, he is at a loss to understand why the European, in a much longer stretch of time, has succeeded so badly. He is indignant at the European disregard for political economy; and the cutting up of Central Europe stupefies him. "Why make it so small?" he asks. "Why make it so complicated? Why don't you follow the American system, which comparisons in wealth and the infrequency of war must certainly prove superior to your violent and barbaric methods?"

The principal complaints against Europe are social and moral. It appears scandalous that, after having lived side by side for so many centuries, people have not learned to tolerate one another. Such an attitude flouts both the precepts of society and the exhortations of the Gospel. Criticisms of like nature appear frequently in the press. In November, 1922, the New York *Times* published an article on Hungary beginning: "Hungary is the most openly mad and revengeful country in a mad continent." In the popular press, the Hearst and McCormick groups, editorials similar to the following are not uncommon:

"The insolence of England, France, and Japan in regard to our righteous and rightful domestic laws is offensive but enlightening.

"It shows first that these foreign nations have no understanding of our ethics, no sympathy with our idealism. Their whole policy is one of immediate material advantage. They try to deceive us by professing at times our high American humanitarian principles, but their real principles are 'grab, greed, and aggression.' Their only ideals are the mailed fist, the iron heel and itching palm." [1]

An English journalist once complained that America fiddled while Europe was burning. To this Arthur Brisbane, editorial writer for Hearst, replied that it was better to play the violin than to set one's house on fire.

It is often denied that such statements are representative or have much influence. Obviously their authors were not inspired by intellectual impulse. But although they do not

[1] New York *American,* January 7, 1923.

appeal to logic, they do something more effective: they play on the emotions. These precise, simple, and vivid outbursts are supplemented by satirical cartoons and often by accounts of scandals in European high society. Add to this a few simple facts—that Europe is poor, does not pay her debts, is always seeking our aid, individually and collectively— and one cannot fail to see why the older continent obtains so little sympathy from the great mass of Americans.

This attitude cannot be formulated officially, for reasons which are primarily domestic rather than diplomatic. Every four years comes an election crisis, during which the highest dignitaries of the government need the aid of the motley crowds. The Jews and Irish of New York must be courted, also the Scandinavians of Minnesota, the Germans of Chicago, the Canadians of Denver, the Greeks of Boston, etc. The negresses must not be forgotten since they "vote so well." Their husbands are more fickle, but the ladies have taken solidly to the Republican Party and they cling to it as an integral part of the old guard. No element can be neglected with impunity. Even the proudest official must stoop to conquer. Once the electoral season is past, the tension is relieved and action becomes less constrained. The four years of administration belong to the Anglo-Saxons just as surely as the six months of campaigning belong to every one. In 1924, to satisfy the former without irritating the latter inordinately, the government conceived of an admirable law. It reduced the annual number of immigrants permitted to enter the United States. Moreover, it scrupulously specified how the choice should be made. A certain portion is taken from each ethnic group which has contributed to the population of the country. And the basis of computation was so formulated as to allow a generous immigration from England while reducing the Italian, Greek, Levantine, and Slav quotas to a minimum. The following table affords an interesting comparison of annual immigration under the new and old laws.

	New	*Old*
Belgium	512	1,563
Bulgaria	100	302
Czechoslovakia	3,073	14,357
France	3,954	5,729
Germany	51,227	67,607
Great Britain and Northern Ireland...	34,007	
Greece	100	3,063
Hungary	473	5,747
Irish Free State	28,567	
Italy	3,845	42,057
Jugo-Slavia	671	6,426
Norway	6,453	12,202
Poland	5,982	30,977
Russia	2,248	24,405
Spain	131	912
Sweden	9,561	20,042
Turkey	100	2,654
United Kingdom		77,342

This is the method by which the dominant race hopes to retain its numerical superiority in the future. It may be indirect, but it is well adapted to a democratic age when numbers are of such importance.

The English are naturally attracted to the United States. Despite all the British government has done to divert the flow to the dominions, where the need of a white population and of English blood is so pressing, the United States still remains the most tempting destination to those whom the native country has rebuffed or discouraged. The industrial crisis in England after the war accentuated this tendency and increased the flow of immigrants. Were the subsidies to the unemployed discontinued, a vast human tide would certainly sweep to the coasts of America.

This is not characteristic of England alone. All over Europe wherever economic conditions make the people restless and oblige them to endure material sacrifices, many a longing glance is turned towards New York and San Francisco. Since the new American immigration law Italy is at a loss to dispose of her over-abundant population. She complains acridly of the restrictions imposed by Washington.

France is almost the only country which remains indifferent, since she too is a center of immigration, not of emigration. But even France feels the repercussion of the new American laws. Many of the poor folk who set out for the United States end up in Saint-Denis, Levallois or some out-of-the-way province where French labor is scarce or too costly. This is not greatly to their benefit, for instead of working in a country with a high exchange where they might economize until they returned home with a comfortable fortune, they are obliged to accept small wages in a depreciated currency. Though earning a decent living while in France, they must abandon all hope of wealth. So both peoples and governments accept the new legislation grudgingly. It is irksome and humiliating—and implies an adverse criticism of the quality of their blood. It is unbearable to the Roman, the descendant of legionaries who conquered and civilized the world, to hear of Italians being treated as an "inferior race" and being excluded accordingly from the new continent which he may look upon as barely civilized.

This is the source of much trouble and embarrassment for the government at Washington. Were the United States less powerful, this affront to the pride of friendly but susceptible nations might result in unpleasant reprisals. But under present conditions, that is to say until Europe attains some degree of unity, the new world republic has nothing to fear but vain and polite recriminations. The one effective

arm which the discontented peoples might employ is the
voting strength of their national colonists who have become
citizens of the United States. Such tactics have been tried
more than once, and not always without success. It is
affirmed that a certain Italian ambassador was recalled for
having concerned himself too indiscreetly with American
elections. On the whole, however, a majority of citizens will
always approve of the immigration law, since it gives reasonable assurance that high wages will be maintained.

As America is in no way dependent upon the Latins and
Slavs for its economic welfare, fearing them on neither
land nor sea and expecting little of them, the government
might continue the restrictive and Nordic immigration policy in peace did it not conflict with one of the nation's
dearest ambitions—that of a Pan-American union. The
citizens of the United States have a variety of material interests in Latin America. They have lent the smaller republics vast sums of money and continue to do so. Commercial relations with them on a large scale are always desirable and are frequently attempted (though not always
successfully).[2] Many efforts have been made to attract South
American students and to impress them with the advantages
of an Anglo-Saxon civilization. This movement has attained
a partial degree of success. The number of young Argen-
tinians, Chileans and Brazilians who come to study in the
United States is increasing yearly, and more and more colleges of the northern type are to be found in the southern
continent. But despite a wholesome admiration for sky-
scrapers, railroads, great universities and charitable institutions, the South American is still led by racial and cultural
affinities to prefer Europe to the United States. The Pan-
American Congresses, which are organized primarily

[2] See J. H. Blakeslee, *The Recent Foreign Policy of the United
States*, New York, 1925, pp. 139-42.

through the initiative of the northern republic, have not always been examples of perfect cordiality or unreserved confidence. The Latins of America still feel tenderly towards the old races of the Mediterranean basin, as they show by frequenting the theaters of Paris and the restaurants of all Europe, and by their attachment to the League of Nations. The supercilious way in which the United States sometimes treated the southern nations has brought about a certain coldness between them and the great Yankee republic. Nordism has its disadvantages.

Racial politics is a thorny problem. It disturbs Europe, upsets South America, and angers Asia. Indeed, the summary exclusion of the yellow races is even more radical and brutal than the attitude towards the Latins and Slavs. The Japanese are not wanted in the United States. Though the issue primarily concerns the Western states, it has become an electoral principle which the rest of the country accepts with more or less enthusiasm, but at any rate with acquiesence. The law alone would perhaps have sufficed to cut Japan to the quick, but the decision was rendered still more insulting by the actions of Congress, which the president and secretary of state were powerless to stem. Spurred on by demagogic zeal, the senators and representatives gave the vote a character so clearly hostile to Japan as to evoke a wave of resentment from the other side of the Pacific. The American administration with its ministers in Tokio and the numerous merchants and bankers having connections with Japan did much to efface the first impression and to iron out the difficulty. But the facts of the case remain in all their brutality. In years to come the Japanese, stifling on their islands, will be more and more tempted by the fertile lands of Australia, Hawaii, and California which the white races occupy without filling. They will be confronted by a resolute and well-armed nation which is negligent about many matters but is ever vigilant on this. It already seems prepared to occupy and protect the Philippine Islands indefinitely, although the natives are impatiently clamoring for their promised independence. This policy is in no wise the result of economic benefits. The United States has nothing to gain by possession of the islands, unless it be the discomfort caused by the exclusion of the Japanese. American opinion, which in recent years had been rather in favor of abandoning the Philippines, seems to have shifted to the point of view that it is perhaps wiser to retain possession of the colony, cumbersome though it is.

Since the discovery of the Americas, the two continents have been a source of disquietude and trouble to Europe. Nations have fought for Western gold and massacred one another's colonists for territorial wealth. The northern continent, being less opulent and less tropical, should not have touched the imagination so forcefully as its southern counterpart, yet it was the source of endless quarrels. Money, ships, and men were lavished upon the conquest of its wildernesses, which were vacant and often frigid, peopled solely by a few wretched, roving Indians. While the Seven Years' War was heavily burdening Europe, the new world acquired an unenviable reputation. It came to be looked upon as a firebrand of discord, a fabulous lodestone attracting thousands of young men who never returned. Men cursed Christopher Columbus. His discovery served only to depopulate Europe and involve the blind and greedy powers in endless disputes. After the discovery of America, wars multiplied, slavery spread and Europe became weakened. Voltaire's capricious remarks about the acres of snow (Canada) express the same disgust and lassitude. With the formation of the United States this attitude was completely changed.

Philosophers and men of good will, of whom there were many in the eighteenth century, looked upon this as the redemption of America and as compensation for so many horrors. A few murmured, "Take care; in time the child will become a giant and dominate you." But such an attitude was ridiculed as the idle fabrication of a dreamer. The probability of such an evolution seemed indeed remote. Sages declared, "America has caused the diffusion of slavery. Now it is becoming a land of liberty. It will shelter the unfortunates of the whole world and will certainly abolish compulsory servitude. The wrong will be more than righted." Such were the words and attitudes of the young French aristocrats who supported the United States in its struggle for independence. The "insurgents" were presumed to be virtuous, moderate in their requirements, rustic, modest and proud. Liberty would reign, aided by her sisters, Fraternity, Justice, Equality, Philanthropy and Natural Religion.

Throughout the turmoil of the late eighteenth and early nineteenth centuries, the doctrinaires of liberty who were working, fighting, and suffering in Europe often looked towards America for encouragement and consolation. Benjamin Constant said, "If things go badly here, I will take refuge in Virginia." When things were darkest La Fayette sent his son to Washington. He himself made a triumphant and consoling visit to his second home. Mme. de Staël thought of going to America to escape the tyranny of Bonaparte. The tradition persisted during the nineteenth century and left a number of monuments as witnesses to its power and fertility. Most remarkable are the books of Tocqueville and Bryce. Like Raynal, Mably, Turgot and the other "philosophers" of the eighteenth century, they looked upon America as a field of human experiment. Intelligently, patiently, and sympathetically they studied all aspects of American life. Their works have become classic in the new world and have exerted a profound influence upon the development of political theory in Europe.

As a matter of fact, however, these two great men are often hampered by the nobility of their own conceptions. The lofty eighteenth-century tone of Tocqueville has disheartened more than one reader. Likewise it often kept him from seeing the men behind the institutions and from going behind the idea of American democracy, which he loved and admired, to perceive the real United States, with its human properties, its passions and appetites. He frequently gives the impression that he is discussing general principles and only turns to actualities for verification. When compared with anything so complex, changeable, and full of vitality as the United States, Tocqueville's writings on democracy and its application in the new world may easily seem cold and limited and even arbitrary. On the whole he is not far from Montesquieu.

Bryce, whose Anglo-Saxon temperament and protracted visits to the United States provided him with more firsthand documentation, suffers also from that extreme preoccupation with the mechanics of government which characterizes the liberal doctrinaires of the eighteenth and nineteenth centuries. A man who writes with too much precision on such a subject frequently gives the impression that he is superficial or is the dupe of outward forms.

The ideas of a Tocqueville or a Bryce may indeed evoke a noble enthusiasm in high-minded and idealistic souls, but they often cause a reaction in more punctilious and argumentative minds. The United States has constantly suffered from the optimism of its advocates and from the legends which they invented or perpetuated. Travelers who came to New York after learning of America through Lafayette, Tocqueville, or Bryce, have more than once expressed surprise and dissatisfaction. None spoke with more candor and blunt frankness than Victor Jacquemont, though he was a friend of Lafayette and an ardent republican. After one night in New York, he wrote to V. de Tracy, in 1827: "As a whole, American customs displease me. . . . Their minds, though not always devoid of severity, and consequently of nobility, are more generally merely cold, platitudinous and vulgar."

Similar passages are frequently to be found in nineteenth-century correspondence. The industrial development and increasing wealth of the land never failed to amaze the traveler who arrived with his head crammed full of noble ideas, convinced that the United States was an idyllic country and the hope of the universe. He was alienated by slavery, the bitter economic strife, and the intensity of work, which he met with everywhere and which seemed to arise from a desire for gain, since he generally failed to appreciate the necessity for outfitting a continent where everything was still to be done. In a word, every detail of daily life in America did its part to rebuff him. The striking absence of artistic life and literature heightened his disillusionment. (Travelers customarily have a taste for literature and artistic sensations.) Stronger and stronger grew the impression that the new world was the land of the dollar and that the sole reason for going there was to make money. America still remained an absorbing spectacle to savants interested in the phenomena of nature and eager to observe animal and vegetable life under primitive conditions, or to sociologists who were studying the problems of population, the aspects of racial distribution, and the development of political education in a young people; but their effect on opinion was slight and indirect. Rare indeed have been men like Claudel who saw the subject from another angle and studied the human greatness of the American type.

In this respect *L'Echange* seems to me to offer one of the most lucid analyses of American character ever written, one of the most generous efforts of intelligence in confronting a new personality. But how many people had read *L'Echange* before 1914? The accepted type in France was the one presented by M. Abel Hermant in *Les Transatlantiques*. That novel, of somewhat low-grade wit, was the only document on America with which the majority of the bourgeois were acquainted. It is still widely read, despite its ungallant and ridiculous imaginings. Such a book has a much more important bearing on the relations between peoples than it is generally credited with. It easily convinces since it makes no pretense at doing so. Consequently no refutation of it is feasible. Moreover, its simple, unsubtle caricatures are readily absorbed. Again there was no obverse side to the comic portraits so flattering to French self-esteem, which delights in moralizing to Anglo-Saxons. The United States was known largely through such works as these and through the investments which were made in America. Every year a goodly sum of European money, a large proportion of it French, was used in constructing railroads, developing mines, and building cities in the new world. The less respect European capital had for the American character, the more it tended to invest funds in America, confident that they were in the hands of men who would get the most out of them, being unhindered by philanthropical concerns or artistic interests.

The belief that Americans were exclusively occupied with getting rich was so well established, that hardly any one in Europe foresaw the coming development of a powerful spirit of nationalism capable of tearing bankers from their desks and workmen from their machines. No one was surprised at American neutrality and the traffic in arms, munitions, and supplies, which engrossed American industrialists in the early years of the war. This was in the order of things. The unforeseen came when a considerable number of young Americans enlisted under Allied colors, when President Wilson protested against German pretensions, and when he backed his statements at the critical moment by a declaration of war. As a matter of fact, the Allied forces, realizing their weakened condition, had been carrying on a dual propaganda for some time. In America they were striving to increase the popularity of the Allies; in Europe they aimed to impress upon public opinion the advantages of an Anglo-American friendship, a Franco-American fraternity, an Italo-American alliance, etc. Intervention became a reality, and while the blood of soldiers flowed on many fields, an immense wave of sentiment brought the Allies and the Americans together, each delighted to discover the other. The opinion of all Europe, which had hitherto been unanimous in a moderate dislike and scorn for America, was now divided along the line of battle. On one side it was transformed into ardent and admiring friendship, on the other into hatred, the latter being the less violent of the two.

With the advent of peace, the United States attained the apogee of glory. In less than three years the nation had passed from a position of secondary importance to world dictatorship. President Wilson had the perilous honor of possessing the greatest material force on earth and the noblest doctrine. He set to work honestly, but the task was too great. From whatever angle it is approached, the Treaty of Versailles seems repellant; nationalists consider it an injustice bristling with dangers, and internationalists look upon it as a monstrosity. Subsequently the Americans retired to their tent, opening a flap from time to time to call out precise though disinterested advice in a loud voice. The difficult years which followed, years of groping, physical suffering, and disillusionment, dealt a severe blow to American prestige. European opinion, still divided in two parts, changed sides. The Allies felt that the United States had abandoned them ungenerously, while the vanquished were well pleased by the renewed state of neutrality, which often worked in their favor. When American pressure brought about the evacuation of the Ruhr and the establishment of the Dawes Plan, Germany saw the dawn of an American friendship, while France cast black looks at the new world. But in all truth, this about-face is not final. Europe is gradually returning to one general opinion which strikes an average between the two extremes.

Despite all that may be argued to the contrary, the United States has been the most ardent and pressing advocate of a League of Nations; likewise the United States since 1920 has been the only dangerous and persistent enemy of the League of Nations. The League exists, however garrulous, limping, incomplete, chimerical, and ridiculous it may be—and it is a useful meeting-place for the most loquacious and sonorous voices of Europe. The prime ministers and foreign secretaries of our parliamentary democracies are intelligent, so I am told, but impressionable and anxious to express what they think rather than what they feel. Though we need not drive this theme to its logical conclusion, it would seem that the United States has been pleased to inaugurate a club to formulate general European opinion—an opinion which will certainly not be favorably inclined towards its founder. And matters are not helped much by the amiabilities of a Medill McCormick taking advantage of a brief stay in Geneva to spread pleasantries about that Areopagus. This factor is not negligible.

But there is a more important consideration. For some years the United States has been settling the question of war debts, that is, has been collecting money which was lent, or is considered to have been lent. (We will not enter into a discussion of the distinction between the two, since the subject is most complicated, and the conclusions, whatever they be, are of no value.) If the sums are to be recovered, the former Allies must pay over large amounts at a time when they are bled white and are tottering under huge taxes. They have no available funds, and will have none for many years to come, save what Germany pays under the Dawes Plan. Fifteen years from now, if conditions remain unchanged, all Europe will be turning over to the United States, with a uniform, monotonous gesture, the money produced by the labors of Germany. The former European Allies and their enemies will, perhaps for the first time, have a definite bond in common, a concrete joint interest. The Dawes Plan, the duration of which is fixed by no treaty, may indeed weigh heavily upon the economic life of Germany for the better part of a century in order to satisfy the demands of Washington. Likewise, the treasuries of the European governments will be constantly disturbed by the problem of procuring funds already promised. That situation will weigh heavily upon a Europe whose social difficulties are acute and which has been seriously handicapped by the gigantic conflict. Despite national rivalries, and despite the pains which Mr. Coolidge's administration has taken to settle each debt separately, these problems are too similar and too intertwined to be treated independently of one another. It is possible to believe, if one is well disposed, that Washington expects to use these settlements as a way of compelling the governments of Europe to collaborate. Such may be the result, but the products of that collaboration may also be far from Washington's liking. At any rate, it is still distant. There is, however, another less noble and less useful form of collaboration in process of development—the collaboration of public opinion.

Despite official pronouncements, the United States has

the privileges of wealth. Every summer the great trans-Atlantic liners unload in Europe hordes of Americans who drift about and penetrate the remotest recesses of the continent, bringing with them a rather noisy gayety enhanced by prohibition, a sense of liberty, a desire for a good time, and much money. These tourists ordinarily do nothing which can be termed exactly reprehensible, and they are nearly all good-hearted at bottom. But they make a show of their wealth and assume that it is unnecessary to adapt themselves to the peoples and environments among which they are temporarily stopping. Consequently throughout Europe Americans spontaneously and unconsciously carry on an annual campaign of propaganda against themselves and easily convince people they are fabulously rich and more or less brutal. Traveling has been advocated for its educational value and its ability to promote good relations between peoples. It would doubtless be more exact to define touring as one of the most deadly engines of international hatred and prejudice. The herds of voyagers pass hastily through countries which they do not understand, and, in general, do not try to understand, and where they always think they have been fleeced. Then on returning home they are ashamed of the excesses for which their trips furnished the pretext or occasion, and which they blame entirely on the lands where these took place. Such pilgrims, who are forever comparing their native towns with those they visit, solely to demonstrate the superiority of the former, and who leave behind them a reputation for conceit, avarice and vulgarity, will never promote good understanding between nations. We should like to propose that the League of Nations bar all foreigners from Europe unless they come to work or to stay for at least six months. We should like to do the United States this service, the importance of which would be appreciated in the next century. At present Americans do not realize the danger. Conscious of their peaceful intentions and free rights, they do not see that behind the European governments, which are obsequious because they wish to exist and cannot do so without American money, behind the upper classes which have preserved some habits of good education and a few cosmopolitan instincts, and behind the banking interests, there is a great mass of human beings, workers, peasants, intellectual proletarians, among whom a hatred of the United States is silently but steadily growing, just as the hatred of Germany grew between 1900 and 1914. A few clear-sighted Americans have perceived this condition and the dangers involved. In an article published July 11, 1926, Edwin James of the New York *Times* called attention to it lucidly and courageously. He wrote: "Leaving aside the effusions of the professionals who make a specialty of international sentiments and considering only the profoundest feelings of Europe, we find that ninety-nine Europeans in a hundred regard Uncle Sam as an egoist, heartless and avaricious. Note this attitude well and compare it with that of six or seven years ago when Uncle Sam was considered an altruist, good, generous, a true Don Quixote." Then he concludes, "May we never see the day when bad news for us will be good news for the rest of the world." James, who knows Europe thoroughly, sees what few other Americans have yet discerned. Are there not the fine speeches of ambassadors at every official ceremony? Are there not everywhere groups of the intelligentsia only too pleased to mingle with Americans in transit and drink their champagne? Whenever a disagreeable incident occurs in Europe, Asia or South America, does one not read in the papers of the United States that "despite the clamor of a few excited politicians, the people remained calm and the nation preserved its deep and traditional affection for the United States"? How can a naïve and unsuspecting public realize that such statements are the baldest of falsifications? For three years politicians, ambassadors, functionaries and professors throughout Europe have taken great pains to prevent the sentiment of anger and indignation against the United States from being formulated and organized. What would happen if the day came when some government found it advantageous to utilize this attitude? What would happen in one or two decades when the smoldering debt quarrel had been fanned by years of venomous polemics, if the administrations should follow their peoples and egg them on?

Such will not be the case for a very long time, let us hope, so that other circumstances may intervene and arrest the development of that profound crisis. But America should not count too heavily upon her "European friends." Among the elements which defend the United States in Europe, there are two principal groups: the first is composed of bankers, merchants, business men, even professors salaried directly or indirectly by American institutions. These respectable and well-considered men can, so long as passions remain under control, play very useful rôles as go-betweens and peacemakers. But their situations render them useless as combatants or courageous advocates. Through force of habit they yield to facts and never resort to force. As discussion becomes violent, they are given little consideration. Public opinion would easily brush them aside.

The second group is more coherent and more energetic in the affection and sympathy it bears for the United States. It is composed of the heirs of the Tocquevilles and La Fayettes, for whom the United States still remains the kingdom of equality. They upheld Wilson and had confidence in his idealism. For the most part they belong to the left wing—radicals, socialists, but with a certain number of Catholics, etc. They contributed much to that halo of moral grandeur which enabled the United States to assume the rôle of world arbiter in 1918. But what can they do in the future? They preached the League of Nations, because it was an American—at least a Europeo-American—idea; they talked of European federation, for they were inspired by the moral and material success of the American federation; they wished to destroy the barriers which separated the European states in the hope of imitating the Americans. But the United States disowned the League of Nations and refused a common settlement of the debt problem, thus obliging Europe to remain divided on an essential point; and it would not ally itself with the other white races in China. As a consequence every word pronounced by these defenders of the United States seems either derisive or false. They can save their face only by having recourse to theoretical idealism or to a superannuated sentimentality. They frequently have the appearance of false prophets. If they are faithful to their doctrines they must condemn the present attitude of the United States; and by championing the latter, they forswear their creed. They hold the odious position of advocating international altruism and the abolition of customs barriers while Washington boasts of its high tariff and sacred egoism. They become irritated and abandon their efforts.

Since her internal policies are at the moment as conservative as possible, the United States might well expect to gain a few friends in the conservative ranks of Europe. This would indeed be possible, were not the phraseology of the American government so revolutionary. For the part which this phraseology happens to play in elections, it must be conserved. Moreover, it contains nothing definite or binding so far as domestic affairs are concerned. Unfortunately words usually have a precise definition in Europe and their constraining logic is not easily avoided in the representative republics of the old world which are so sensitive to the slightest reflex of public opinion. Thus the different conservative parties—except that of England, to which the national disposition leaves a greater degree of freedom—continue to regard the United States sourly. Doubtless they perceive the admirable refutation of communistic ideas which the United States provides by its mere existence, but fear of communism is not sufficiently acute at present to make this argument convincing. And the United States still remains the product of the first experiment at grafting a democracy upon a traditional society. European conservatives for the most part are weary of democracy, or would like to lay it quietly aside, and they hardly feel equal to the task of extolling America. Indeed they experience rather a sentiment of irritation with the United States and with Americans in general. Moreover, the conservative parties of Europe draw their members largely from aristocracies of long standing (nobles, bourgeois, intellectuals and industrialists) in whose eyes American society, with its millions, its luxurious motors, and its French, English or Italian palaces, is a hasty, avid, and unobliging upstart. It is impossible to be on good terms with such people. They moralize too much; and when they do not, such a vivacious and happy aristocracy is a reproach to the others, who are fallen, battle-scarred, or fighting desperately for life.

The gulf which separates Europe from America is profound. No one has yet found an effective means of bridging it. The method most persistently employed—recourse to sentiments—is certainly unworthy. Nothing is more laborious than trumped-up sentiments, nothing disgusts the sincere, young or strong more than forced emotions. A great deal of benefit would result if Europe and America should refrain from talking sentiment for several years. Such tactics, far from destroying those sentiments which may and should exist, would restore them to their freshness and truth, and thus to their effectiveness. In this respect Europeans are more at fault than Americans. Their phraseology is more florid and hollow. They wrongly hope to make good in this way for what injustice they have done; and what is still worse, they think that they are erasing the injuries which they themselves have suffered. What they really do is to add misunderstanding and sullen, undignified, and hypocritical rancor to a situation which a direct and precise disagreement might clarify and bring to a solution.

It is to be regretted that no one in Europe seems to have a logical and practical point of view from which he may consider this subject devoid of vain illusions. Why do Europeans, whatever their complaints, fail to remember that the Western republic is their offspring, that they are responsible for it; that its successes and its failures (whether they wish it or no) are the successes and failures of Europe; that the defects and qualities of America are those of the old world, carried farther and more freely expended; that the forms of American life are the dreams of Europeans, realized in the face of improbability or expectation? Finally, how is it possible not to see that in spite of all contrasts, the two continents are ordained to understand each other and to work together? Europe is wrong to judge itself solely by its own standards and for its own ends. America is the outgrowth of some of its best accomplishments and a few of its transgressions. America still depends upon its initial point of departure and original impulse. It cannot be denied that Europe is jealous of America, but such feelings are naïve and shocking. A mother envious of her daughter. Why should Europe be jealous of her most brilliant achievement? And why should she denounce so haughtily those passionate instincts of action and material domination which she alone cast upon American soil, until then a land of peace and silence?

A philosophical idea rarely deflects the course of history or calms the hatreds of men. But there is more than an abstraction in the belief that Europe and the United States possess their civilization and purposes in common. It should serve as a hope, and should point a direction.

CHAPTER X

THE LESSON OF AMERICA

Liberty enlightens the world and New York harbor. Her statue is seen when one arrives from Europe, gigantic yet minute in comparison with the liners. With her torch aloft she seems to cry aloud, "Remember, now you are in the land of democracy." At the same moment you are accosted by the tribe of journalists in search of prey, who ask, "What do you think of America? How do you like American democracy?" Then they explain that whether you are poor or rich, famous or unknown, you will have the same cordial reception which has always been given to travelers and refugees. While they are telling you this, the medical authorities treat you with some show of courtesy if you come by first cabin, or hustle you into the Ellis Island barracks if you arrive in the steerage. The first-class passengers disembark in a few minutes, the third-class in a few hours—if they are lucky. The beacon of liberty shines always, but it shines more brightly for the rich than for the poor. Every step you take in the great city convinces you of this. And the longer your visit, the more embarrassed you will feel in speaking of liberty, equality and democracy. You then appreciate the wisdom of the reporters in gathering your impressions of America before you have had any, before your preconceived notions have been obscured. You are constantly asked the same questions, for Americans are eager to know what people think of them. When embarking again, you yourself will try to formulate a profound impression of the country, and you will find it difficult.

Certainly the democratic vocabulary is current today in America, as it has been for two hundred years and will undoubtedly be for some time to come. But does it correspond to the facts or is it simply a façade? How can one arrive at a precise formulation when confronted by so complex a reality? Even during its first courting of democracy did not America owe its salvation to forces which were alien to such a doctrine? What would have been the outcome of the Revolution without the fleet, troops, and money of the King of France? One cannot make a very optimistic answer on recalling the drastic steps taken by Franklin at the French Court to obtain, at any price and under the threat of an immediate cessation of hostilities, the subsidies which he knew were indispensable. In that crisis it was neither the majority nor general suffrage which saved the United States, but the valor of a few hardy and courageous leaders, and the opportune assistance of a foreign power.

Between 1788 and 1790, when the democracy was vacillating between a despotic demagogy and a landed aristocracy, it was again the prudence of a distinguished few which preserved national unity by inducing the leaders to support principles of federation and compromise. There was one more great crisis in 1860-65, when the nation was saved from disaster and dissolution by the keen-sighted and heroic dictatorship of one man.

The country fortunately took its first slow and arduous steps under the monarchical protection, first of England, then of France. National development took place under the aegis of federalism, which prevented more than one calamity. With such assistance, democracy was able to make headway. Moreover, conditions were exceptionally favorable. Immense territory containing infinite natural wealth enabled each person to make a place for himself. Thus democracy could proceed directly to the enrichment and social uplift of the

humblest, while avoiding the odious process of the Tar-
quin, that work of leveling and obliterating, of destroying
the great and reducing the strong and active, which nearly
all other democracies have thought necessary to accomplish
at the outset and to keep in view as a cardinal principle.
Instead of employing jealousy, this democracy utilized
emulation by rewarding its heroes and strong men royally.
Thus limited and tempered, it grew great, still faithfully
repeating the phrases of its childhood (liberty, equality,
government of the people by the people, inalienable rights,
etc.) but quite willing to attach no precise meaning to these
high-sounding words which are so helpful to internal peace.
The nation has triumphed over its enemies and over time,
but who would dare say whether its triumph should be
attributed to democracy or to other forces? We do not.

What is the present political trend of the American nation,
with its great navy and a chief executive whose powers and
prerogatives, though sometimes arrested by the Senate, do
not appear to be declining? On the contrary, they may be
expected to increase as the sense of power and authority
becomes more instinctive with the United States. And will
the cultivation of such tastes give rise to a second Rome
where the apparent maintenance of democratic forms is
discreetly subverted by other tendencies and other principles? As an instance of this could we not point to the
curious and unexpected way in which the mass of the American people became reconciled with the trusts? Americans still
intensely dislike to hear any disparagement of their democracy. When a journalist craves distraction, he need only
affirm that such and such a prime minister, or professor, or
chorus girl declared that democracy has not made the world
any happier. Then a hue and cry is raised and the unfortunate heretic would be stoned if any one had the time to
spare. Yet it was found quite natural in 1917 for Mr.

Wilson to employ every device and trick ever used by the most absolute and militaristic of governments in order to stir up enthusiasm for the cause he had espoused. Indeed without such methods the United States would never have acted so magnificent a rôle nor created such a splendid army —facts to which no one objected at the time. The revolt came later. But at any rate the venture sufficed to demonstrate what can be done with a democratic people, when press, diplomacy, police and ideals are all controlled by one brain.

America, like Rome, runs the danger of falling in love with its own mass and power, thereby forgetting its obligations and losing its sense of proportion. Confronted with the complexities of international rivalry, it feels that it is fated to become an instrument in the hands of the rich and powerful, and particularly the president. Hence it is quite natural that politicians who are sagacious enough to realize this menace to themselves and to democracy should endeavor to suppress all international relations and should refuse to admit that the United States requires a foreign policy. They deny all semblance of autonomy to this aspect of government, considering it merely as an unimportant adjunct to domestic politics. Though this attitude may cause embarrassment, still it is feasible in times of peace. But at critical moments it is so cumbersome as to make all negotiations impossible. The only way out is for the president to take entire charge and assume the very powers which had been jealously denied him.

As the Americans amass more wealth than they can possibly utilize at home, a sincere functioning of democracy becomes increasingly difficult. Officials no longer dare admit that secrets of state are kept from the voters, but every sane man will readily concede that important economic secrets cannot be handed about the market place without

ruining the divulgers. The American government broadcasts
its views on Mexico and China, but the Standard Oil, which
presumably works in accord with it, is under no obligation
to publish its agreements with the Royal Dutch even though
such agreements—or disagreements—may have an infinitely
more vital bearing upon American destinies than incidents
on the Mexican border or along the Yang Tse Kiang. How
many Americans are acquainted with the political aspects of
the United Fruit Company, or of J. P. Morgan and Co.?
Yet they form essential cogs in the national machinery;
they are indispensable adjuncts to the government, as was
clearly shown during the debt negotiations. With the passage of years, American democracy, preoccupied with ideas
of comfort and greatness, is becoming neglectful of its authority and tends to surrender its prerogatives to any one
who will produce a durable prosperity and a stable power.

Impelled by its own mass and its delight in the grandiose,
the republic of the new world seems to be steering inevit-
ably towards hegemony. Everything appears to be pointing
in this direction. The circumstances which struck down
Europe when she was about to attain the acme of prosperity, have shifted the axis of commerce from the Mediterranean to the Atlantic and on towards the Pacific. Its geographical position, by making the United States the one
great white power on the Pacific Ocean, selects it as the
sole champion of the young Anglo-Saxon peoples developing in that vast area. Thus, despite its own moderation,
despite the prudence of England, it is bound to become the
center of Anglo-Saxon economic and maritime power. Each
day draws Canada, Australia and New Zealand closer to the
United States. Were she to permit it, they would all send
ambassadors to Washington to sit beside an English emis-
sary greatly diminished in power and prestige. To date,
the United States has wisely resisted temptation and has

held aloof from this imperial destiny which will mark the end of democracy and the transformation of federalism. Federalism, with its conceptions of prudence, compromise, and moderation, should have resisted the expansion of material power. At the outset it envisaged a conscientious but weak central government which, though able to defend the nation in crises, would be incapable of involving it in national adventures. Federalism could not withstand the pressure of democracy and ambition. Bit by bit its tangible features have been brushed aside, though some of its intangible precepts still retain their vigor. It was a step in the development of a nation; it facilitated transitions, cooled the fervor of democracy, and averted crises, but it never appealed strongly enough to the imagination and passions of men to endure. It was an instrument, an expedient, without which the United States could never have attained its present greatness. But further expansion demands new principles and new formulas.

It is very difficult to say precisely what political doctrines the United States is now developing. American intelligence is better able to invent forms and materialize them than to define or justify them by logic. To peoples with a less spirited capacity for action and a more acute power of analysis, this may appear hypocritical. But it is unjust in this case to adopt an attitude of censure. The democratic vocabulary is still maintained for convenience sake, somewhat as the thalers of Maria Theresa are still in use along the Red Sea. The merchants were ejected from Trieste, but they clung to the silver pieces to which they were accustomed. The case is no different with the democratic jargon of America.

Another factor which attaches Americans to democratic traditions is the conservative aspect which the word "democracy" and its institutions have tended to assume since the rise of socialism and communism. The democratic system is the one under which the powerful nations of today arrived at their present position and wealth. The less prosperous peoples, which are only at the outset of their careers or are going through periods of contraction or metamorphosis, have no reason to extol the virtues of democracy, as its diffusion brought them little profit. To establish their titles in good faith, the United States, Britain and France should explain, along with their principles, the methods for applying them and the social conditions which have made it possible to reap such huge dividends from democracy. In the United States at least, even should the jargon cease to have a meaning, it will be defended as an integral aspect of the nation's wealth.

But phraseology will not alter conditions. With the civilized world at its feet, with interests to be protected in every corner of the globe, with huge debts to collect, the United States faces imperialistic temptations which will be difficult indeed to resist. Moreover, one must not credit her with an asceticism which she does not possess. Americans do respect the rights of others, and they are not oblivious to the meaning of power. Were they confronted by a compact and coherent world which formed a solid and resistant group, they would take great care not to enter into difficult enterprises or hazardous adventures. But for the last ten years Europe has apparently been doing its best to remove all obstacles from the American path, has endeavored to leave the field clear for an exploitation which it expected, desired and could not forgo. The Americans were told the war could not be ended without them, that they were needed to make peace, that post-war conditions could be reorganized only with their aid, that the financial restoration of Europe depended upon their collaboration. They were constantly called upon to act as arbiters, judges or experts.

The great nations as well as the small auctioned themselves off to American capital and went out of their way to obtain American intervention. The most deplorable instance of this is the Dawes Plan, which regulates the transfer of money from Germany to its former enemies. It was prepared and put into operation by American experts, even though the American government had withdrawn from the Allies. The latter justly resented the fact that the United States had left their ranks, but such being the case it was manifestly absurd to ask for American aid in settling the financial problems of Europe. But since 1918 a kind of vertigo has led Europeans to turn to America for help at every new crisis. Despite their difficulties in coming to an understanding with one another, they feel an ardent desire to have things settled—and these factors have made the peoples of the old world blind to their own errors. They have put the United States in an artificial and abnormal position, while involving themselves in embarrassment and peril.

Enfeebled by the war, the nations of Europe were immediately placed at a disadvantage in relation to the United States. This inequality galls the former, which were accustomed to absolute supremacy at home and were used to being regarded as co-directors of the world at large. And the latter has not yet learned how to turn its power to the best advantage. The debts constitute a vast mortgage upon Europe which will require constant supervision. Sooner or later Washington will be obliged to direct officially and officiously every political and economic congress of Europe for the balance of the century.

The European democracies are wearing themselves out with party quarrels and worries over theoretical defense. Their parties are like churches, with their dogmas, and their hierarchies having the power of excommunication. They exhaust one another and scatter national energy to the winds.

No sooner has the necessity for international collaboration been established than a party politician arises to address his constituents, "Yes, but you were right, O Lord Major- ity, when you told us to hate such and such a nation." European democracies are obsessed with the idea of rights and privileges. They cannot renounce the principle of elec- toral infallibility. As a result the quarrels left by past cen- turies are continued indefinitely without hope of ameliora- tion: radicals against conservatives, Saxons against Franco- Latins, Greeks against Turks, etc. Every democratic insti- tution leads the voter to believe that he can decide and settle whichever of these problems directly or indirectly concerns him. Demagogy and the belief in Utopian miracles still pre- vail over his reason and the weight of experience since the French Revolution.

Such is the chaotic state of democracy in Europe. Aggra- vated by post-war difficulties, the old world may well be reduced to a condition of economic servility, or at least to political and financial tutelage. It seems a defenseless, and even willing prey. Blinded by its resentments, it yields to the hypnotic attraction of the United States. But there is still a way out, a possibility of maintaining independence and recapturing something of its former prestige, provided Europe is willing and able to reconcile all its national units and to alter the alignment of its discordant factions. The federalism which rendered such great aid to the youthful United States would now be of invaluable assistance to the ravaged continent of Europe. It would teach the nations that their interests in common are not the least important, and, if studied and cultivated, would bring greater happiness, peace, wealth and prosperity. It would impress the voter with the fact that, after all, his ballot is a very small thing and that his opinion is generally quite negligible. In the long run the important thing is not what he thinks and desires, but what will net him the most advantages. But the inculcation of such ideas cannot be effected on the high roads and in the market places. The voter today demands sentiments bordering on the sensational. And that is precisely what should most carefully be avoided. Local and regional disputes, likewise, should be relegated to the background. Nothing but coöperation can infuse life into the amorphous body of Europe; but not a coöperation of words and declarations which would merely reproduce the present evils on a larger scale. A super-parliament will only inflate the troubles born in local and national assemblies.

As is too often stated with disarming candor, this regeneration will not be attained, or a truly European consciousness evolved, by a few Genevan institutions, appended to the present national structures and flooding Europe with their sub-committees. There must be a new trend to take the place of sterile democratic dogma; principles must be found which are better adapted to modern requirements. Banish the myth of the omnicompetent voter and the omniscient majority. The entire world offers both theoretical and practical proof of the absurdity of such doctrines. On the other hand, for several decades Europe might derive salutary results from a sincere trial of federalism, from organized collaboration aiming at the reconciliation of conflicting interests, from obligatory arbitration, and from a resolve to suppress, once and for all, the political considerations born of the French Revolution. Such a course promises much to Europe; likewise it would spare America many illusions and blunders. Nothing would have so profound an effect upon the American masses as the establishment of some form of European federation. The propaganda which the nations of the old world have carried on against one another in America has reacted against them all. The current must be reversed.

Assuredly every plan for a European federation has its difficulties and inconveniences. But those who declare the remedy worse than the disease do not appreciate the gravity of present conditions. And a necessary task need not be abandoned because it is hard, particularly since many of the difficulties may be foreseen and taken into account at the outset. The first danger is that of an arbitrary, hasty and artificial unification. A continent led by demagogues into a precipitous collaboration without rules or restrictions would be legitimately in danger of a brutal reaction to particularism. The United States is, it is true, accomplishing a complete unification through the suppression of individual and regional variations. But this is only possible because the territorial rivalries of Europe have never existed there and because racial animosity has been in some measure emasculated by transplantation. Moreover, the basis of Anglo-Saxon stock is naturally adaptable. Even so the success of the experiment is not assured. In Europe the variety of civilizations results from centuries of effort. Neither Greece, Rome, nor the Papacy could subject Europe to one artistic, literary and social ideal. After every attempt at political unification, new variants appeared. Every political power which attempted to suppress them has reaped disastrous results. Even the Roman Empire foundered in a sea of blood after trying to abase and unify the people of Europe. No race, no conqueror, no system has ever succeeded in this Augean task. That indeed is one of the triumphs of the continent. This rich and fertile land, full of vitality and spiritual qualities, marvelously propitious to human originality, has consistently refused to subject itself to the impoverishment which results from unity of type and habit. To neglect this essential characteristic would be folly, and that alone suffices to condemn all projects for European communism or super-democracy. Such methods would give the appearance of triumph over particularism, but they would create new hatreds to be allayed.

The weakness of federalism lies in its intellectual character. This moderate and intelligent principle has at its disposal none of the forces and passions which democracy and communism can rely upon. If coupled with any such elements, it will eventually become a dupery or else be cast aside. If all questions are presented to the nations of Europe in elective form, an experimental federalism will never succeed. The strongest nation will sooner or later use its mass to win over the other ethnic groups. Federalism will only make the condition of Europe still worse if the governments and peoples do not, first of all, invent the requisite instruments or borrow them from the past. In the eighteenth century, when Europe was nearest to that harmonious unity which we dream of today, and which might have been accomplished but for the democratic and nationalist precedents of the American and French Revolutions, there were enlightened groups which acted as bumpers between popular masses and ethnic groups. Above each government there was a guiding principle independent of the irritable and evanescent opinions of men, a principle characterized by clarity and stability. This was the principle of authority, conferred upon one leader, who alone should discern what was useful. In our complicated world of today no one save economists and bankers has the right to speak unequivocally and to make demands. There is no aristocracy in the true sense of the word, except for a number of Jews, whose international situation and technical knowledge place them apart. The fate of nations, in the final analysis, is decided in the private offices of business men, who alone may dictate and alter conditions. This is a cruel, derisive and ludicrous fact.

The god whom we adore is the lord of economic laws, whose priests are alone invested with the right of pronouncing oracles and enforcing them. The only grandeur worthy of veneration is that born of the manipulation of money and of the laws governing the ebb and flow of gold. Bolshevism, despite its barbarity, is estimable as a reaction against this unworthy fetichism, as an effort to liberate new human forces, as an attempt to find sounder principles of discipline. With good reason it terrifies the bourgeois world which has been reduced, voluntarily or not, to such a wretched code. But it suggests analogous ways which might be pursued. Unless there be a spiritual renascence (and there are some indications of such) Europe must construct new political doctrines and form a younger aristocracy if she is to attain a salutary and logical federalism. As the social structure of the Middle Ages was based upon the possession and protection of land, so in centuries to come the center of authority should be vested in a group of men who understand international necessities and national realities, who in a word are capable of adapting themselves to a vast and varied milieu. Herein lies the heroic and highly difficult rôle of Europe. America has created an aristocratic bourgeoisie to which the art of figures and the love of homogeneity, discipline, and tolerance suffice. That is not enough for Europe, which requires a superior class with a sense of quality and relative values, and which can appreciate, utilize, and enjoy such privileges. If the press, educational institutions, and great industrial organizations were more far-seeing they could—and they still can—accomplish the work of education and selection, directing peoples and even majorities towards a resignation which the dangers and sufferings of subsequent years will make more acceptable.

If the task is well done, Europe may again turn towards America without fear or jealousy. Then only will the two continents arrive at a true friendship, born of mutual appreciation and respect for each other's qualities. America, with the power of its great mass; Europe, sovereign in its variety and fertility—these two successful creations of one race, endowed with tireless energy, rich imagination, and keen desires, will enjoy the status in the world which befits their ambitions and their greatness.

What a magnificent possibility! With the United States providing the final glory of Europe, after having restored her to her youth. It may come to pass—and many other things besides.

At any rate, America will have served some purpose, if there is any purpose to life and the multiplicity of its forms.